Actors Organize

Actors Organize

A History of
Union Formation Efforts
in America, 1880–1919

KERRY SEGRAVE

McFarland & Company, Inc., Publishers

Jefferson, North Carolina, and London

Library of Congress Cataloguing-in-Publication Data

Segrave, Kerry, 1944–
    Actors organize : a history of union formation efforts in America,
1880–1919 / Kerry Segrave.
        p.   cm.
    Includes bibliographical references and index.

    ISBN-13: 978-0-7864-3283-7
    softcover : 50# alkaline paper ∞

    1. Actors — Labor unions — United States — History — 19th
century.   2. Actors — Labor unions — United States — History —
20th century.   3. White Rats of America — History.
4. Actors' Equity Association — History.   I. Title.
PN2016.S44   2008
331.88'117920280973 — dc22   2007033757

British Library cataloguing data are available

On the cover: "White Rats of America" badge by Kate Irwin;
clown actors ©2007 Shutterstock

Manufactured in the United States of America

McFarland & Company, Inc., Publishers
    Box 611, Jefferson, North Carolina 28640
    www.mcfarlandpub.com

Table of Contents

Preface

This book is about the attempts of actors to unionize in the period 1880 to 1919, a period of intense activity in the trade-union field as workers throughout America flocked to unions in response to poor employment conditions and the growing control of industry after industry by employer combinations, or trusts. Actors were slow to unionize relative to other professions, mostly due to the structure of their workplace. The book concentrates on the White Rats Actors' Union of America (vaudeville) and the Actors' Equity Association (legitimate stage).

Chapter 1 outlines the trials and tribulations often experienced by actors in the period 1880 to 1900, such as being cheated out of their payment, or being stranded on the road, or being arbitrarily dismissed with no notice and for no reason. Sunday performances, offering no pay for the actor, were often forced on the players. Other abuses included sudden changes in a performer's schedule (with increased transportation costs) and sexual harassment, an abuse all too often a part of the theatrical industry but rarely mentioned.

Chapter 2 looks at early efforts by actors to resist the employer, and to organize, up to 1900. Groups such as the Actors' Society sometimes set out as quasi-unions but were usually co-opted or destroyed by the trust. The formation of the first real actors' union one that would last at least for a time, took place in 1900 with the appearance of the White Rats. Its first two years, and the strike it spearheaded, are the topics of chapter 3. Chapter 4 is about the decline in organization efforts that occurred in 1902 to 1907 following the beating back of the Rats. The subject of chapter 5 is the arrival of Harry Mountford in 1908, who lead the Rats toward being a coherent and militant trade union, and his sudden removal from power in 1911.

Chapter 6 outlines three more years of stagnation in the efforts of players to organize, while chapter 7 focuses on the return of Harry Mountford to the White Rats near the end of 1915 and the first half of 1916, when an increasingly bitter war of words took place between the union and the trust (with the latter preparing to crush the union). The White Rats' strike in Oklahoma in the last half of 1916 is the subject of chapter 8. Covered in chapter 9 are the Rat strikes of 1917, its defeat that year, and its decline to the point of being an effectively dead organization (although it would officially linger on for some time).

The formation of Equity in 1913 is the topic of chapter 10, along with its activities up to the middle of 1919. During that time its experiences were similar to those of the Rats, with the trust in the legitimate theatrical industry as determined to destroy Equity as the vaudeville trust had been to eliminate the Rats. Chapter 11 covers the Equity strike of 1919. Although the managers fought it with a strategy identical to one employed by the vaudeville managers, the legitimate trust failed to see the differences in the circumstances and situations. As a result, the outcome of the Equity strike was quite different compared to any outcome achieved by the White Rats.

1 | General Conditions, 1880–1900

"The rascals must go! It will require plenty of hard work, perseverance and energy to purge the stage of the swindlers that fatten on actors, but it can and it shall be done."
— *New York Dramatic Mirror*, 1892

"Conditions in vaudeville around 1900 were pretty bad.... [Management] had gypping agents, grafting bookers, cancellation clauses in the contracts, and switching of routes...."
— Joe Laurie, Jr., 1953

Actors were slow to attempt to form unions, relative to many other occupations. It was 1900 before actors formed a true trade union that would last at least a couple of decades. One reason for the slow start had to do with the nature of the profession. With so many actors being on the road regularly, it was difficult to gather a lot of them together at the same time. Another reason had to do with the perception that actors were too egotistical, too bound up in themselves to engage in the solidarity believed to be one of the necessary hallmarks of an effective union. Craft and technical workers in the theatrical industry organized long before the actors did. But actors in the latter part of the 1800s faced a variety of oppressive and exploitative working conditions, as did all members of the working class, no matter what the occupation. While the bad conditions affecting actors were often unique to the theatrical industry, the solution for the workers was always the same no matter what the profession — organize. The theatrical industry near the turn of the twentieth century was an industry no less than the steel industry or the shoe manufacturing industry. In all cases the ruling class organized and rationalized activities within each industry according to the same principles.

Of the many problems faced by actors, one was the propensity of some managers to avoid paying them. At the Academy of Music in Richmond Virginia in November 1872, the musicians were not in their places in the orchestra pit until late in the evening, and then declared they would not play a note until they had received at least some of the back wages due them. Forced to respond, the manager took $14 out of the box office and gave it to the musicians on account. Apparently satisfied, the musicians settled in and prepared to accompany the play. However, the actors were also owed back pay. Annoyed by what they had witnessed, the troupe notified the manager that if they did not each receive $10 on account they would not perform the play. But the manager would not, or could not, comply, and so the evening's performance was cancelled. Audience members were told they would be given a refund. With the box office now short $14, it meant some spectators could not get an immediate refund; they were told to come back later. That led to much shouting, cursing, and threats from audience members. Finally, the spectators all left the theater, as did the actors, who took their luggage with them. A little later that evening, Mr. Jones, owner of the venue, took possession of it for rent due him and locked out the theatrical management.[1]

Unpaid salaries at the Germania Theatre in New York in July 1882 led to a rumor that the actors would stage a walkout. Based on that rumor, a reporter went to the venue, where he interviewed an unidentified person who admitted salaries were overdue. Management had stalled the company a few times with promises to pay the next day but never did so. An exasperated troupe then threatened to strike. At the time, some 60 performers in the large-cast opera were owed for one-and-a-half weeks' work.[2]

In 1887, for the first time in the history of the National Theatre in Washington, D.C., an advertised performance was not given. On August 26, with the audience assembled to see the play *Russia*, an announcement was made that the curtain would not rise and money would be refunded at the box office. That action occurred because of a strike by the actors. During the week the troupe had noticed the houses were not very large and began to fear that the management would not pay their salaries. Thus, on the 26th, actors Colton and Ambrose (men) and Livingston and Waldren (women) took the initiative and demanded the company be paid the wages due to that point. The fact that the actors worried about a problem that might arise, and had even demanded an early payday, perhaps indicated how pervasive the problem was generally.[3]

Company manager E. E. Hume informed the actors that as the salaries were not due until Saturday (two or three days later), he would on no account pay them until the usual payday. Because of that response the actors went out on strike. Hume explained to a reporter, "We have been doing a poor business, it is true, but the members of the company had no right to demand their salaries until they were due, and I preferred to have the performance stopped rather than accede to their demands." One member of the company told the reporter that another catalyst for the action was the fact that two members of the troupe, Miss Behrens (Mrs. Hume) and Mr. Bangs, had received a salary payment early that week.[4]

Emmie Parker joined the Annie Mitchell theatrical company at Chatham, New York, late in September 1893. She remained with the company for two weeks as it toured the state, but during the whole time she received only $2 and was left stranded and penniless in Port Jervis when the troupe was suddenly disbanded. On a Saturday night [the usual payday in the industry], at the end of Parker's second week with the group, Mitchell closed her season without notice but reorganized her company under another name immediately afterwards. It was a thinly disguised ruse, as the company, with a new cast, opened the following Monday at Hawley, Pennsylvania. Mitchell's reorganization gambit was fairly common in the theatrical industry, as it prevented unpaid and disgruntled actors from obtaining a legal attachment against the company, since it no longer existed. Percy Lindon was another cast member. He was owed $32.30 at the time of the sudden closure at Port Jervis. Another of the men in the company refused to go on stage on that last Saturday unless his back salary was paid to him. According to a news account, "His part was cut out and the play promptly proceeded with."[5]

Hadjali's Troupe of Arabs — an act consisting of eight acrobats — brought suit in court in New York in 1893 to recover $150 for one week's salary and $100 for extra performances they were requested to give. They sued the Matthews and Bulger company. For performing at Providence, Rhode Island, they were to receive $150 per week for the usual number of performances. But, said a reporter, "The management compelled them to parade about the town in their Arab costumes, much against their will, and then wished them to perform twice a day. This they rebelled against, but finally submitted with the understanding that they would claim extra compensation for the additional performances." In the end they were paid nothing at all. Judge Moore in the Third District Court rendered judgment in the performers' favor for the full amount and costs.[6]

Frederic Melville was a member of Springer and Welty's *Black Crook* company until he left it at Danville, Illinois, late in January 1894. According to him, at Columbus, Ohio, on January 1 the actors in the company received notice that the season would close in two weeks. Three or four days later that notice was rescinded after the company consented to continue at reduced salaries. Melville was especially incensed because he said he had already submitted to a large salary cut earlier in the season with the proviso his salary would stand for the rest of the season, as long as the company remained out on tour. Upon reaching Danville a couple of weeks later the managers asked him to take yet another salary cut — his third. He refused and demanded his passage home; train fare was $20. Most contracts actors signed in this period required the manager to pay the actor's fare back home or to the city where the actor first signed on with the troupe. When the managers refused to give Melville his train fare he threatened to take legal action and have the box office receipts attached. Finally, Melville succeeded in securing $12.50.[7]

While on tour in October 1895, the Diamond Dramatic company closed down suddenly at Red Key, Indiana, because of the unexpected and sudden departure of owner Walter Newman. Salaries were unpaid and company members were left to their own devices to make their way home. Actors in the troupe wanted to hold a benefit show to raise money for themselves, but the use of the one hall in Red Key was refused them. Around the same time, in a separate incident, players in the *Maloney's Rattle* company were stranded on tour at Binghamton, New York, after being on the road for two weeks. All members of the company were owed one week's salary. Company managers skipped town on a Saturday night, leaving unpaid the board bills of the troupe, whose members had no money to pay their fares to New York.[8]

Jewish actors of the Adler Theatre on the Bowery in New York began a strike near the end of 1895. For several weeks salaries were not paid, and when the Adler manager's only compromise was to give the leading lady $18 on account, and the villain $6.75, all players in the company agreed to strike. After the walkout the manager recruited substitute actors for the play, *Cardinal Richelieu*, but it was a move that did not sit well with the audience, who "hooted and hissed" the replacements, said a journalist. It was such a fiasco that all the money had to be refunded; the house was dark the next night. But on the night after that the play was staged again with yet another set of actors; it played to "very small" business.[9]

Most of the actors with the Hodges Dramatic company, playing at the Third Avenue Theatre in Seattle, struck in July 1896, demanding an assurance their salaries for the previous week would some day be paid. That walkout came just before a performance, with the audience filing into the house. Some type of agreement was reached, and the performance went ahead as scheduled. However, after the show, manager Walter Hodges announced that the actors who had struck were all dismissed, as he had engaged others to replace them.[10]

Players could also find themselves suddenly consigned to the road without their knowledge. Theatrical producer Mr. Palmer signed up with a Mr. McConnell to take his Union Square company of New York and play in San Francisco in the summer of 1882. Palmer did not tell his company, and many of the players were upset, with several of the principle players refusing to go. Still, despite the fact no notice had been given, the editor of a trade paper, the *New York Dramatic Mirror*, felt the actors should not complain because, "the chance of filling in an idle spot in the year at terms they are accustomed to receive at the busy time should gratify rather than displease even the artists of the Union Square Theatre."[11]

Conditions of dressing rooms were often another sore spot for the actors. Through its editorials and letters to the editor columns, the *New York Dramatic Mirror* often exposed the appalling conditions of the dressing rooms found in so many theaters. One of its reporters said, in January 1883, "the arrangements pertaining to that department are made with a lamentable disregard for the comfort and health of the artists." And, he continued, "In squalor and filth they exceed the wretchedest tenement-garret that the imagination can picture. In the front of the house there is an air of elegance and refinement." One unnamed venue had, in addition to its poor quality dressing rooms, a manager who rehearsed his people for a new play three mornings a week, put them through the regular performance (of a different play) each evening, and ordered night rehearsals as well, "which began at twelve o'clock midnight and lasted until five in the morning." Calling for a sweeping reform in the area of dressing rooms, the editor added, "Either through carelessness or callousness, the managers entirely overlook the rights of the actors in respect to accommodations behind the scenes, and the latter put up with surroundings of the most abominable nature without a word of complaint. It is a singular characteristic of players that they will submit meekly to grievances that other people would not tolerate for an instant."[12]

Actors were also commonly stranded on the road. In mid–September 1888 when the editor of the *New York Dramatic Mirror* reviewed the new theatrical season — then less than one month old — he remarked that the "usual percentage" of stranded companies appeared in the season's early accounts. While he said managers were mostly to blame, "because they have led truthful people into trouble by false pretenses that are censurable; if not actionable," he went on to chastise the actors for often being credulous and rash because they "place themselves with persistent regularity in the position to be swindled."[13]

Octavie Barbe was hired for one of the lead roles in *A Modern Heroine* in 1894 by manager David Traitel. Her contract called for a specific salary and the traveling expenses for herself and her mother (who was to travel with her). The contract contained the usual and standard two-week clause wherein either party could end the contract by serving two weeks' notice. After rehearsing for two weeks (unpaid — actors at the time were never paid anything for time spent rehearsing, no matter how long), the play opened on September 1 in Hartford, Connecticut, under an agreement by which the company was to play the first week for no salary, as the drama was a new one and needed time to catch on. At the end of the second week Barbe got one week's pay but also received two week's notice. By that time the company was in Rochester, New York, from which city Barbe had to pay train fare for herself and mother home to New York City since the troupe manager refused to live up to the contract and pay the transportation costs. No reason was given for serving notice on the actor. Barbe had received consistently excellent reviews for her work in the play.[14]

The Comstock Mammoth Minstrels of New York City were stranded in Port Jervis, New York, after their manager skipped town in October 1895, leaving the 25 members of the trope — it was a mostly black company that included 11 women — stranded without funds. With nowhere to go, the group reportedly spent all night walking the streets of the town. By next morning local authorities were talking of advancing them money from the poor fund of Orange County so they could get back to New York.[15]

A 1906 report from St. Louis detailed the plight of a dozen women and 100 men, all members of Parker's *White City on Wheels* company, who walked the streets of East St. Louis one night in October because they had no money to pay for lodging. Their managers had skipped town owing some $8,000 in back wages due the players and employees. Individual claims ranged from $50 to $900; some in the company had not been paid for months.[16]

Since either a manager or an actor could end a commitment by serving two weeks' notice, that clause, found in virtually every acting contract, seemed to be fair to both sides. The reality, though, was quite different. Actor Maida Craigen was given two weeks' notice in the fall of 1890 after her first performance in a play for a company led by producer Margaret Mather. Earlier she had signed up for a salary of $100 a week, but Mather suddenly decided the amount contracted for was too much and asked her to work for $75 a week. Craigen declined and was promptly served the two weeks' notice; and, wrote a commentator, "the actress seems to be without legal redress for the injustice."[17]

Craigen's experience generated a number of letters to the *New York Dramatic Mirror*, which caused its editor to remark, "We have said that the usual two weeks' notice clause in contracts between managers and actors was not only inequitable, but iniquitous. It is neither the one nor the other in theory, but it is both in practice." With respect to the supposed equality of the clause — a point frequently stressed by producers and managers — the editor remarked, "As to the mutual advantages of that clause we cannot see that they are particularly in evidence.... Does not the record of the last five years show that the convenient loophole for terminating contracts has been resorted to more frequently by managers than actors?" It was also pointed out that it was not unusual for a company to stop on the road for "reorganization," and that "the euphemism means simply that the manager has taken advantage of his clause in the actors' contracts to dismiss his company for the express purpose of reengaging them at reduced salaries? Are we not constantly hearing of cases of individual discharge, under that same elastic provision, growing out of frivolous pretexts or accounted for by no reason or pretext at all?" That notice clause was open-ended and did not require a reason for notice, or cause, be given to the recipient. Declaring the clause to be "flagrantly unjust to the actor," the editor concluded, "Under the present arrangement a theatrical contract insures an actor no more than two weeks employment. He might as well have no contract at all." Given the nature of the acting profession, which always had more members of the fraternity unemployed than employed, it was highly unlikely that a player who had managed to secure a job would invoke the two weeks' notice clause.[18]

Besides the rules of the game, which favored the producer and manager over the actor, there was the problem of the swindling manager — that is, the manager who set out to defraud his actors, as opposed to managers who stiffed their players after poor management or some such, but had not started the project with a clear intent to do so. In June 1892 the *New York Dramatic Mirror* thundered that it was time to institute drastic measures to "crush out a crying evil" and eliminate the crooked manager, as the newspaper launched one of its periodic campaigns to achieve that goal. It had requested that ex-judge A. J. Dittenhoefer draft a bill designed to protect actors from such larcenous individuals. It was to be a bill to make swindling a misdemeanor, punishable by fine and/or imprisonment. With respect to managers in that category, the newspaper's editor declared, "the rascals must go! It will require plenty of hard work, perseverance and energy to purge the stage of the swindlers that fatten on actors, but it can and it shall be done."[19]

Back in October 1891 one of the *Mirror*'s regular features — the Dates Ahead column (which outlined where companies would be playing in the future) — published the names of 392 traveling theatrical companies. Between October 1, 1891, and March 1, 1892, 100 of those companies collapsed on the road, leaving the players stranded (35 troupes in October; 28 in November; 14 in December; 18 in January; and five in February). And those were only the ones the newspaper knew about; the editor was certain "the number of wrecks was in reality considerably greater."[20]

Dittenhoefer submitted a draft of the bill to the *Mirror* in July 1892. Called "An Act to Punish Frauds Committed Against Actors," it was intended to introduce the measure to the New York State Legislature during its next session. Actor Louis Aldrich contacted the newspaper to report that he had been engaged by a fraternal group called the Actors' Order of Friendship to lobby that same legislature to have them enact a law that would have made an actor's salary the first lien upon the receipts of each performance — just the same as a mechanic's lien held before all other debts upon the buildings that tradesmen were engaged in constructing.[21]

Overwhelmingly, according to the paper, actors supported the bill, and many letters to the editor in support were indeed published in its pages. The *Mirror* also was busy circulating petitions for actors and other interested parties to sign, which were to be presented to the Legislature when the Dittenhoefer measure was finally introduced.[22]

Around the same time Dittenhoefer was submitting his bill, the story of producer Lydia Thompson and her last season's company had just come to light. Cast member Emmie Fossette was hired by Thompson in December 1891. She had a verbal understanding but no written contract, which was not unusual for the time. That company opened its season on December 21 in Cincinnati to poor business, and business continued to be bad until the season closed in April 1892. All seven players in the company received their salaries promptly at the end of the first and second weeks. But at the end of the third week Ernest Hutchinson (manager of the troupe and Lydia's husband) explained to the actors that the lack of business meant he could not pay the salaries but he had cabled London for funds (Thompson supposedly had property in England) and expected a draft shortly. Thereafter the actors received nothing but excuses of various kinds, and no salaries were paid, although traveling and room and board expenses continued to be met. At the end of the season's final week in April — the company played New York that week — Emmie and the others each received $15. They also received more promises, stalls, and delays as to why Lydia could not pay her debts (such as her English property being in a legal dispute, and so on). Fossette said the amount due her was $336 for 17 weeks. She was left penniless at the end of the season but was helped out financially by friends. To verify her story the reporter tracked down another member of the company, stage manager Louis F. Howard, who confirmed the story as related by Fossette. Howard added that company member Lea Jarvis was left in the hospital at Rochester without a cent after she was suddenly taken ill while the troupe was performing in that city. He later discovered Thompson and Hutchinson had sent her no money after she was stricken, even though they assured the company on several occasions that they had done so.[23]

Some four years later, in 1896, the editor of the *Mirror* brought up the subject of fraudulent managers again, complaining the situation was still bad. Briefly, he pointed to the paper's past efforts to bring about reforms, including the Dittenhoefer draft bill. Regarding that bill, he explained that the majority in the industry then were "indifferent" to that effort and that many in the industry were against such a law because they believed it would be a hardship on many managers of small companies and the people employed by them. "In these circumstances, although there was every prospect of the successful passage of the bill, it was dropped," said the editor.[24]

Sunday performances were another bone of contention for actors. Theatricals on Sundays flourished in some cities, but were opposed in many others. In some cities all such performances had been banned. Throughout this period of time there were battles in cities all over America as to what to allow on Sundays and what not to permit. So-called sacred concerts were allowed in most cities, while theatricals were completely taboo in some of those municipalities. Rules were complex and loopholes often large, and soon the whole question of Sunday entertainment was an almost hopeless muddle. Players were caught in the middle.

Typical of the forces opposed to Sunday entertainment was the Law and Order League of Cincinnati, which had been fighting to abolish such entertainment completely. Theatricals were often mounted on Sundays in cities that banned them because the producer felt he could get away with it, and sometimes the rules were so vague and hazy that he really thought he was obeying the letter of the law, if not its spirit. When such performances were raided and shut down by the police — and they sometimes were — it was usually because citizens had complained; it was the actors who were hauled into court and charged. Usually the manager was not taken into custody. Many actors had a clause in their contracts calling for Sunday performances and were thus compelled to appear when the manager decided to schedule one. As of 1886, Sunday theatricals were said to flourish to the greatest extent in Cincinnati, Chicago, St. Louis, New Orleans, and Milwaukee. Actors were overwhelmingly opposed to performing on Sundays. Objections were not religious in nature; the players argued they were entitled to one day's rest in every seven, just like other workers.[25]

A decade later the *Mirror* editor termed Sunday performances "deplorable," stating that they should all be banned. A few of the more prominent stars had the power to refuse to perform on the Sabbath, "but a majority of stars and companies are forced by the will of local managers, who believe in this feature of an engagement, to play on that day," he explained. One of the worst aspects of such performances, he continued, could then be seen in Cincinnati, "where the habit of playing on that day has developed a method of injustice of which actors are the victims." By this time Cincinnati had passed a law banning theatrical performances on Sundays. However, an understanding had emerged between managers and the police by which no performance was interfered with, but as soon as the show was over the police stepped in and arrested the actors concerned, leaving the managers untouched.[26]

An example of vague laws with respect to Sunday shows could be seen in New York City, wherein, through 1900, Sunday theatricals were clearly and definitely banned. However, a permissive law with respect to concerts (supposedly sacred) had led to violations in the form of vaudeville performances on Sundays that did not materially differ from the vaudeville performances given throughout the week. For years such performances had been illegally given under the guise of "concerts." When no one complained, the police always looked the other way. If a complaint was lodged, the police may have grudgingly and reluctantly done something. That may have caused the venue to go dark for a Sunday or two, but it quickly returned to business as usual.[27]

Three years later, in 1903, the New York Police Department took a sudden interest in Sunday concerts. Under instructions from Police Commissioner Greene, two men were assigned to visit each theater where a Sunday concert was given in order to see if it really was a concert, and to make arrests for any violations of the Sunday law. A few arrests were made in March of that year. At the Circle Theatre, Harry Taft, the whistling, dancing comedian, in the judgment of the police officers, overstepped the line that separated the sacred from the secular, and they arrested him. They also took the venue manager into custody. To help make the distinction between a concert and a theatrical program a little less murky, the Sunday law forbade any performance that used costumes and wigs, and any that involved a change of scenery. According to the *Mirror,* "Whenever the police take these sudden spasms, the performances are altered so as to conform to the law. When the officials are inactive, as they usually are, the entertainments are very little different from those given from Monday to Saturday."[28]

In New York on Sunday, January 3, 1909, Aaron Kessler, assistant manager of Hammerstein's Victoria Theatre, and the Avon Comedy Four were placed under arrest for an alleged violation of the Sunday law. The Avon Comedy Four appeared at the matinee performance and did their usual act, which, according to the police officers present, came under the heading of sketches (a banned category) and thus could not lawfully be performed on a Sunday. All those arrested were quickly bailed out. Two arrests were also made at the Thalia Theatre that day. Rose Rappaport and Anna Herwitz were charged with a violation of Section 277 of the Penal Code; they appeared on the stage in something other than street clothes. Meanwhile, at other venues, "sacred" motion pictures with an alleged lecture were presented unhindered. During this period of crackdown, some of the city's vaudeville houses were closed on Sundays owing to the lack of acts that had some probability of falling within the generous loopholes provided by the law. Producer Willie Hammerstein remarked, "Don't blame the police. They have to use their own judgment in such matters, but we selected that act [Avon Comedy Four] especially for a Sunday performance as one that would surely come within the law. But the laws will have to be radically changed if the Sunday performances are to continue. The public want more than the law allows."[29]

Women in the theatrical profession were on their own more frequently and enjoyed greater autonomy, independence, and so on, than did most women during this period. They also paid a price by being subjected to increased sexual harassment. Its extent remained unknown, as the subject was almost never broached by the media. In a rare exception, an account in *Variety* in June 1913 reported, with no names or details, that a vaudeville actress had been sexually harassed [that term, of course, was not then in use] or worse. Said the account, "There have been many complaints by women in vaudeville against this sort of thing from booking men, but it is seldom if ever one reaches the light. A very big vaudeville star (female) is said to be now harboring an extreme grievance against a well-known vaudeville manager for something along these lines."[30]

Around the same time, *Variety* reprinted an article from a New York newspaper that summarized the problems faced by vaudeville actors. It noted that almost all vaudeville actors' contracts contained a clause that permitted any theatrical manager to dispense with the actor in the event his work proved unsatisfactory. This was almost never done on the basis of quality, as managers and bookers were well aware of all the acts signed up; none that played the first-class vaudeville circuits were unknown quantities. According to the account, "It appears that each house [chain] has a local manager whose special business it is to find fault with acts in order to can them and send them on their way." So common was the practice that a generic name was applied to such places — in the trade they were called "canneries." Vaudeville actors were independent contractors, and if they developed an act with elaborate props and scenery they had to buy or make such items and pay the freight costs of sending them from town to town as they toured. At each venue, of course, stagehands erected and struck any sets an actor might use. Managers were also known to fine an act — and reclaim part of the act's salary by the indirect method — for all sorts of spurious reasons. For example, a player performed his act in a brown suit in one theater for almost one week. Late in the week he changed to a black suit; the actor was fined $10 by the manager for appearing in "street dress."[31]

Continuing on with the list of problems, the reporter observed that some theatrical managers and agents made no contract at all, giving the actor a mere slip of paper that stated the name of the theater or theaters at which the player was to perform. And there was a reason for that. "All irresponsible vaudeville managers — and nearly all acts sooner or later come into contract with them — unhesitatingly book more acts each week than their houses can play. Of necessity many must be canned or canceled, while those retained are not the best, but the cheapest. Sometimes the best acts are retained but only in the event the actors will consent to cut their salaries." One manager told actors he wanted to play them in two New Jersey towns, half a week in each venue. Because those places were not highly esteemed by the players, the manager added the inducement of bookings in New York, Boston, Philadelphia, Chicago, and so on after the New Jersey run was completed. However, at the end of the New Jersey run the acts were informed their work was not satisfactory.[32]

A certain manager owned a vaudeville house in a rural city where Sunday shows were not allowed, but he still got seven days' work out of his acts. Those acts played six days at his venue, and then he hired them out for a fee to a house in a nearby city where Sunday shows were allowed. The performers got no money for those extra shows. Actors were never paid until the end of the week and so were forced to comply. Normally the actor got paid on Saturday night after the last show, but if he was told to play on Sunday, in the original venue or another one, he did not get paid for the week until late Sunday night. To add insult to injury, the player farmed out to another house for Sunday shows had to pay all the transportation costs involved.

Crooked agents also abounded in the industry. For example, an act may have told his agent that $250 a week was the minimum salary he would work for, taking into account travel costs, room and board, and so on (all such expenses were borne by the vaudeville actor). That agent then offered the act around at $250 but might agree to a manager's offer of $200 a week, without telling his client. Only at the end of the week at settling up time did the player learn the truth.[33]

An agent sometimes told an act he had booked him to play two performances a day at a remote theater, when he knew the manager insisted on four performances a day. In such cases the act was forced to finish the engagement on the manager's terms. Few vaudeville actors could afford to pay the expense of a long journey and lose a salary besides. Another method used by a manager who wanted to get rid of an act before it had started was to collude with the freight company that serviced his venue. If on some Monday morning the manager of a circuit wanted to get rid of an act, he got the expressman to lose the baggage belonging to the act. When the luggage was not found until the following day the manager explained that he was sorry but inasmuch as the act had missed its Monday performances the booking had to be canceled. Vaudeville actors usually worked for a week in a particular venue (sometimes half a week in smaller centers), and at the start of each new week they were required to "check in" at their new venue on the Monday morning, usually no later than 10 A.M. The reason for that was to allow the house at least a few hours to get a replacement act if any player was a no-show.[34]

Later in 1913 an account observed that in the legitimate theater field many, and perhaps most, of the contracts had a clause calling for the actor to be paid half-salary for certain weeks in the season, such as around Easter and before Christmas. Managers explained this was done because business was traditionally slower in those weeks than at other times during the year, hence the lower pay. It need hardly be said that actors did not receive any extra pay with respect to weeks that had larger than average attendance. While this news story remarked that most contracts contained a two weeks' notice clause, and that transportation costs back home had to be paid if the production closed on the road, it was also noted that such clauses were "widely ignored."[35]

As the 1900s began, the industrialization of the American theater led to a radical transformation in the relations between actors and managers. As historians Don Wilmeth and Christopher Bigsby pointed out, "The rapid shift to contractual relations and clashing perspectives and business practices was accompanied by significantly worsened working conditions for the journeyman performer and, in many cases, wholesale abuses." As the producing companies merged and consolidated, they formed combinations, or trusts, leaving a much smaller number of independent entities, but with each entity being much larger. Those large outfits worked together quite openly in restraint of trade and made life even more difficult for actors. Managers realized the actor's only recourse when a contract had been violated was for the actor to sue for breach of contract. That was an expensive and impractical course of action for someone who spent most of the year on the road. Also, many managers had incorporated, thus insulating themselves from lawsuits. As a result, noted Wilmeth and Bigsby, the abuses players were subjected to "became increasingly frequent near the turn of the century." All of these events paralleled what was occurring in the larger society. Trusts were everywhere — the oil trust, the steel trust, and so on. Articles on the dangers posed by trusts, the need for trust-busting, and so forth filled the media and eventually resulted in federal laws designed to curb trusts and limit their powers. However, more show than substance was involved in moves by governments to curb trusts. Yet it clearly demonstrated that the theatrical industry was merely one component of the capitalist system, no different from the widget manufacturing industry: A widget was a play was a widget. Identical rationalizations and reorganizations were applied to each industry and each obeyed the same "natural laws."

One of the theatrical industry trusts was the United Booking Offices (UBO).[36] "Conditions in vaudeville around 1900 were pretty bad," wrote historian Joe Laurie Jr. in 1953. "The U.B.O. had things their own way. They had gypping agents, grafting bookers, cancellation clauses in the contracts, and switching of routes, which meant they would lay out a nice route for you, with short jumps [when a vaudeville performer finished his week and traveled on to his next city that trip came to be known in the industry as the 'jump]' which you could afford to take at the salary they offered, then would switch dates where you had to make big jumps that ate up a lot of your salary."[37]

Given the situation in the acting profession, it was not unusual for the players to start to think about organizing, about forming a union.

2 | Early Efforts to Organize, 1880–1900

"But all attempts to regulate or improve or benefit the actor from the industrial point of view merely will be abortive, because the conditions of his labor do not permit of any such regulation."
—*New York Dramatic Mirror*, 1888

"The duty of this young [Actors'] Society is now to find out the cause which makes it necessary for actors to organize, and when they have found it, to strike boldly for its removal."
—James A. Herne, 1896.

To exploited and oppressed workers in many segments of American society the solution to intolerable working conditions and adversarial relations, by 1900, lay in unionization. By the end of the nineteenth century, the resistance of labor to capital had become a common occurrence. Industrial expansion after the Civil War, paired with the increased immigration that flooded the market with cheap labor, led to lessened opportunities and rapidly deteriorating conditions for the average American worker. A great deal of labor strife took place in the period from 1873 until the end of that century. Events such as the Homestead Strike, the Pullman Strike and the Haymarket Square Riot became etched for all time in the American memory. Consistent with that trend, craft and technical workers began to unionize late in the nineteenth century, all before the actors took similar action. Stagehands formed local unions in the 1880s to demand that managers employ them, and not actors, to change stage scenery. Those locals became the basis for the National Alliance of Theatrical Stage Employees in 1893 and later the International Alliance of Theatrical Stage Employees (IATSE).

Stage painters formed the Protective Alliance of Scenic Painters in 1885, and Yiddish actors formed the Hebrew Actors' Union in 1899.[1]

While they were slower than workers in other fields to organize, actors had considered the subject for some time. Back in July 1864 a group of actors in New York City, said to represent all the city's theaters, held a meeting at which they passed a resolution directed at the managers in which they asked for a salary increase. It was an "appeal to the liberality and sense of justice of the managers, for a prompt and adequate increase of salaries, placed on a specie basis." Another resolution passed at that meeting was one to "establish, for the future welfare of the profession, a Protective Association or Union...." They hoped that such an organization would "be a strong and invulnerable defence for [actors] against the dishonest machinations of outside speculators and dishonest traders on other people's talent...."[2]

The *New York Dramatic Mirror* lamented, in 1886, that there were no associations for actors, as there were in other professions. As far as the editor was concerned, the actor's business was still in a nomadic stage of development, with "the gypsy taint" still clinging to it. Still, the editor was advocating not a real union but something along the lines of a fraternal organization that also got involved with helping players in some sort of vaguely defined business way.[3]

Even when actors engaged in informal, union-like activity, the *Mirror* was distressed. The newspaper grumbled in 1882 about what it viewed as a fairly dramatic increase in salaries for actors. Much of the blame for that situation was laid off on manager Mallory of the Madison Square Theatre, who, for example, had recently signed Carrie Turner for $80 a week when "From any other manager Miss Turner would have been lucky to receive twenty-five dollars." The rise in salaries, said the account, "although of course not resulting from concerted action, has all the effects of a strike; there is said to exist among the most influential professionals a firm determination to yield not a jot in their demands." While most managers were said to refuse to meet inflated demands, the editor went on to urge that actors realize each side was "helplessly dependent" on the other, "and that in embarrassing the men who employ them by striking for exorbitant salaries they are committing a deed about as foolish as killing the lamented goose that laid the famous golden eggs."[4]

Although the editor of the *Mirror* seemed reluctant to endorse anything that was obviously a union for actors, he went on in that same year, 1882, to note the large amount of litigation that went on between actors and producers or managers, without making any connection between unionization and increasing exploitation. "A pestilence of litigation has descended upon the profession, and the lawyers who make a speciality of theatrical cases are reaping a generous harvest," he explained. "During the past fortnight actors and managers have thronged the courts, and a spectacle of wholesale legal contentiousness is the result." As a solution, the editor suggested arbitration, where persons of the trade involved rendered judgment in the case of disputes. Advocated was the standard arbitration system wherein each side (actor and manager) picked one person to represent them, and those two together picked the third and final member of the panel.[5]

Two and a half years later the same newspaper again bemoaned the amount of theatrical litigation and the need to somehow end it. "Unquestionably the manager has very much the advantage of the actor in the terms of the contract," especially if the player was not a big star, admitted the editor. And, he added, "The actor resorts to the law in vain. Unless he is well provided with means, he gives up in despair and contemplates an empty pocketbook."[6]

Pervasive litigation finally led to a formal proposal to organize in 1891. However, it contained only arbitration as a solution and was proposed by the management side. Producer/manager Mark Klaw (one of the biggest names in the business then) had taken an active interest in paving the way for a Mangers and Actors League to relieve its members from costly and slow litigation. Arbitration was to be the motto of the proposed new organization. It was estimated a complaint could be settled in two to three days by the League, compared to six to eight months in court, and save a lot of money. Not surprisingly, the *Mirror* was very enthusiastic about the idea of using standard arbitration to resolve disputes. But the editor admitted that comparatively few people had taken an interest in the idea to that date, and those were "chiefly managers and actor-managers." Dealing with the obvious flaws and faults in the proposed League the editor remarked that if "the notion gains ground that the League is merely the outcome of the loss and chagrin sustained by a few managers in courts of law and that it is intended chiefly for the protection of the manager against the actor, the organization will not be likely to become either extensive or influential." Klaw insisted the object of the League would be to protect actor and manager through a binding arbitration clause that would be a feature of the uniform contract.[7]

One month later an initial meeting of the League was held at which Mark Klaw was elected President. However, by that time most observers understood that the League was simply a thinly disguised management device to further control the actor. Fraternal associations, such as the Actors' Order of Friendship, vigorously opposed the League, as did, by then, the *Mirror*, which described the League as an organization "thought to conceal ulterior motives and objects." Nothing more was heard of the League.[8]

The Actors' Order of Friendship (AOF) was the promoting organization behind a petition delivered to the U.S. Congress in 1888 urging an amendment to the Immigration Law of 1884 so that none except "star" players could come to America as contract labor and perform on the native stage. So many actors had signed the AOF petition that the *Mirror* thought the total must have represented a majority of the native players. Noted, too, was that most newspapers were editorially opposed to the proposal. Part of the AOF's petition observed that all classes of wage earners, except actors, were granted legislative protection against foreign competition arriving as contract labor. With respect to that issue, the *Mirror* editor adopted something of a neutral stance and declared, "It all depends upon the actors themselves and in what light they regard, or are compelled by circumstances to regard, their vocation. If they view it as an art in whose temples they are votaries the very idea of employing legal protection jars. If they hold it as a trade they should enjoy every advantage which the law extends to other trades. There is the whole matter in a nutshell"[9]

A week later the *Mirror* abandoned any neutrality it may have previously shown to exclaim that the AOF was "only regarding the rights of the actor as a working man, somewhat oppressed by combinations, trusts, syndicates, foreign cheap labor, etc., etc., and puts itself on the plane of the shoemaker, the longshoreman and the rock blaster who, being weak in his skill individually, naturally looks for strength in association and cooperation." As far as the *Mirror* was concerned, though, any attempt by actors to form a union, or engage in union-style activities through a fraternal organization, was doomed. "But all attempts to regulate or improve or benefit the actor from the industrial point of view merely will be abortive, because the conditions of his labor do not permit of any such regulation," concluded the newspaper.[10]

One early and short-lived attempt to organize occurred in 1894 when 250 chorus girls of the Eldorado company's ballet then on the road in Illinois were said to have organized themselves into a union so they could act in concert "if a question concerning their salaries rises again...." No other details were provided.[11]

Chorus girls were regularly subjected to exploitation. One anonymous woman who got a chorus position in the production *Polly* a few years earlier, in 1885, had to sign her contract at the agency used by the manager who secured her services. She was to receive a salary of $20 a week. But at the end of the first week she found, to her dismay, that she *owed* the manager $9. There was an agency fee of $6, tights cost $7, shoes cost $6, and she was fined that week a total of $10. All actors (men and women) in this time period had to pay for all clothing items necessary for the play (except for period pieces, for which costumes were supplied). For example, if an actor appeared in a play wherein the character essayed wore several sets of evening clothes during the play, the actor had to buy them. Often an impoverished player did not have the requisite outfits at home in his closet, so it became a major burden. Of course, women were usually hit harder than males, since female characters tended to have more elaborate costumes and more frequent changes. Chorus girls (and boys) all had to buy their matching, uniform-style costumes and shoes, yet would probably have no use for them when the production ended.[12]

During September 1894 a report surfaced that a new organization, the Actors' Association of America, was then being formed by an actor named F. F. Mackay and one or two others. Sympathetic to the plight of actors, the *Mirror* editor commented, "That the condition of the rank and file of the profession is far from happy; that the business side of their existence is fraught with loss and hardship; that the means of earning a livelihood are becoming more precarious every season, are facts which no person familiar with the subject will dispute. Whether these and other evils of the actor's career at the present time can be removed by such an Association as Mr. Mackay proposes only time can determine." Noting that organizations for mutual strength and an improvement of conditions had proved successful among the industrial classes, the editor went on to muse, "Whether the stage is a field where individualism only controls the pecuniary and artistic relations of its followers, or whether the same benefits that the men of the trades enjoy from combination can be secured by actors, has not yet been established satisfactorily." Reportedly, the new organization was modeled on the existing Actors' Association in London, England.[13]

Slow getting started, the Association did not formally organize until sometime in 1896. Early that year it had about 100 actors enrolled, with Wright Huntingdon serving as interim President. The purpose of the organization was said to be to provide protection against both irresponsible managers and irresponsible actors.[14]

As of early May 1896 the group changed its name and officially became the Actors' Society of America (AS). One reason for its name change was reported to have been to avoid confusion with the Actors' Association of

Britain. By this date the group had over 600 active members. According to this account, "the chief aim of the society is to secure contracts for its members with responsible managers."[15]

One of the "cardinal principles" of the new organization was that none of its members would knowingly perform in a pirated play (pirated works in which unscrupulous managers staged productions without paying any author royalties were rampant and a major problem in this period). Somewhat optimistic about the AS, the editor of the *Mirror* felt that if it acted with care, fairness and deliberation it "may solve at least one vital question of the moment" as to irresponsible management and unconscientious actors. "In that aim it should receive the aid and cooperation of every manager in the country," continued the editor, "because the interests of reliable and well-meaning actors and of fair-dealing and respectable managers are identical...." Naively, the newspaper continued to argue — in the face of the increasing amounts of litigation it had often bemoaned, and in the face of increasing abuses of actors it had often documented — that the interests of the two sides were identical, despite that unions everywhere, in all industries, came into existence precisely because interests were diametrically opposed.[16]

When the AS held its first annual meeting in August 1896, it had nearly 1,000 members. Yearly dues were set at $3, and John Malone was its first elected president. In the previous few months the organization had been active in examining complaints, brought by either side, and had arbitrated many when both sides agreed to the method. Some of the cases were against managers, others were against actors; decisions sometimes favored the actor and sometimes favored the manager. Also by this time, the AS had produced a standard form of contract for use by members of the group in their dealings with managers. Use of such forms, of course, was purely voluntary on the part of management.[17]

As of November 1896, AS membership was still listed at 1,000. Notable was the fact that women as well as men were on the membership rolls, apparently as equal members. It was not uncommon for females to be barred from membership in such groups. According to the AS constitution, its objective was "to promote and improve the actor's calling and its conditions of mutual benefit, dramatic, artistic, economic, and social means." Still strongly behind the AS was the *Mirror*, which described the society as "one evidently destined to work powerfully for the future good of the native theater." Especially admired was what the publication described as its "moderate and conservative stance."[18]

Yet just a week later all that would start to change, as the *Mirror* and others suddenly became opposed to the group. It all began in that same month of November when the AS held a public meeting in New York City to explain what the organization was, what it stood for, and so on. It was a meeting open to anybody who was interested. One speaker was prominent actor James A. Herne, who told his listeners he wanted to offer a clear view of the labor question in general and how it related to the actor. He spoke about capital and labor and the myth that capital created labor. As he canvassed for actors to join the AS, he related that of those he contacted many said to him, "If we do this (that is, if we organize), we will antagonize the managers, and they will close their doors against us, and, indeed, refuse to employ persons who are members of our Society." Herne added, "The duty of this young Society is now to find out the cause which makes it necessary for actors to organize, and when they have found it, to strike boldly for its removal."[19]

After noting the AS had the "earnest and hearty countenance" of the *Mirror* from the start, the editor, based on the November public meeting, issued a warning that a critical moment in the history of the AS had been reached. It was a warning to take heed lest a wrong impression of its scope be given, "and by every means must it safeguard itself against influences that may insidiously hinder its plans and injure its prospects." Two things at that meeting particularly concerned the *Mirror*. One was a suggestion made for affiliation with the Musical Protective Union, in the form of an overture from that body. The second irritant were the views of Herne. "But the meeting of the Actors' Society was no place for socialistic propaganda or for a political harangue," explained the editor. "As individuals, actors may properly cherish and expound the ideas that appeal to them, but the Actors' Society of America has other subjects than socialism to consider and other business than politics in hand."[20]

As 1897 began, the AS made a formal declaration and protest against theatrical agents who recruited actors for productions that contained, unknown to the players when signed, immoral acts, indecencies, and so on. The AS promised it would extend every possible assistance to the police and district attorneys to suppress such examples of vice. All this was at a time when one of the periodic public and media campaigns to eradicate "filth in the house" was in full bloom. In the opinion of the *Mirror*, that was a "proper protest" for the AS to make, and it would "inspire new respect for that body."[21]

Internal dissension had hit the AS by 1897. Some wanted the group to be little more than a fraternal organization with occasional protests left to topics such as smut — something that did not and could not alter control within the theatrical industry, or threaten the distribution of power between capital and labor. Others wanted the AS to come out of the closet, admit it was indeed a union, and affiliate in a formal way with the organized labor movement. Said the *Mirror*, "It is now in the throes of an agitation, the results of which will fortify and strengthen it as a professional body or change it arbitrarily to an organization on the lines of trades-unionism." An even sterner warning was issued by the editor to the AS: "If it becomes an indistinguishable element among a mass of simple trades-unions, it will lose all character as an association that ought to uphold artistic ambition and purpose ... but must also yield sympathetic allegiance to and subordinate its own welfare to other merely mechanical organizations that have nothing in common with the profession of the stage."[22]

But having pointed out the abuses suffered by actors for so long, the editor apparently felt compelled to address the issue of how those were to be redressed, if not through the actions of a union. Vaguely he argued that the individuality that made the actor valuable would somehow correct those excesses "through the natural law of supply and demand" with a greater degree of probability than if the actor submerged his individuality to that "of a mere mechanic." Among other activities in which the AS was then engaged were the establishment of an employment bureau for actors, and enlisting the boards of health in various cities in a crusade against unclean and unsanitary dressing rooms in theaters.[23]

When the AS held its annual meeting in August 1898, Charles Le Barbier, Assistant District Attorney of New York County and AS counsel, told delegates that under the society's constitution and by-laws it could not possibly affiliate with a labor order. He expressed the personal opinion as the legal advisor of the society that such an affiliation would be detrimental to the best interest of the society. F. F. Mackay, an AS delegate who had been appointed to attend the convention of Stage Employees at Omaha, read his report. The AS had applied to the National Alliance of Stage Employees for a charter under the American Federation of Labor. That charter was refused to the Society after the National Alliance had considered the application and had voted on it. They advised the AS to apply directly to the American Federation of Labor for a charter.[24]

Division over the issue of whether or not to affiliate with organized labor so split the AS board and its members that membership in the group fell in 1898 to half of what it once had been. Finally, after being rejected by the Stage Employees, the AS returned to its original concept of being a fraternal organization, with some aspects of a business society concerned about its members and the acting profession in general. However, the AS would remain completely ineffective in regards to the basic and fundamental grievances of players. It settled into a program of moderate and peripheral reform, such as protests against smut productions and agitating for better conditions in dressing rooms. When it behaved that way it was supported by the likes of the *Mirror*, but never if it tried to function in a union-like fashion. Over time the AS became even less relevant. Its membership dropped and its influence decreased. A few more half-hearted and unsuccessful attempts were made later to obtain an AFL charter, but by 1912 the AS was effectively dead. While it lingered on until 1916 it was essentially supplanted by the formation of Actors' Equity in 1913.[25]

A news report from March 1900 revealed that a large cigar manufacturer had been struck by its 2,000 cigar makers, members of a radical American labor union, the Knights of Labor. Outside the mainstream of the organized labor movement, and not part of the AFL, it was soon to disappear entirely from the scene. During that strike, as time dragged, at strike headquarters someone suggested a communication be sent to the actors' branch of the union asking that some performers be sent to entertain the strikers. Apparently some vaudeville players were affiliated with the Knights of Labor, though probably only briefly.[26]

At the very end of the 1890s the issue of trusts received more and more media attention. Starting with its November 13, 1897, issue, and continuing for several months, the *Mirror* devoted a huge amount of coverage to the Theatrical Trust (Mark Klaw, Abraham Erlanger, and Al Hayman were among its principles). It was all intensely negative coverage, and the newspaper railed against the Trust with special supplements, each several pages long, in many of its issues. Outlets such as the *Mirror* opposed the Trust for different reasons than those registered by actors. Players worried about a smaller number of jobs available, about salaries being held down, about the Trust membership being more easily able to generate blacklists and enforce blacklists (because of information shared among its members), and so on. With respect to media outlets, combinations such as the Theatrical Trust often tried to control the press and muzzle critics by threatening to withdraw ads from any media outlet that offended it. Also, the existence of trusts worked against all other outsiders in the capitalist class, as it was harder for anyone else to break into the business. To greater or lesser extents, both groups worried that combinations in general reduced the number of plays available, thereby limiting culture access, and that trusts drove the quality of plays down, as the Theatrical Trust was much more likely to pander to the lowest common denominator.[27]

Thus, as the 19th century gave way to the 20th century, a major problem for actors was the centralization of theatrical management and how the players might deal with it. Several fraternal organizations and professional societies then existed for actors, but none were effective, and whatever little value they had in engaging in union-like activities became even more insignificant in the face of the trusts. Theatrical circuits began to appear as early as the 1870s, when groups of theaters in a particular area joined together to sign their attractions. Centralization in the industry moved further along with the creation of booking offices. The booking agent served as a middleman for hundreds of houses in arranging for players. Charles Frohman, along with his partner W. W. Randall, controlled the bookings for more than 300 houses in the 1880s. As a next step, the major booking agencies consolidated, forming the Theatrical Syndicate in 1896, "an organization that virtually monopolized the booking of first-class theatrical attractions in America," observed historian Benjamin McArthur. Six men, three sets of partners, made up that trust: Charles Frohman and Al Hayman; Abe Erlanger and Mark Klaw; and Samuel Nixon and J. Frederick Zimmerman. McArthur also remarked, "No theatrical institution has every been as vilified as was the trust."[28]

One early and short-lived act of resistance by actors to syndicate control came in 1898. Several players declared they would not deal with the trust, stating that their stand was for artistic control. However, the lure of big money offered by the syndicate caused most to quickly experience a change of heart. Richard Mansfield, for instance, was a very prominent actor and among the most energetic of the trust's foes; he was also among the first to defect after a big money offer was made to him. His defection demoralized other resisting actors who attempted to avoid all dealings with the Trust by appearing only in independent venues. One by one players such as Goodwin, O'Neill, and E. L. Davenport capitulated. Francis Wilson surrendered only after the syndicate blacklisted him and almost ruined his career. (But he would never lose the desire to organize or forget the importance of unions. Some 15 years later he emerged as the first president of Actors' Equity.) Only one major star held out against the syndicate during this brief period of rebellion. Mrs. Fiske (backed by her husband's newspaper, the *New York Dramatic Mirror*) quietly resisted the syndicate and steadfastly refused to play in any of its venues. Turning down lucrative offers from the Trust, she performed in second-class houses, dance halls, and on one occasion at a skating rink. Fiske's solitary stand only emphasized the lack of organization and the weakness of the players.[29]

Trying to deal with such situations through fraternal or business organizations in the acting community had not worked. If actors had difficulty in relating their situation to those of a mechanic or steelworker, there was a successful example closer to hand, and perhaps one they could more easily empathize with. Within the theatrical industry competition from contract musicians from Europe and from native military bands prodded musicians to form local associations, which in 1886 joined together to form the National League of Musicians (NLM). All theaters, be they legitimate, vaudeville, large, or small, had a house band that was an integral part of the performance and experience. They varied tremendously, of course, in size and scope. Like the AS, the NLM tried to combine the features of a professional or fraternal organization with some aspects of a trade union. And like the AS, the NLM discovered the two functions to be incompatible. When the American Federation of Musicians (AFM) organized in 1896 with an open and avowed trade union policy, the NLM withered and soon faded away. The AFM adopted a strict closed-shop policy and paid vigorous attention to practical issues to win gains for its members. Over time, the musicians of the AFM were repeatedly held up to actors as exemplars of protective action, as a model to follow in how to deal with the Theatrical Trust.[30]

Combinations in the theatrical industry continued. In May 1900 a news report surfaced that the heads of many of the major vaudeville circuits in various American cities had met in secret in New York to begin taking steps to form an alliance for "mutual protection" and to regulate the dates and salaries of performers. Managers, it was explained, were unhappy with what they considered to be the constant increase in performer salaries. The UBO was taking shape — the Theatrical Trust previously mentioned controlled the legitimate stage — and would soon control vaudeville. Finally, it was time for actors to organize into a true union. Still, those first steps were hesitant and tentative enough that the new organization would start its life by pretending to be something else — just another non-threatening fraternal society.[31]

3 | The White Rats
Emerge, 1900–1901

"The White Rats intend to make themselves felt in every city in
the country ... you can imagine what a fight we can make against
such managers as encroach on our rights."
— Edmund Day, secretary of the White Rats, 1901

"The Rats who struck will not be let into any of our places hereafter. Nor will they get their salaries for the week in which they
have made their kick."
— B. F. Keith, manager, 1901

"[The Rats are] not controlled by anarchists or agitators, but by
level-headed, God fearing men, who, knowing their cause is just
and right, intend to fight to the last ditch."
— George Fuller Golden, president of the White Rats, 1901

Early in May 1900, the managers of the principal variety theaters in the
U.S. established the Vaudeville Managers' Association (VMA), which later
evolved into the United Booking Offices of America (UBO). After one of
its early meetings it announced actors would be able to get 40 weeks of work
through the year, thanks to the size and booking capacity of the syndicate,
but that they would receive less pay per week. During this time it was customary for vaudeville to close for the summer (about 12 weeks), as, for one
thing, a lack of air-conditioning tended to discourage business. As well, the
VMA declared that outside agents (actors' independent agents) were to be
eliminated and acts booked directly through the VMA. Therefore, the agents'
old fee of 5 percent of the actors' salary would be collected by the VMA
instead. All of these changes in the industry caused enormous anger among

the players and led to a meeting of a small group of actors on a Sunday in June 1900 in New York City.[1]

On that day eight vaudeville players assembled in the café of the Parker House, according to George Fuller Golden, who led that meeting. They were: David Montgomery, Fred Stone, Sam Morton, Thomas Lewis, Sam J. Ryan, Mark Murphy, Golden, and James F. Dolan (Dolan actually was not present for the first meeting but attended all that followed and was therefore elevated by the others to being listed as one of the "original" eight). Golden also said, ignoring math difficulties, that David Craig and Charles Mason were among the eight who attended that first meeting but did not say why they did not become part of the official founding group. Perhaps they lost interest and attended no more meetings. It was a meeting held to find some way of combating the power of the VMA (headed by vaudeville's biggest names, B. F. Keith and E. F. Albee). Golden related what the Water Rats of London, England [a theatrical fraternal group], had done for him — how they had helped him out when he was on tour in Britain and found himself broke. A decision was made to adopt that name for the fledgling group, but with a variation. As there was some joking about Murphy's prematurely snow-white hair, the men called themselves the White Rats (WR). They were aware that the last word came out "star" when it was spelled backwards.[2]

The *Mirror* saw the Rats as a fairly innocuous group when the newspaper commented on its formation, at the end of June. It related that several well-known vaudeville artists had met and formed an organization to be known as the White Rats of America, modeled after the English group, "and the object is the promotion of good fellowship among the members." It continued the story by declaring, "An idea that gained ground, to the effect that the White Rats were organized to enable the performers to take a firm stand against the salary cuts of the new Association of Vaudeville Managers is declared by the members of the White Rats to be entirely erroneous. According to one of the members seen yesterday, the new club is purely a social organization." That account listed the names of 20 players supposedly at the founding meeting. Named were the original eight (including the absent Dolan), Mason (but not Craig), and 11 others: Harry Dillon, John Dillon, Nat Haines, William Robyns, Joe Pettingill, Edmund Hayes, Charles Grapewin, James J. Morton, Al Stinson, George W. Day, and Mark Sullivan. Still other accounts listed different people as being in attendance, and some even listed different dates for that founding meeting.[3]

Two weeks later the *Mirror* reprinted an article from another New York newspaper that compared the actors' responses in vaudeville and legitimate to the trusts formed by managers. Argued in the piece was that the vaudeville actors had set a brave example to their brethren in the legitimate branch of the profession. Recalled was the brief rebellion of 1898 wherein "there were a great many vociferous members of the profession who made grandiloquent statements as to what they would and would not do. To-day there is barely one member of the crowd brave enough, independent enough to stand out. All the others have been wheedled or whipped into the line — have become willing workers in the field of trust productions." Regarding the Rats, the piece said, "Just what these artistic trades union men intend to do is a little hazy yet," and, "they are acting upon the hypothesis that evils will appear, and are preparing to meet them." At the birth of the Rats the *Mirror* saw a harmless social group; the New York *Daily Sun* saw a trade union with potential.[4]

A full page ad placed by the Rats in the July 28, 1900, issue of the *Mirror* announced their existence, and stated their aims and objectives. That ad began, "The Society of Vaudeville Stars lately organized in New York City called The White Rats of America wish it understood by all to whom it may concern, that said society is a social order founded on the same principles of brotherly love as The Water Rats of London, England, and composed of vaudeville players who combine such excellence in their art as public entertainers, with such stable heart qualities as men, and such high standing as good fellows, that they may justly be called Stars from all points of view, 'Rats' being the word 'Star' spelled backwards." Having a desire to gain more respect for actors and to make the calling a more dignified one, the Rats hoped later to lobby Congress to have laws passed for the benefit of the profession. Members and potential members were expected to lead clean and moral lives, for the ad warned, "Knocking and scandal must be unknown in 'Ratland' and less than wholesome living could get a member expelled, or not admitted." Perhaps worried by what had happened to organizations in the past that came to be seen as behaving like unions (such as the AS), the Rats moved to set aside and put to rest any doubts about their agenda. "It cannot be too strongly impressed that we are not in any sense organized to fight or seriously consider any combination of Capital or form ourselves into a 'trust' of any kind for the purpose of incurring the enmity or displeasure of any person or persons connected with our profession or any other calling," reassured the ad. At the bottom of the advertisement were listed by name the 124 members in good standing, and the names of 45 others who had been unanimously passed and elected to White Rats' membership but were yet to be sworn in. Prominent names among the members included George M. Cohan, Lew Dockstader, Charles Aldrich, and Eddie Foy. Of course, publishing a list of members was not the wisest move, as it made it so much easier for managers to compile a blacklist and/or to harass.[5]

A packed house turned out on September 2, 1900, for the Rats' first testimonial benefit, held at the New York Theatre. Gross receipts totalled about $7,000, with much of that total coming from performers who paid premium prices for a seat to the event: comedy team Weber and Fields paid $300 for a box; Tony Pastor paid $25 for a seat; James J. Corbett shelled out $100; De Wolf Hopper handed over $50 for a seat.[6]

Like many unions of the era, the White Rats was both racist and sexist. Membership in its ranks was limited to white males only. That was a problem for the group because many women, of course, were involved in vaudeville, from superstars down to chorus women. Some of these females were part of acts involving men but many worked on their own, or with one or more other women. For years the Rats wrestled with the issue. In October 1900 a report was published that a number of vaudeville women had formed a society along the lines of the White Rats — calling themselves the Little Mice of America. A first meeting of that group reportedly was held at the residence of Sadie Cushman, of Cushman, Holcombe and Curtis. While a number of prominent vaudevillians were said to have already paid their dues, this group was apparently very short-lived.[7]

As of January 1901 the membership in the WR was over 500, and the organization's Board of Directors were considering the admission of female players to join as associate members. A week later it was reported the Rats had decided to admit women as members. Female members were to be known as "Ratlambs," with the first women already then admitted, including Lillian Russell, Jennie Yeamans, May Irwin, and Flo Irwin. All these women were said to have been chosen by unanimous vote. Some 200 membership applications from women were then on file. White Rats membership was then 508, and the group had $20,000 in the bank. However, that report was premature. Frank Lalor, secretary of the WR, declared a week after the above report surfaced that no method had been adopted by the Rats for the admission of women, but, "They will, however, eventually have nearly all the privileges at present enjoyed by the male members."[8]

As February 1901 began it was announced that, because of action taken at the most recent WR meeting, after June 24, 1901, no member of the organization would accept an engagement unless it was made through the White Rats Vaudeville Agency, their in-house booking agency or employment bureau. Said WR secretary Frank Lalor, "It is a strange thing that performers are the only class of professional people who are forced to pay for being allowed to work. As long as this is the case, and commissions must be paid, we feel that we ought to have the benefit of the custom. We are doing this to increase our revenues." Lalor then added a comment designed to ease managers' fears: "We are anxious to act in harmony with the managers, and we have no wish to antagonize them in any way. We don't intend to dictate salaries, as that is a matter that rests entirely between the manager and the performer; nor do we wish to interfere with bookings in any way." Membership then was reported as 568. What enraged the players was the 5 percent commission extracted by the VMA. Outside agents had not disappeared but continued to book their clients, at their request. As a result an act might have to pay 10 percent in commissions — 5 percent to each of two agents. During this time many players did not have an agent, handling booking themselves. They had to pay 5 percent to the VMA, whereas before they had no booking fees to pay. To make matters worse, the VMA demanded that some of the outside agents (whom they allowed to continue) pay half of their commission to the VMA for the privilege of booking their clients through the VMA office. Many of those agents then charged their clients 7.5 percent commission (in order to clear 5 percent for themselves). Thus, some players found themselves losing 12.5 percent of their salaries to commissions, whereas only a few weeks earlier it had been no more than 5 percent.[9]

When Epes W. Sargent, an editor with the trade publication *Variety* reported on the situation, he observed that the WR were patterned after London's Water Rats with the latter — in theory, if not always in practice — a social group and not a belligerent organization. Sargent explained that the WR "were also started with the idea of promoting sociability, but it soon developed into an organization to bring about needed reforms." As membership grew in 1900, a decision was made to make a show of power. A general rally was arranged for the middle of the summer in 1900, said the editor. Some members did attend, even cancelling bookings to be there, but other Rats scabbed and took up the cancelled time "and gave a black eye to the proceeding."[10]

Then suddenly on February 14, 1901, action was taken. Reporting on the activity in the *Washington Post* a journalist declared, "What is probably the most powerful organization of theatrical performers ever formed has recently attained eminence and influence with amazing strides." According to the journalist, the theatrical managers never realized what a "powerful association" was taking shape until the executive committee of the WR declared a boycott of the four vaudeville theaters in the Keith circuit, located in Philadelphia, New York, Providence, and Boston. Those houses were closed for nearly five hours, until the problem was adjusted, and, said the reporter "The settlement was a great victory for the White Rats, the managers surrendering unreservedly." By this time the WR had determined not only to fight the managers over salaries and conditions but to form vaudeville bills of their own. Ultimately they wanted to rent venues where they could run their bills. That is, they had it in mind to compete directly against the existing vaudeville circuits.[11]

Cause of the boycott was the single issue of the much despised 5 percent commission charged by the managers' trust. Notice was first served upon the Keith management that the commission had to be abolished. Receiving no reply, the executive committee ordered every WR member playing in a Keith house to leave the theater and await orders before returning. "The programmes at the four Keith houses were almost ruined, seven out of nine acts leaving in one case," remarked an observer. Almost instantly after the strike was put into effect the Rats received a request for a conference, and after several hours the objectionable commission was reportedly to be abolished. As a result, the WR notified players to return to work.[12]

Secretary of the VMA, P. B. Chase, of the Grand Opera House in Washington, D.C., did not believe the WR would last long. "The Association of Managers, of which I am secretary," he said, "has signed an ironclad agreement that if we cannot conduct our business without interference of the performers we employ, then we will convert our theaters into stock companies or combination houses, abandoning vaudeville." Chase added that his group was willing at first to relinquish the commission, but it would fight the Rats if they persisted in their announced policy that as of June 24 the Rats "will go on what may be called a general strike to force us to engage acts through the society, but we most emphatically will not agree to such a proposition."[13]

By then the Rats had booked one of their vaudeville bills to play in Washington for one night on March 3 at the Columbia Theater — in direct opposition to Chase's house. However, he claimed to not be worried because, "with 3,500 vaudeville acts in the business and only 600 of them in the White Rats Society, I think we can worry along without submitting to the arrogant terms of what is practically a labor union, organized not for protection, but for aggressive measures."[14]

In that brief strike of a few hours the manager of the New York house affected (the Union Square Theatre), managed to find a few substitute acts and kept the show going, according to the *Mirror*. However, the newspaper did admit that many acts did walk out, and, "In the other cities the houses were severely crippled and chaos reigned for several hours." When the conference was called that Thursday afternoon, managers in attendance included B. F. Keith, F. F. Proctor, and E. F. Albee. Five members of the Rats were in attendance, including Golden. With the temporary truce in place, performers returned, and Thursday night shows went normally (it was the Thursday afternoon performances that had been affected). On the following day, Friday, a final agreement was reached wherein the managers consented to remove the commission and book artists in the future without charge. One seemingly innocent and additional proviso was that a general meeting of the Eastern and Western managers would be held in New York on March 6, when the agreement would be officially ratified. (The VMA had two branches, Eastern and Western, one headquartered in New York, the other in Chicago. It was all one organization, but it divided itself into two parts for ease of administration. At the strike meeting only Eastern managers were in attendance, as only Eastern houses were affected.)[15]

George Fuller Golden said, just after the settlement was reached, "We gained our point, and there is not much need to add anything to that statement.... Any one who doubts the fact that actors can stand together, when necessary, has only to reflect on the unity of action that characterized the movement on Thursday." Golden added, "Our action was not in the nature of a strike. Our organization is very strong but we do not intend to take any stand that would seem to be arbitrary or unjust."[16]

At a jubilant WR meeting a few days later the members celebrated their victory, but already there were worries as a "large, comprehensive doubt" surfaced about the sincerity of the deal. Rumors circulated about discord between Eastern and Western members of the managers' association over the agreement. More ominously, a communication from the managers declared, "The commission business would be kept in force until June 3 anyhow."[17]

At the same time, the *Mirror* reprinted an article from the *Springfield* (Illinois) *Republican*, which enthused, "The combination movement on the part of theatrical managers, which has been the chief feature in American stage drift of late, has received its first check at the hands of the White Rats of America." According to the *Republican*'s assessment, "A year or two ago the vaudeville managers formed an association to keep down salaries ... and it came about that the commodity of vaudeville entertainment was largely controlled by syndicates." Then the managers established a booking agency "and compelled the performers to pay 5 percent of their salaries for the privilege of being given engagements, which were equivalent to a cut in salary."[18]

When the Springfield editor compared the situation in vaudeville with that in legitimate, he declared it to be "quite different," because the legitimate theater syndicate of managers was "all powerful," but no semblance of a protective organization existed for actors. All the well-known players in legitimate, with the exception of two — Mrs. Fiske, who had fought the Trust for years, and newly emergent independent star Henrietta Crosman — "are completely dominated by the syndicate of theater managers." Superstar Sarah Bernhardt, one of those under the control of the syndicate, in the view of the editor, remarked on Trust control: "I think it is abominable, and all honor is due to those who fight it, as it seems to me it is a direct menace to the drama, destroying personal freedom of action, without which art cannot exist. Such a thing would not be permitted in France. It would be absolutely impossible. If it is persisted in here it must affect the future of the drama in this country."[19]

Edmund Day, secretary of the WR board of directors, arrived in Washington on February 22 in connection with the engagement of the White Rats' Vaudeville Company, scheduled to play at the Columbia Theatre on March 3. Said Day, "The White Rats intend to make themselves felt in every city in the country, and as we have among our members more than three-fourths of the vaudeville stars of the country, you can imagine what a fight we can make against such managers as encroach on our rights." Day added that one of the objectives of the group was to band players together to assist each other. One of the WR goals was to establish homes for actors without funds at the end of their careers. To raise money for such goals, the WR meant to put on the road companies it controlled, with the effort slated for the Columbia being the first such production. Players on that bill included George Fuller Golden, James J. Corbett, Bonnie Thornton, Casedo the wire king, Alice Shaw, the Dillon Brothers, and several others. "The White Rats and the ladies branch, known as the White Mice, are so well organized that we can make it uncomfortable for such managements as do not accede to our reasonable demands," declared Day.[20]

Back on February 14, when the WR had launched its boycott — members involved did not actually refuse to report for work; rather, they all called in sick — Albee was informed there would be no show the following day unless conditions were adjusted and that the performers might be sick for a very long time. At the meeting later that day Albee said he was powerless to abolish commissions until the Eastern and Western managers met on March 6. He did promise that commissions would be abolished, though, at that meeting. Also promised by Albee was that until the March 6 meeting no more commissions would be deducted. But the managers refused to sign a written agreement to that effect, although the WR requested they do so. All the managers were prepared to give was their word.[21]

In the days after February 14 commissions continued to be deducted by the VMA exactly as before. Despite the fact the WR sent representatives to the managers asking them to honor the understanding, the managers refused to keep their word. On February 21 organizers for the WR were sent to the principal cities east of Chicago to issue a strike notice for that day. Many White Rats failed to appear on vaudeville stages that day in the East or Middle West.[22]

With the strike one day old, Golden stated, "Our object is to down those managers who are getting rich by using us. Before long there won't be any Association of Vaudeville Managers at all, for we are going to run our own shows from now on and ruin them." The Rats would organize vaudeville shows all over the U.S., he promised. J. Austin Fynes, press agent for the Proctor circuit, said the strike of Rats had not hurt his chain: "We are not having a bit of trouble. Already we've had 200 applications for jobs today...." B. F. Keith thundered, "The Rats who struck will not be let into any of our places hereafter. Nor will they get their salaries for the week in which they have made their kick. They can sue as much as they like. They have broken contracts and the law is with us." Fynes added, "Why, we make money by the disturbances. For instance, the amount I owed the strikers for their services this week in our theaters was about $9,000. The expenses incidental to the fuss will, of course, not be that much, so you can see that we come out ahead on the deal."[23]

On February 23 the VMA said the total number of acts that struck venues, both Rat members and Rat sympathizers, amounted to 80, with 60 of those acts being in New York City. According to Mr. Hennessey, VMA secretary, in preparation for such action the VMA had prepared a total of 523 substitute acts, assembled them, and had them ready and waiting to be sent to any venue short of performers, if and when it was necessary. But things were not as the managers wanted people to believe.[24]

Like the brief strike earlier in February, the one started on February 21 also began on a Thursday afternoon. It affected no less than 23 vaudeville houses in the East. And, also like the earlier action, this one was not officially a strike but another "sick-out." All WR members who chose to follow the call booked in sick. A few houses had to close and dismiss audiences, being unable to round up sufficient talent on short notice. Among them were Keith's theaters in Boston, Philadelphia and Providence; Proctor's in Albany;

Lothrop's in Boston; Well's in Richmond and Norfolk; Shea's in Buffalo; Ehrick's in Cleveland; and others in Syracuse, Pittsburgh and Atlanta. Effects on New York City houses were as follows: Proctor's venues — Fifty-Eighth Street Theatre (seven acts out); Twenty-Third Street Theatre (six); One Hundred and Twenty-Fifth Street Theatre (10); Fifth Avenue Theatre (six); Keith's Union Square Theatre (nine); Percy Williams Orpheum in Brooklyn (five); Hyde and Behman's (seven); and Percy Williams Novelty Theatre (four).[25]

Meanwhile, at the VMA office, a mad scramble was underway, with an estimated 25 messenger boys kept constantly busy to scrounge up possible talent and hustle them to a stage door. "Performers who had been turned down time after time by the managers were now implored to come and play," said a reporter. One young woman who had produced a sketch two years earlier but bombed with it on stage and never got near a theater since "had no fewer than four appealing offers within as many hours." Some bizarre programs were presented that day, continued the journalist. Bills that "brought wonder and consternation to the audiences. All sorts and conditions of queer unprograms were projected upon the amazed public.... The substitutes were arriving in cabs and automobiles and dashing out on the stage without even time to speak to the piano player about the music." And, "Young men who for years have done naught mightier than to dazzle the Y.M.C.A. circuit with primitive feats of legerdemain, suddenly found themselves thrust into the best places in the bills of great metropolitan theaters. It was a strange day." Fuming with rage, B. F. Keith told a reporter, "All this trouble has been caused by agitators, irresponsible persons who are unable to get good work to do themselves...." It was also observed that "Some managers announced that none of the actors who had struck would ever again work in their theaters."[26]

Golden again told the media the 5 percent commission extracted by the managers was "nothing short of robbery." But he also pointed out the players had other grievances. In his view the contracts used by the managers were not equitable, as they gave the managers the right to cancel the players' engagements without giving them the same right. Also, the manager could cancel a player's engagement if he personally did not like the performance, or on a whim. Players and acts were all well-known before they were booked, and for that reason, Golden argued, contracts should stand unless cancelled by mutual consent. Trying again to downplay any radical image, Golden explained of the WR organization: "It is not controlled by anarchists or agitators, but by level-headed, God fearing men, who, knowing their cause is just and right, intend to fight to the last ditch."[27]

As the strike continued, independent theaters in various cities were offered to the WR rent free for weeks so they could put on their own bills. The Rats did engage the Academy of Music in New York City for 10 Sundays to hold benefit shows. On Sunday February 24 the first benefit was held there; it played to a packed house and grossed nearly $10,000 (much of that came from people again paying a voluntary premium for their ticket). Players on the bill included Maurice Barrymore, Weber and Fields, and De Wolf Hopper. Maurice Barrymore had been an active supporter of the Rats, even prior to the strike and going back to the group's formation. He wrote letters on behalf of the WR, made speeches at their rallies, and composed messages for their circulars.[28]

A reporter who covered that benefit remarked that the 5 percent commission was the only visible issue in the strike, but he speculated the strike might also be directed against the VMA itself and that it might end only with the annihilation either of the Trust or of the Rats. He felt that idea was brought out forcefully at the Academy benefit by Golden in his speech there to the audience. In that oration Golden said he knew the managers would be forced to abandon the commission, but there was an issue involved that went deeper and was more far reaching. That issue, said Golden, was the "dictatorial power" the syndicate would have if it was allowed to continue.[29]

With respect to the managers' explanation of the troubles, a reporter for the *Mirror* remarked, "The managers neglect to state, however, that the White Rats did not organize until the Managers' Association was formed.... The managers have repeatedly denied that reduction of salaries were contemplated when they came together, but the evidence has not been overwhelmingly in support of this denial." In an ad explaining its position, the VMA declared:

> By their action in wilfully breaking their existing contracts, and attempting to prevent the Managers from serving the public, by going on strike without notice on Thursday, Feb. 21, the White Rats have openly and wilfully violated the above agreement [to wait until the March 6 meeting] and in consequence we wish to publicly announce that we will have no further dealing with the White Rats as an organization, nor will any of the undersigned managers accept any contracts other than those made through the offices of the Association of Vaudeville Managers.... We will deal with individuals only....

That ad was signed by the full membership of the VMA: Benjamin F. Keith, Frederick F. Proctor, Max C. Anderson, George Lothrop, Hurtig and Seamon, M. Meyerfield Jr., George Middleton, Charles E. Kohl, Enoh W. Wiggins, J. H. Moore, Michael Shea, Louis Behman, John D. Hopkins,

Louis M. Ehrick, John J. Murdock, John K. Burke, Edward F. Albee, Antonio Pastor, Plimpton B. Chase, Jake Wells, R. Coley Anderson, Lee Shubert, P. F. Shea, and Percy G. Williams.[30]

When the editor of the *Mirror* analyzed the strike after its first couple of days he concluded that if it was right for the managers to organize for their own protection it was certainly right for the performers to organize for a similar purpose. He concluded there would have been no performers' organization "if the managers had not made such an organization necessary by their own combination. As it is, the performers soon found that the managers' organization was inimical to the performers' interests, and were forced as a measure of self preservation to combine as they did combine." Still, it was the opinion of the *Mirror* editor that combinations were "the curse" of the American theatre:

> The chief combination, the Theatrical Trust, which all who have the best interests of the stage at heart abhor, is the father of all these troubles. No combination in theatricals is necessary for any legitimate purpose. But if there be any combination to be commended it is that of actors or performers in self defense against the aggressions of those wholly concerned in the theater's material interests.[31]

As the strike dragged on over the following two weeks, not much happened. Rats on strike remained out while the venues continued to use substitute acts. The trade publication *Billboard* commented that if the sympathies of the public were with one particular side, they had not yet become obvious. The editor of *Billboard* declared he looked on the struggle "with complacency and absolute impartiality. It is a fight apparently to the bitter end." But he understood where the power and the money rested, and concluded, "The managers have the money and the theaters, and that is a wonderful advantage. If the White Rats should succeed in their struggle for what they believe to be a vital principle, it will be a famous victory."[32]

After an all day meeting on March 6, the strike was settled, with the managers agreeing to abolish the 5 percent commission — or so they said. After disposing of that point the managers had to decide what attitude they should take toward the players who had walked out. It was decided that since they believed the strikers had, generally, been deceived and misled by a few men, in the future the VMA would deal with each individual on his merits and treat him "fairly and justly." Also decided was that under no circumstances would the VMA recognize the White Rats as the performers' union. That is, acts would be booked individually on the VMA's contract forms. No bookings would be made through the Rats' booking office, the one proposed to start in June.[33]

Striking Rats were busy getting back to their circuits on March 7. Managers reiterated that day that by abolishing commissions the day before, the VMA had kept its promise and that even though the players had acted in bad faith in going on strike, all would be forgiven. An unnamed WR officer commented, "All contracts must be made between the actor himself and the manager. We do not wish to be recognized as a labor union. Our mission as an organization is that of a benevolent society."[34]

At the end of the strike Willard Holcomb, a reporter for the *Washington Post,* declared, "The latest phase of the vaudeville war is apparently a victory for the White Rats." The players in the union were inclined to agree, but the passage of time would put a different conclusion to the episode.[35]

Not long after the strike ended the WR took out a full page ad in *Billboard* that was addressed to managers of all outdoor enterprises, such as carnivals and circuses, listing some of their members (those with specialty acts, such as acrobats and jugglers). It was meant to be a reminder to those managers to book those acts through the WR's own booking agency for the coming summer season. But soon thereafter that in-house booking agency was closed for lack of business. Any idea the Rats had of sending their own vaudeville bills on the road to compete directly against the Trust houses was also dropped.[36]

Before the month of March 1901 ended the WR learned, it was reported, "that certain minor managers of the association were disregarding the managers' concession of five percent commission."[37]

Writing five years after the strike, *Variety* editor Epes Sargent offered a bleak assessment of the strike. "Within three months every promise made by the managers had been broken, and the sole lasting result of the strike was that certain artists were marked as anarchists and some of them even yet feel the effects of their partisanship." Sargent was not impressed with the action of the WR executives during the strike, feeling they had bungled and lost the strike because they had gotten carried away by the turmoil and the excitement of their own speechmaking.[38]

Many years later, historians Armond Fields and L. Marc Fields said that as soon as the strike ended and the players returned to work, "Albee continued to tempt actors away from the White Rats with long-term contracts, targeting those he knew to be financially pressed or habitually scared of being blacklisted. Many of the new contracts included a five percent commission for booking. By the end of the [1901] season Albee's crafty behind-the-scenes maneuvering reduced the White Rats to token opposition."[39]

In their book, Abel Green and Joe Laurie Jr. remarked there was little

unity or courage within the WR, and what little existed was quickly dis-
solved when the WR leaders were sent on long and distant tours after the
strike. "Many of the leaders, including [Dave] Montgomery and [Fred] Stone,
were blackballed forever in vaudeville, to the gain of the legitimate stage.
Others, like George Fuller Golden, who was the real leader of the Rats, were
kept out of every Keith-Albee house until seven years after the first strike."[40]

In a different book, Laurie declared the strike was a bust because many
of the players double-crossed each other. While some turned down lucrative tour offers to stay on strike, other players took up the offers and went
out on tour, further weakening the Rats. Because the WR had not achieved
a union shop out of the strike, or for that matter even achieved recognition,
very quickly over time they surrendered individually what they had won collectively.[41]

George Fuller Golden surrendered the presidency of the WR around
1902. He hailed from Alabaster, Michigan, and at the age of 12, while living at Bay City, Michigan, he and James F. Dolan ran away from home and
started performing, doing sketches in the South. The pair separated, but after
several years of hardship they reunited in Chicago. Once again, though, they
split up, with Golden working for the next four years or more with other
partners. At one point he went to England with Cliff Ryland as his partner.
Golden remained abroad for four years, working as a single for the last two
years. It was during that time that he became acquainted with the Water
Rats of London. When he returned to America in 1895 he soon became one
of the country's most popular monologue artists, with his services being in
constant demand.[42]

One of the reasons Golden removed himself from playing an active role
in the WR was his failing health. Golden died on February 17, 1912, of tuber-
culosis at his home in Los Angeles. An obituary in *Variety* described him as
"probably the best known and most beloved actor who ever appeared in
vaudeville." Noted was the fact he had founded the WR and gave up a prosperous stage career for several years to devote himself "to benefiting the conditions of variety players with rare and unqualified selflessness, and was alone
responsible for the fundamental principles on which the order of White Rats
is based." With regard to his activities in the 1901 strike, the obituary
remarked, "Mr. Golden, then the moving spirit among the artists, was pronounced 'wild' in his views, and his opinions were set down by managers as
impossible and impracticable, but even the same managers have since admitted the White Rats in those troublesome days had a victory within their
hands, but didn't know it, although Mr. Golden undoubtedly did."[43]

By the end of 1901 the White Rats' challenges to the Trust had been beaten back; the organization was weakened, directionless and dispirited. Membership in the organization dropped dramatically. It was business as usual for the Trust. Union activity by actors entered a period of decline and stagnation.

4 | Years of Stagnation, 1902–1907

"A lot of men and women who are on the stage won't join a union because they think it lowers their dignity."
— Joseph Lawrence, Actors' National Protective Union president, 1905

"The time is coming when the artist will either be organized or beaten without a fight. It remains for the artist to decide which condition it shall be."
— Epes Sargent, editor, *Variety*, 1906

"American artists are too mercurial; possess too much the artistic temperament to bring to a successful conclusion an organization of artists alone."
— Percy Williams, manager, 1906

While the White Rats declined dramatically in this period, there was a small amount of union activity in other areas, but it did not amount to much. The Actors' Society (AS) remained on the scene and reportedly had 1,548 members in June 1902, the largest total in its history. Yet it did little outside of its self-imposed mandate to work on such items as the problem of unsanitary dressing rooms. During its most recent fiscal year it had received 119 complaints on that topic, all of which were referred to the relevant Boards of Health.[1]

Chorus women occasionally tried to organize a union, but had no success. Three young women, members of the chorus in *The Chaperons*, called on American Federation of Labor president Samuel Gompers in Cincinnati in March 1902 to ask his cooperation in their efforts to organize a chorus girls' protective association. They told him their work-related troubles, and Gompers assured them that if they succeeded in organizing, their association would be supported by the AFL. However, he extended them no real help of any kind.[2]

Three months later a delegation of chorus women in Chicago called on Lee Hart, secretary of the National Alliance of Theatrical Stage Employees, at his Chicago office and asked him to help them organize. They wanted to be in a position to demand $25 a week instead of the $10 to $18 a week they then received. As well, they wanted to be paid 50 cents extra for each rehearsal; they were then paid nothing for rehearsals. Hart said he would do what he could.[3]

One actors' organization that did surface at this time was the Actors' National Protective Union (ANPU). It had actually been formed as the Actors' Protective Union in May 1894. On January 4, 1896, the American Federation of Labor (itself founded in December 1886) granted the first actors' union charter to the ANPU. Yet the organization was so low-profile that it apparently did not surface in the media until about 1903. ANPU membership was likely fairly small and did not seem to include any well-known names in the acting profession. Apparently it did not organize any performers who played the first-class vaudeville circuits. That is, it was never involved with the Trusts. It would be merged into the White Rats in 1910. Although it was a small organization, it definitely functioned as a union. A number of vaudeville performers employed at Rob's Casino in North Beach, Long Island, went on strike in June 1903 because a woman who was prominent in the media then in connection with a famous murder case was booked on the bill. (It was not uncommon for people who were notorious for being notorious to appear on vaudeville bills. People such as those, or sports personalities, without the usual talents, were known in the trade derisively as "freak acts." Regular performers generally deeply resented freak acts.) James L. Barry, an executive with the ANPU, warned management that if the woman in question appeared, the others would walk out. When management refused to remove the freak act some artists did walk out.[4]

One year later a number of vaudeville performers who played the 10-cent circuit (less than first-class) in the West established a branch of the ANPU in Seattle. It was organized on July 11, with Samuel Wheeler as president. Two days later the Seattle branch (No. 11) became affiliated with the Western Central Labor Union. It was planned to ask the managers to employ only members of the union in good standing, and if none were available then to hire non-union acts, provided such performers applied immediately for membership.[5]

At the beginning of 1905 Joseph M. Lawrence was listed as the ANPU national president, with Harry De Veaux president of ANPU Local No. 1 (New York — its biggest branch). A mass meeting was held in New York under the auspices of the ANPU for the purpose of interesting everybody connected with the profession in the enforcement of the Employment Agency law. That statute had been passed at the last session of the New York State legislature and was designed to curb abuses committed against actors by among others, agents.[6]

That meeting was attended by representatives of many labor groups, such as the AFL, the Central Federated Union, the AS, the WR, and the American Federation of Musicians, among others. Every speaker, incidentally, advocated unionizing the stage. Such sentiments prompted Lawrence to tell the assembly, "A lot of men and women who are on the stage won't join a union because they think it lowers their dignity. They say they don't want to be classed as cooks and washerwomen. 'We are artists,' they say. They are, in their own estimation, but many a laboring man and woman is better off than are the members of our calling."[7]

The chorus of the New York Metropolitan Opera presented Heinrich Conreid, president and managing director of the company, with the demands of the chorus union in December 1905. Officially it was Local No. 14 of the ANPU. Chorus members wanted $25 a week in salary, and requested that rehearsals be limited to no more than two per day, totalling no more than four hours. Further, rehearsals would be held for a maximum of two weeks before opening a new production, and chorus members were to receive a salary of $12.50 a week during that rehearsal period (then unpaid, rehearsals could last indefinitely). Among other demands were that the maximum number of performances per week be five (Sundays excluded). Besides no pay for rehearsals, chorus members received a salary as low as $15 a week for performances.[8]

Conreid responded by stalling for months and refusing all demands. Finally, all contracts of the chorus members expired on April 8, 1906, at the end of the season. Then he told all the chorus people to call at his office in 10 days time to sign contracts for the next season. While he claimed he was happy with his chorus and would re-sign all, he insisted he and he alone would set all conditions of employment. As those people began to turn up at the office, the staff claimed to know nothing of the new contracts — Conreid had suddenly gone to Europe. Soon thereafter officials of a German chorus union sent G. E. Marchand, ANPU secretary, an ad from a German newspaper for chorus members. Conreid had gone abroad and recruited an entirely new chorus for the Metropolitan Opera Company.[9]

Vaudeville artists in Philadelphia formed Local No. 6 of the ANPU at the end of 1906; it was called the Association of Vaudeville Artists of Philadelphia.[10]

ANPU locals established in several Eastern cities were said to have prospered sufficiently enough that ANPU general organizer Ed Howard was sent to the West in early 1907 to organize more locals. Howard was slated to go to Chicago first and then on to Western cities, including San Francisco, where it was hoped he could re-establish the local there, whose charter had been revoked for reasons not stated. It was a trip expected to last four months.[11]

Later in 1907 the ANPU was in the midst of preparing a campaign for further amendments to the Employment Agency law of New York State. Details were not given, but a bill containing amendments was expected to be presented at the next sitting of the Legislature. At that time the ANPU had some 40 locals, with the new St. Louis local (then six weeks old) having 400 members. It drew its membership from acts playing the "smaller circuits" in the Middle West. The ANPU had supplied vaudeville talent for eight strike benefit performances given for the locked out telegraphers. Players donated their services, with their expenses paid by the ANPU.[12]

When the AFL held its annual convention in November 1907 at Norfolk, Virginia, the position of the ANPU as a labor organization was strengthened further with the passage of the resolution that follows:

Resolved, that it is hereby conceded that all parts of a theatrical production occurring behind the footlights and in front of the scenery after same has been placed in position by the stage mechanics, the same being specialties, acts, illusions, acrobats and any and all form of entertainment presented as such in any theater, music hall, circus, fair ground or park in which any form of entertainment is produced, shall be under the jurisdiction of the Actors' National Protective Union.

That made it impossible for the AFL to grant a charter to any rival actors' union that wanted to affiliate with the AFL. Such a union would be unable to affiliate directly with organized labor; rather it would have to receive its charter from the ANPU.[13]

Vaudeville artists were arranged in several classes of performers. One class contained those whose talent was limited to the extent that they only played their hometown and its immediate area. They worked more sporadically than first-class performers because the local audience got tired of seeing them, so they had to sit out for a time every now and then. Such acts and performers rarely appeared at the major venues; they never would have played on the same bill as a George Fuller Golden, for example. Nor was their talent enough to support the higher salary they would need to go on the road and pay transportation costs and room and board. Likely, these were the people the ANPU mostly recruited from, which perhaps explained why the union got so little attention. Also, it was organized inappropriately for an actors' union. For example, it made no sense for a local to be in Boston, or Detroit, or Seattle unless the members mostly worked there. An actors' union that tried to appeal to the first rank of players, who were all on the road for much of the year, needed to structure itself like the Rats did, just one union and no locals. Of course, that did not preclude the Rats from having offices in cities outside of New York, but they were not locals.

On June 2, 1906, the Comedy Club was formed. It was to be composed of the comedy acts of vaudeville, and reportedly had 50 such acts as members at the time of formation. Will M. Cressy was chosen president of the group whose purpose was the protection of its members — social, fraternal, and protective. Cressy explained its philosophy by saying, "It is for the benefit and protection of members. For the gaining of an equitable contract between the manager and the artist.... No 'down with the managers' or strikes. It is strictly a mutual benefit scheme. For our protection and the manager." By way of elaboration, Cressy continued, "Vaudeville today is a different proposition from fifteen years ago. The artists are of a different calibre. They are business people now, capable of doing business with businessmen in a businesslike way. No labor union idea prevails. Any concession that may be won by a strike may be won without one." Speaking of the problems players faced in vaudeville, Cressy added, "Playing six days in one theater and then paying carfare and baggage transportation to give a gratuitous performance in another [on a Sunday] is not right and is going to result in trouble. Canceling acts on Fridays and Saturdays before the following opening Monday is another wrong to right. It can all be remedied in fifteen minutes by proper representatives, without trouble or strike, when a reliable organization is had."[14]

Soon after formation, the group changed its name to Vaudeville Comedy Club (VCC). The idea for the group was credited to Louis Simon, of Simon and Gardner. Around that time a merger of the Keith-Proctor-Poli vaudeville circuits had caused considerable anxiety among the players — and agitation by many players to organize for their own protection. Simon concluded it would not be practical for an attempt to be made to enlist artists indiscriminately at short notice, and hit upon a society composed of comedy acts only. Discussion of Simon's scheme followed and led to the June 2,

1906, formation meeting held at the Empire Hotel in New York City. Carleton Macy suggested the name "Comedy Club," but the similarity of the title to the name of another group caused the name change. As its first anniversary neared, its membership was said to be almost 400, including the most prominent stage comedians.[15]

At the same time, the *Mirror* declared VCC membership to be 350. Reviewing the group's first year the publication remarked that the VCC's first efforts were directed at protecting players' material, as piracy in vaudeville was then rife and a major problem for many of the artists. Reportedly, the VCC then had an agreement with virtually every house in America that, upon notification from the VCC, when an act belonging to one of its members was being pirated by a person not entitled to it, the manager would refuse to allow the pirate to perform the stolen material in any of his houses. "One year ago the cheaper vaudeville houses of the West were full of people giving stolen versions of Eastern successes," explained the account. "At one time there were seven different acts presenting Dida [material], three were presenting Filson and Errol's 'Tip of the Derby,' three of Cressy and Dayne's acts were being pirated."[16]

The next matter taken up by the VCC was the issue of fair, binding contracts. According to the account, "Up to this time every manager had his own form of agreement. This agreement ran all the way from Mike Shea's one-line contract, stating, 'you are engaged for the week of Feb. 1, at Shea's Theatre, Buffalo,' to F. F. Proctor's two solid pages of rules, regulations, bylaws and items.... If the manager found another act that he liked better he thought nothing of cancelling at twenty-four hours' notice." After negotiations, a contract between the VCC and UBO was drafted and accepted. The *Mirror* liked the VCC because it was "conservative, not militant, and insisted actors live up to their contracts as vigorously as management was required to." With respect to those contracts it was said that binding arbitration was used to settle all disputes.[17]

Whatever effectiveness the VCC had in its union-like activities was quickly eliminated, however. Writing in *Variety* in 1913 a journalist remarked, "The Comedy Club admitted lay members a few years ago and since that time has been dominated by the outside influence, which has practically been in control of the club, originally organized for the protection of the actor. The footing gained by the outsiders has been working for the benefit of the big time vaudeville managers, two of whom are even now on the Comedy Club's Board of Control, the last place in the world where they belong." Any attempts made to restore the VCC to its original function as an aid to the artist had been blocked "by the members in it who are not actors but apparently command control."[18]

Meanwhile, the White Rats went into a precipitous decline in the period from 1902 to 1905, with one account claiming membership had fallen to 63 at the beginning of 1904, and with the group having a debt of $17,000. Another account declared that membership dwindled to 28 men in 1905.[19]

While the actors had no real, effective union in this period, it did not mean problems for players had lessened. The VMA grew in strength, and in 1906 Percy Williams and S. Z. Poli, after pressure was brought to bear on them, added their circuits to the combination; then the United Booking Offices came into being. This was not just a renaming of the then defunct VMA, but a restructuring as well, as the Trust, or UBO, was even bigger. The lack of a union and the persistent abuses of actors caused *Variety* to launch a campaign in 1906 on its editorial pages that would last about half the year. It was a campaign that urged the players to organize. It started with a brief message on the editorial page of the January 20, 1906, issue. Set off in a distinctive box, in large type, the message declared, "To the Vaudeville Artists of America: *Variety* has received numberless complaints in reference to the pernicious evils now existing in vaudeville detrimental to the interests of the artists. We suggest the advisability of all artists whenever assembled discussing the formation of an organization embracing the artists of America for mutual self-protection and co-operation.[20]

A month later Epes W. Sargent began the first in a long series of editorials, almost weekly for many months, urging vaudeville performers to unionize. Explained Sargent, "Ever since its initial issue *Variety* has urged upon the vaudeville artists the need of an organization." He added, "It is true that there is at present an organization known as the Associated Vaudeville Artists of America [the ANPU], a large but quiescent body, but what is needed is a society along somewhat different lines." Sargent did not name the White Rats as an existing union, which it was, but did go on in his editorial to detail the "fiasco" of the 1901 strike.[21]

One week later Sime J. Silverman, the head of *Variety,* penned the editorial; he and Sargent would take turns. Following on Sargent's piece, he remarked, "The White Rats as a body is still in existence, and although that should be the logical society to be enlarged and become the permanent organization of the artists, the present principles governing the leaders forbid it. The policy of the Rats has been changed since the strike. It is no longer aggressive, but passive, and the moving spirits believe in 'headliners' only." He added, "The White Rats to-day is a benefit order conducted more on social than business principles in so far as the welfare of the artists at large is concerned." Nor did he have anything good to say about the ANPU, which "is allied with a labor union and there have been so many rumors in the past regarding the management that it is out of the question." Silverman argued that the vaudeville artists needed an organization that was thoroughly independent, acting under its own orders solely, and not subject to any control other than that appointed by the members. That is, he did not want to see it affiliated in any way with the organized labor movement.[22]

In the following week Sargent returned to argue that perhaps nothing had contributed so greatly to the need for an organization of artists as the booking system then in force. "The methods now employed are manifestly unfair to the artist, and in the general trend toward concentration the artists sees his greatest menace ... and especially to be condemned is the practice of managers combining to book acts through a central office for the purpose of deducting five percent from the artist's salary." Because of combinations, said the editor, an act in trouble with one chain could not so easily book with another circuit. As well, those combinations exerted downward pressure on salaries. He concluded, "The time is coming when the artist will either be organized or beaten without a fight. It remains for the artist to decide which combination it shall be."[23]

Silverman returned the next week to discuss difficulties players had with the contracts they signed. "With two or three exceptions they [managers] have no regard whatsoever for their written signature engaging an artist for a stated period, and contracts in this country today amount to no more than so much waste paper. No artist expecting future engagements gives any thought to enforcing a written agreement...." But, he felt, with a proper organization, that could be remedied by having the name of any manager who failed to live up to his contracts posted among the artists, who would then, presumably, boycott the offending manager. "The present contracts amount to so much data or memoranda of where the artist is expected to appear. No artist cares to bring suit on any ground, for he would stand alone." Despite the obvious need for an organization, Silverman expressed doubts as to the practicality of the artists in America organizing. That was mainly because they were constantly traveling, and relatively few of them, out of the total, were ever in the same place at the same time.[24]

When Sargent returned, he said the best solution to the organization question might be in the formation in the U.S. of a branch of the International Artisten Loge (IAL) of Berlin, if such an arrangement could be made. Twice, he said, an effort had been made to induce the IAL to establish a branch in America, but the IAL had decided the idea was not wise. The IAL was founded to overcome contract and other abuses in German theaters, said to have worse conditions than those found in U.S. houses. Reportedly it had been fairly successful in achieving that goal.[25]

In yet another of his editorials, Sargent detailed what he saw as another problem in getting the players organized. "The great trouble is that there is no one who appears to be willing to come to the front and take upon himself the burden of forming the society with a possible chance of failure and blacklisting by the managers.... All that is needed is a leader. Who will it be?"[26]

In his editorial of April 28, 1906, Sargent presented the views of Percy Williams, owner of the Williams circuit, with venues in Greater New York, and a member of the UBO Trust. He said, "American artists are too mercurial; possess too much the artistic temperament to bring to a successful conclusion an organization of artists alone. The German and most of the other Continental artists are business men as well as performers, the American for the greater part is merely the artist...." So Williams wanted artists, managers and businessmen in any organization. With those three groups in an organization, Williams continued, "conflict between the artistic and business ends would be entirely avoided.... More than all this, it would bring into a fraternal relationship the employer and employee, both of whom are merely servants of the public, and rightly run such an organization would be of incalculable advantage to all concerned."[27]

By May 1906 Silverman began to have second thoughts as he entertained the possibility that the WR could be the organization he so much wanted to develop. What led him to entertain such a thought was that he had heard the Rats had shifted direction and were prepared to equally welcome all variety players into its group, and not just concentrate on headliners, as he believed they once had done.[28]

A few weeks later Silverman argued that the B. F. Keith vaudeville organization [the major component in the UBO syndicate] was watching the WR as it took tentative steps to revive, and was worried. He was convinced Keith intended to cut performers' salaries, and nothing short of immediate organization could prevent that. Yet, Silverman cautioned, "Organization at the present does not mean strike. There is now nothing of sufficient seriousness to strike for." The Keith Booking Agency charged a 5 percent commission on all the acts it booked for its 37 houses. According to Silverman, the Keith company grossed $175,000 to $200,000 a year from those fees, while the cost of running that office was just $60,000—"The balance is Keith profit." Attached to Silverman's editorial was a letter from Harry De Veaux, ANPU national president. He, too, urged organization and gave the following background on the WR: "Four years ago they had a powerful association, and would have gained every contested point, but lacked the strong protecting power of affiliation with the other professions employed in the theaters, with the musicians, stage hands, electricians, calcium light operators. The combination of these forces would command the respect they would be entitled to."[29]

Finally, in the June 23 issue of *Variety*, there appeared the last editorial urging players to organize — at least the last for 1906. Silverman declared his message had gotten through, and the revival and restructuring of the White Rats into the effective organization he had been calling for was well underway. As well, he urged a merger between the WR and the VCC. At about the same time, R. C. Mudge was elected president of the WR. He had been a member of the Rats since February 1901 and was the third leader of the group. Ezra Kendall had led the WR for a couple of years after George Fuller Golden had stepped down. Mudge appeared professionally in the West during 1879–1880, but other than that had not been active in connection with the variety stage except for the management of his daughter's (Eva Mudge) tours.[30]

Mudge claimed he started to take an interest in the Rats, and increased its membership from a low of 63 at the beginning of 1904 to 130 during the early part of 1905. He continued to work away informally and unofficially, receiving no salary or expenses until he was elected president in June 1906. He received 50 votes; 27 were cast for others. Still, he received no salary until around March 1907 when, with membership at 450, he began receiving a salary of $50 a week. Thus, Mudge became the first paid official of the Rats.[31]

As the WR tried to revive and become a force on the scene again, it held a meeting in September 1906 that was attended by three representatives from each of the following organizations: the Comedy Club, the Variety Artists' Federation of England, and the International Artisten Loge of Germany. Plans were discussed for the linking together of all those bodies under an international agreement. Nothing ever came of it. However, while those people were in New York, E. F. Albee, general manager of the B. F. Keith circuit, sent for Willie Zimmermann, a representative of the IAL. After the latter was given a tour of the Keith circuit, Albee told him that no artists' society anywhere was needed as far as the Keith office was concerned. Albee pointed out the magnificent Keith houses and how well the players were treated by the Keith circuit, and, said a reporter, assured Zimmermann of "Keith and Albee's friendly, almost lovable regard for the artist."[32]

Discussing the philosophy of the WR, Mudge wrote, at the end of 1906, "It is our desire to enroll every high-class vaudeville artist, with a record for honesty and integrity, and to refuse membership to the unreliable trouble makers." The purpose of the organization was to improve the general conditions existing between managers and artists. The main points were: "First, an equitable contract; second, the abolition of tips to theater employees; third, the regulation of contract cancellations by both manager and artist; fourth, protection for originality." Pirated acts remained a sore point, with the cooperation of managers needed to quell the copy acts. Concluded Mudge, "It is not the purpose of the White Rats of America to in any way dictate to the managers as to how they shall conduct their business. We expect, however, that by earnest, honest efforts and by consultation with managers to do away with the present grievances, which are as well known to the manager and to the artist as to myself."[33]

When the UBO had formed, both E. F. Albee and Percy Williams told *Variety* that there would be no salary cuts for acts, no clause compelling Sunday performances, and no two-weeks' notice of cancellation on arbitrary grounds. However, they said they would require the artists to perform in up to 14 shows a week. Both declared they wanted to see an equitable contract drafted and would do so, in consultation with the players.[34]

Thus, after several years of near complete dormancy the WR became active again, to some extent. By the end of February 1907, both the WR and the VCC had named representatives to jointly call on Williams and Albee at the UBO to work on drafting an equitable contract.[35]

As evidence of good faith the UBO sent a letter to the WR and the VCC dated March 16, 1907, signed by E. F. Albee (general manager of the UBO), B. F. Keith (president), Percy G. Williams (business manager), and J. J. Murdock (representing Western managers). In part, that letter stated there was a distinct understanding between the parties that an equitable contract was to be agreed upon; there would be no cutting of salaries; that there would be no blacklist; that if the changing of any artists' tour route resulted in extra transportation costs for the player "the manager shall bear his share of the railroad expenses." And, "that we shall endeavour in every way possible to establish the most friendly relations between the artists and the managers and in the case of disputes to arbitrate matters."[36]

A version of a contract Percy Williams had used on his circuit was accepted by the VCC and the WR in March 1907, and was expected to shortly be put into use across the full UBO system. In that contract no mention was made of Sundays, although one clause stated performances would be two a day, to a maximum of 14 in a week.[37]

About a month later, on another front, a delegation from the AFL and the Central Federated Union appeared before the WR at one of the latter's meetings with a communication from their respective bodies, calling on the Rats to make some declaration of principle as to its attitude toward unionized labor in the U.S. Generally, that move was viewed as the opening shot in an attempt to draw the Rats into some sort of affiliation with the ANPU, which held a charter from the AFL and was represented in the Central Federated Union. It all came about after the ANPU had complained over certain WR activities. The Rats had a formal agreement with the Variety Artists' Federation (UK), which was registered as a labor union and held a charter in the British Labour Council. Because the British Labour Council was closely federated with the AFL, the ANPU contended that the Variety Artists' Federation had no right to treat with the WR in a formal way since the Rats had no official existence, within the AFL, as a labor body. Thus, the AFL was trying to smooth over the situation. Some time earlier the ANPU had offered a charter to the WR under its banner, but the offer was not accepted.[38]

During the summer of 1907 the WR appointed a committee of five to investigate the many complaints received regarding the illegal and unprofessional dealings of vaudeville agents. A New York State law brought agents under the control of the License Commissioner of New York City. The first target was to be agents who booked for the summer season, for places such as amusement parks. Many agents booked artists under blanket contracts (for example, booking an act for 12 weeks at $x per week) before the opening of the park season. However, it was often all done on speculation, with the agent, after booking the acts, then going to the parks and fair managers to try and place the artists. As a result, the player did not look for summer work because he had a contract, but often found late in the year that the booking was an illusion, as the agent could not live up to the pact.[39]

Sunday performances remained a sore spot. In that same summer a move was in the works to get a bill introduced in the New York State Legislature making it illegal to open any theater on a Sunday for amusement purposes. A similar bill introduced in the Legislature the previous year had been quashed. Church people were said to be behind the movement, but theatrical managers blamed actors, insisting they were really the force behind the efforts. Actors were still often forced to perform on a Sunday (either in the same city they had played that week, or brought in to one city from another) with no extra pay. A reporter commented that there was no definite proof the artists were behind the movement, but the managers declared they were "and have enlisted the church element, ever ready and anxious to go to the front in a crusade of this sort and always a powerful body in securing action from the capital. The advocacy of the church people also gives the movement the color of disinterestedness, while the participation of the artists would rob it of public interest as a religious movement." It was conceded by the reporter that the push to establish such a law was doomed to failure.[40]

Women continued to pose a problem for the Rats. Toward the end of December 1907 the WR sent out a letter to all women in the variety branch of theatricals, at least for whom an address could be obtained. For a nominal fee of $5 a year, explained the letter, a certificate would be issued to a woman player granting her the rights of an active member. "The by-laws of the White Rats forbid that women shall be received into full membership, and this expedient has been hit upon to tide over the difficulty," added the communication.[41]

Around the same time, a reporter exclaimed, after Mudge had been WR president for some 18 months, that over that time, "the theatrical world has seen the White Rats society spring up with bounds and leaps until at present it is the leading variety artists' body." According to that reporter, the Rats had advanced "on Mr. Mudge's theory that arbitration, backed by the force of numbers, is the best road to future greatness." Full of praise for Mudge, the journalist declared that the president had been called upon personally to arbitrate many times between artist and manager, with the final decision left to him, "and his impartial rulings have brought to him unsolicited the post of general mediator for various vaudeville circuits throughout the country."[42]

But little had been accomplished by the Rats by the end of 1907. The contract put into use by the UBO had corrected none of the abuses players were subjected to, regardless of its language. It was business as usual for the Trust. Membership in the Rats had increased — one estimate put it at 700 in April 1907 — but it remained a small, not-very-militant, ineffective organization. However, it was at least alive once more and active to an extent. Then, near the end of 1907, Mudge was accused of corruption by some of the Rats. Such accusations, always denied by Mudge, were never pursued in any formal sense, but under increasing pressure from the membership, Mudge resigned as president early in February 1908.[43]

Suddenly the Rats were not just weak, they were leaderless. Not long before, Epes Sargent had complained of the lack of a leader for an actors' organization and wondered where a leader might come from. In the last days of 1907 that leader was on a boat in the Atlantic, in transit from England to America. A very tiny piece in *Variety* in the publication's last issue of the year commented on the trip, although no one, including the man involved, then knew his destiny. Harry Mountford, the English artist who, with his wife, comprised the act known as Mountford and Walsh, were reported to be on their way to New York, having sailed from England earlier in the week. While they were in America the couple were going to look for bookings, ended the account. Mountford was perhaps a mid-level talent, unknown as an artist in America. He had been active in players' unions in the UK. Soon he would be very well known in the U.S., but not for his artistic abilities.[44]

Those years of stagnation quickly came to an end once Harry Mountford arrived on the scene and took control of the Rats, which he did less than two months after he arrived in America. Over the period 1908 until the very early 1920s Harry came and went as the dominant force in the union. When he was absent the union lapsed back into stagnation but while he was in charge the Rats uttered threatening noises and flexed their muscles, but did not actually accomplish a great deal. However, it could be argued that the tactics and strategies used on Harry and the Rats by the trust to subdue Mountford were exposed and thus became less effective when a different trust tried to use the very same ploys on the much stronger Actors' Equity during their strike.

Mountford was the focus of a fierce attack by the capitalist class in the entertainment industry and by virtually every media outlet. Two primary responses were made to Harry by the media outlets of the day; either he was ignored completely or he was attacked hysterically by libelous and slanderous accusations. Few figures of the American labor movement of the era provoked such extreme rage from the ruling class as did Harry. Certainly no such reaction was provoked by Golden, Harry's main predecessor in the Rats, or by Francis Wilson when he took the helm of Equity.

Part of the extreme reaction to Harry was the result of Mountford's own acerbic personality. He was given to extreme rhetoric, wild accusations, and lies himself. His pleas to actors not yet members of the Rats to come into the union fold consisted not in logical, rational pleas but, more often than not, in insults and sarcasm directed at the uninitiated, calling them traitors, parasites, and so on. In short, Harry was never one to play nice. Another part of the reaction was due to the fact that Mountford left no doubt about what the Rats were; they were a union and were ready to use any tactics to wrest some control from the trust and to right what they perceived as wrongs. And that was at a time when many groups set up for actors tried to hide any aspirations they may have had to be unions under the cloak they were nothing more than harmless social or fraternal organizations.

Looking back at the verbal assaults on Mountford one was struck by the lack of fairness involved. No matter how outrageously false were the attacks made on Harry in the press, his side of the story was never aired. Whether a media outlet ignored Mountford or attacked him they all boycotted him in unison in never allowing him to respond to the attacks. It was an example of how the capitalist class of the time could and did band together in a display of solidarity never matched in any union. Harry Mountford was fated to go on to become one of the most hated and reviled figures in the American labor movement, at least from the perspective of the ruling class. He was fated to lose his battles, to be beaten down and to finish his life in obscurity. Perhaps, though, he made things a little easier for actors to organize in his wake.

5 | Mountford Arrives; the White Rats Resurface, 1908–1911

"[Managers] have refused the olive branch of peace, conciliation and arbitration, and if the actor now takes steps to protect himself by employing capital against capital ... they should lay the blame upon the shoulders of those to whom it rightfully belongs — the managers themselves."
— Harry Mountford, 1908

"The idea to circumvent managers and agents at their own game was bellicosely belched forth, but quickly flared up, with its originator [Mountford] long since discredited."
— *Variety*, 1912

In the wake of the resignation of R. C. Mudge as president, the White Rats held an "Emergency Committee" meeting in the middle of February 1908 to deal with the situation. One of those present was Harry Mountford, then secretary of the WR board of directors. He had been in America for perhaps six weeks at most. Never would he be president of the Rats; nor would he ever seek that office, content to be secretary of the board and later International Secretary. Some of his positions were by appointment, while he seems to have been elected to other posts. Whatever title he held in the Rats, though, he quickly came to dominate the organization. It was Mountford who determined strategy; it was Mountford who made the public pronouncements for the group. Always, the president of the WR took a back seat to the English performer. Harry was described as an orator of high calibre who had been especially prominent in the UK in 1907 in the Variety

Artists' Federation during that group's clash with English theatrical management. As the UBO flexed its management muscles, the battle with the Rats was joined. During this period the WR was a militant union, the only such actors' organization around.[1]

By the end of March that year the Rats announced they had drafted an equitable form of contract and were then having it printed. Plans were to submit that contract form to managers whenever requests were made for it. Reportedly, one manager had already agreed to use the contract; other circuits were expected to accept it within a short time. However, the Rats did not intend at that time to try to make the use of that instrument compulsory.[2]

Early in June a meeting was held between E. F. Albee, general manager of the UBO, and Mountford at which the issue of contracts was discussed, specifically the one used by the UBO, which the Rats contended contained many clauses unfair to the artist. One was a clause that gave the manager the right to cancel an act if it should prove "unsatisfactory" to him. Effectively, it meant a manager could dismiss a player for no reason at all. Another aspect of the contract disliked by the performers was the "barring" clause. Under the provision, once an act contracted with UBO it was forbidden from playing within a certain distance of the venue named in the contract (for example, within 20 blocks of the house, within five miles, and so on) for a certain period of time (for example, for the six months preceding the starting date stipulated in the contract).[3]

At the annual general meeting of the WR, held on June 18, 1908, Harry delivered the Board of Directors report — but not for the fiscal year of the organization (June 17, 1907 to June 17, 1908), but only for the period when the emergency group, led by him, took control (February 6, 1908 to June 17, 1908). According to him, most of the independent theater managers, most of the burlesque managers, and even Ringling Brothers circus management, for the first time in the history of vaudeville, preferred to come to the WR offices and settle there any differences that had arisen between them through the use of a three-man arbitration panel. When a proposal to do the same was put to Albee, added Harry, "it was summarily declined...." He declared it was significant that the UBO had a working agreement with the musicians' union but had refused to have such an agreement with the WR. Overly naively, Mountford told the assembly that was all the Rats needed, "a working agreement in the shape of a board of arbitration between this Order and the United Booking Offices, which shall arbitrate simply upon contracts and conditions." Then he mentioned the WR's newly established

Investment Fund. He hoped it would "have great power as a lever in attempting to compel managers with whom we are at variance to come into line. Money can only be fought with money, capital can only be opposed by capital, and the larger the Investment Fund is the better will be our chance of final success, at least such is the opinion of the Board of Directors."[4]

Later that month special representatives, duly authorized by the Rats, were announced as being in the process of appointment to become traveling adjusters for the group, empowered to settle "slight differences" in cases coming to their attention while in territory removed from the New York headquarters. First to receive such a commission was Edward Keough, who opened at the end of June in Winnipeg for a trip over the Sullivan-Considine circuit.[5]

A day before Keough hit the road the Rats elected Fred Niblo as president (or "Big Chief," as he was called in WR parlance). Immediately he sailed for Europe, not to return until near the end of October, some four months later. It only served to emphasize the superfluous nature of the position of president in the WR, as long as Mountford was involved.[6]

When Harry, along with other WR officials and additional guest speakers, addressed a mass meeting in Chicago on July 3, 1908, the crowd was said to have been 1,000 people. Earlier, when Mountford arrived at the train station, he was met by a local delegation of 150 labor union types, with the automobile procession led by Charles Horn's band — a 20-piece aggregation provided for free for the occasion by the musicians' union. At the assembly Harry called on people to join the Rats, and at one point said the group had 2,500 members. Speaking of the shady practices of agents, and of managers' power to cancel a contract in a few days, he added, "The general public has a wrong conception of the show business. Actors don't drink champagne, smoke big fat cigars, lie abed late, bully the managers into fabulous salaries. This is all a popular fallacy." Another speaker was S. L. Lowenthal, Western legal representative of the Rats. "The nomadic condition of the vaudeville artist makes him a prey to unscrupulous mangers," he said. "It is the intention of the order of White Rats to make arrangements for a powerful brotherhood, and place in its hands the weapon of co-operation for its protection throughout the United States. It is their aim to have laws enforced to prevent conditions that would be a disgrace to the Middle Ages."[7]

One of the first major shots in the conflict between the Rats and the UBO took place in July 1908 when the WR announced one of the first uses for the money in its Investment Fund. The Rats stated they had an agreement whereby they were buying a share of the Mozart vaudeville circuit in order to interest artists in the management side of vaudeville. Owned by Edward Mozart, the circuit controlled a number of houses, the greater portion of them being in Pennsylvania. There were enough venues in the circuit to reportedly supply an artist with 20 weeks or so of work. As well, the Rats were said to be actively looking for other circuits to buy into. Mountford verified that story for reporters and said a contract had been drawn between the Rats and Mozart by virtue of which the Mozart circuit agreed it would not connect, associate or affiliate during the coming five years with any manager, circuit or booking agency. Further, it was agreed the contract used by the Mozart houses to book acts would be an "equitable" one, to be approved by both sides.[8]

Coming as a surprise, the story about the WR buying into circuits and becoming managers enraged the establishment. For the managers, Martin Beck of the Orpheum circuit ominously warned, "Any organization of actors that tries to invade their employers' field will surely defeat the great fundamental object of the order behind it, and be an unqualified failure. Furthermore, it might turn influential friends into necessary foes." Replying to Beck, Mountford remarked that if the managers agreed to the Rats' proposals for arbitration, and had they agreed to remove "illegal" clauses from their contracts, the need to buy into circuits might never had arisen: "They have refused the olive branch of peace, conciliation and arbitration, and if the actor now takes steps to protect himself by employing capital against capital, by fighting fire with fire, they should not lay the blame upon the actor; they should lay the blame upon the shoulders of those to whom it rightfully belongs — the managers themselves."[9]

At the end of July the WR announced it had four managers and 30 houses under the control of its Investment Fund, and that the fund had $100,000 in cash to operate with. No names or particulars were given, although, of course, one chain was the Mozart circuit. At the same time, the Rats announced they had formed their own in-house booking agency — the Independent Booking Agency. An advertisement was placed by the Rats in *Variety* announcing their latest foray into a management area, and inviting vaudeville managers to book acts through its new facility. According to the ad, it had enough artists signed up to provide a manager with 30 weeks of performers.[10]

When the *Mirror* spoke to Mountford about the plans of the Rats to become managers he pointed out that vaudeville circuits worked against the development of acts because they did not pay enough. Thus, it did not make sense for an actor to devote time and money into developing an elaborate act with intricate sets, and so on. Also, the managers' attitude to piracy worked against the artist. Many managers encouraged performers to steal an act, said Harry, telling the pirate to just change the title of the piece, and so on. Many of those managers turned a blind eye to piracy. Such attitudes also discouraged artists from developing new acts.[11]

Especially outraged over the idea of the Rats becoming their own managers was the *Mirror*. In an editorial in its August 15, 1908, issue it warned the WR of the folly of pursuing their plans for an opposition circuit as a way to force a more equitable contract from the managers. Recalling the strike of 1901, the editor said, "Once before the White Rats attempted to compel a decision from their opponent in their favour. The rats struck; but the strike failed ... another strike, if it occurs, will likely have the same fate."[12]

Three weeks later another editorial attacked the same idea, and then went on to attack Harry. In the opinion of the editor this plan was an abrupt change in direction on the part of the Rats, one which started only when Mountford got involved with the group. What worried the editor was, "that Mr. Mountford, with 'much power,' may be directing rather than being directed by the Board of Directors."[13]

Such attacks on Harry prompted a letter to the editor of the *Mirror* from George Fuller Golden, the founder and first president of the WR. He pointed out the monopoly position in vaudeville and that one of the original purposes of the Rats was to fight such conditions and eliminate them if possible. Protesting what he saw as a personal attack on Harry in the publication, Golden declared that Mountford was merely carrying out the original intention of the Rats. "That he is performing his duty courageously and conscientiously will be proven by the amount of abuse and vituperation he will probably have to endure from those theatrical scribes who can be subsidized into the servitude of syndicated greed," he wrote. "Therefore the position of your paper, if one may judge by this article, is as remarkable as it is obviously inconsistent."[14]

Plans of the Rats to compete directly against the Trust with its own venues and its own booking agency pushed ahead. It was announced at the beginning of June 1909 that over 50 of the small vaudeville theaters had combined to book their shows under the banner of the WR as represented by the Independent Booking Office in New York. In the new combination were (besides Mozart) the Feiber, Shea and Coutant circuit, with seven weeks (that is, houses); M. R. Sheedy, 11 weeks; and John J. Quigley, a Boston agent who claimed to have over 25 houses to book for in New England. The Mozart circuit had about 12 houses, bringing the total to over 50 venues.

Some of those houses played shows only three days a week, changing the bill twice a week, so the net time to be offered totalled around 40 weeks. Each of those houses was to use the WR form of contract. However, rumors of a blacklist circulated in the industry. A blacklisting threat had been made to Carita, a toe dancer who was then on the Feiber circuit and was booked to play their Bayonne, New Jersey, theater the next week. Carita said Joe Wood, a UBO agent, told her if she played Bayonne she need expect no more time from the UBO because that organization would blacklist her. When questioned about that story by a reporter, Wood said, "I may have told an act about to play some of the smaller time it would be barred in the United offices if it did so.... I have said nothing to acts that other agents have not told theirs."[15]

Yet the idea never got off the ground and was soon dead. The Independent Booking Agency ceased to exist shortly after its formation. WR control of venues had dwindled to two of the houses in the Mozart chain (one house in Elmira, New York, one venue in Lancaster, Pennsylvania) by February 1912, at which time they passed into other hands. And the experiment was over; lack of business being a chief reason for the demise. And that was due to the blacklisting power of the Theatrical Trust. At a time when the capitalist class was virulently anti-union, it was a risk to join or support a union or any such group the capitalist class declared to be acting like such an organization. However, it was possible to join a union and keep that fact hidden, perhaps. But it was not possible to perform in a union house and keep that a secret. Any artist who performed at a Rat venue was a very easy target. A reporter who noted the demise of the plan declared, "the idea to circumvent managers and agents at their own game was bellicosely belched forth, but quickly flared up, with its originator [Mountford] long since discredited."[16]

During 1908 the Rats drafted an "equitable" contract, which was used by its own Independent Booking Agency, although not by many managers and certainly not by any connected with the Trust. That contract provided for binding arbitration to adjust disagreements that arose out of the contract, something the WR had long wanted in a contract. As to the question of Sunday shows, the document contained only the vaguely worded clause that the player would give "the usual number of performances as in accordance with the law." As well, the WR contract allowed for no arbitrary cancellation and provided that if any change of route imposed upon the player entailed any additional transportation cost, that cost was to be borne by the manager. In the "distance limit barring" clause it was provided that in cities of over 75,000 population the act under agreement would not perform within one mile of the theater contracted for during the six months prior to the start of the engagement. For smaller towns a three-month time limit was imposed without regard to distance. According to a reporter, this WR contract was the first ever prepared, issued and used by American artists.[17]

During August 1908 the WR formed the White Rats Political League "for the object of advancing the interests of artists by every legitimate political means," according to the resolution establishing it. It was to work with other actors' societies in pursuit of its goals.[18]

The first meeting of the WR Political League was held in September that year, reportedly the first political gathering ever called by actors. Leading political figures from both the Republican and Democratic parties were on hand as speakers, along with representatives from the Actors' Society, Greenroom, Players, Lambs, and Comedy Club. Without formal affiliation to any political party, the Rats hoped its political arm would be able to influence State governments to correct what it saw as abuses of actors that were possible under existing statutes. An early attempt was to be made in New York State, where the players wanted to amend the existing agency law so that it was not possible to extract a commission greater than 5 percent in total from an act.[19]

Other groups, such as the ANPU, also were involved in actors' concerns from time to time. A huge controversy broke out over Salome dancing (women in veils, harem pants, exposed belly buttons, and so on) in the summer of 1908. One example occurred in Newark, New Jersey, where Acting Police Captain Brown refused to stand for "the 1908 bunk" at Electric Park in August when artist Carola was slated to do a Salome dance. She was one of the acts in a festival for the benefit of a German hospital, but Brown told the management to cancel Carola, which it did.[20]

That same month the ANPU bowed to the pressure and declared it had set its face resolutely against Salome dancers in any and all forms. Clubs and private entertainments by the score had made application to John Barry, general manager of the ANPU New York local, for exponents of the new vogue (listed on its artist registry) but all were turned away. Barry said no less than 40 entertainment committees had approached him to find Salome dancers, and the number of women who had expressed a desire to emulate Gertrude Hoffman (one of the more prominent Salome dancers) had already reached 30, with the season just barely underway. "This Salome thing," said ANPU president Harry De Veaux, "has gone to a point where it does not deserve the serious consideration of any body of artists. I am more than willing to concede the talent of some of the dancers who are interpreting Salome, but the really artistic performance stands in relation to the worthless trash that is being foisted upon the public in the ratio of about 100 to 1."[21]

John E. McCarthey, president of the National Vaudeville Managers' Association and manager of the Grand in Hamilton, Ohio, issued an order in September 1908 barring all Salome dancers from that circuit of about 150 small houses in Ohio, Indiana, West Virginia, Kentucky, and Pennsylvania. McCarthey condemned the dance as being against "the higher aims of vaudeville."[22]

Among its other activities, the WR had established a loan fund to help out artists. Any artist in immediate need of funds for travel, and so on, had only to present evidence to the Rats of having a contracted engagement, and an amount sufficient to take him to the opening city of his tour was advanced to him. The WR had advanced about $20,000 (over an unspecified period of time) to needy members. But the group was strict about those loans being repaid. Members who failed to repay the loans could be, and were, expelled from the organization.[23]

At the close of 1908 Harry Mountford reviewed the union's progress over the calendar year of 1908, his first full calendar year in effective control of the group. After noting that at the start of the year the WR had only one organization and office, located at 1553 Broadway, in New York, he pointed out that by December it had the White Rats' Publishing Co., the White Rats' Investment Co., the White Rats' Political League, a permanent Arbitration Board, and a Board of Directors elected by the WR members. Also, the Rats had an attorney in New York, an independent booking office in New York, an attorney in Chicago, an independent booking office in Chicago, and a branch office in Chicago headed by Harry Knowles.[24]

If any doubt remained as to whether the Actors' Society (AS) was a union or a fraternal organization, that doubt was put to rest early in 1909. On occasion it had managed to collect back salaries due its members, but mostly it concentrated on solving sanitary problems in the houses wherein its members appeared. AS president Thomas Wise declared, "The unionism of actors, in the sense of a labor union, akin to those organizations of mechanics and artisans, with all their harsh and dictatorial measures, is a thing I don't believe in." He added that every man had the right to run his own business, and that arbitration and peaceable measures accomplished more than did severity and force. "But an association of actors for mutual help and benefit, maintaining the friendliest relations between the managers, producers and actors is a help to all those factions, and that's what we want our society to be."[25]

At a mass meeting attended by representatives of all the actors' societies in New York on March 7, 1909, all in attendance pledged their support of New York Assemblyman Voss' bill. Speakers also included representatives from the AFL, the Society of American Musicians, and other labor groups. Voss' bill was designed to amend the existing Theatrical Employment Agency law and was endorsed by the Actors' Society of America, the Actors' Church Alliance, the ANPU, the Society of American Magicians, the Vaudeville Comedy Club, the White Rats' Political League and the White Rats of America.[26]

Late in April 1909 the amendments proposed by Voss passed both the House and the Senate and went to the Governor for action. The Voss bill amended the agency laws of New York State for the cities of the "first class" (the largest ones) and was introduced by Assemblyman Voss after he was lobbied by the combined forces of the actors' societies of New York, led by the WR and the ANPU. Both Harry De Veaux, the original sponsor of the measure, and Mountford gave much time and effort to the proposal. It was reported that Denis F. O'Brien, attorney for the WR, practically drew the amendments himself and was instrumental in securing the speedy action the bill received in the Legislature, along with the strong backing given the bill by organized labor in general. Among other amendments, the Voss bill limited the amount of money agents could collect to 5 percent of a performer's salary in total, no matter how many agents were involved. Under the existing law commissions were limited to 5 percent, but there was no limit placed on the number of different agents who could collect 5 percent from a performer. Thus, most players were then paying out 5 percent to the UBO and 5 percent to their own personal agent. When that personal agent was forced to pay half of his 5 percent to the UBO he sometimes raised his fee to his client to 7.5 percent, calling the extra 2.5 percent something other than a commission to get around the existing law. Thus actors regularly were hit by commissions totalling 10 to 12.5 percent. Also, some agents then acted as contractors who agreed to supply entertainment for a show for a fixed sum and then bargained individually with acts themselves. As a result, their share was often much more than 5 percent. Under the Voss bill that procedure was no longer allowed. Mountford said of the probable effect of the bill, "I believe the bill, if it becomes a law, will mark the beginning of an era of peace and friendship between the artist and manager." Whether the UBO could continue to "split commissions" with the outside agents under the Voss bill was unclear. Many observers felt they could do so by simply calling the excess they received over 5 percent (the 2.5 percent from outside agents) something else, a fee for the use of the UBO offices for booking purposes, for example. It was already being assumed that outside agents would charge their entire commission to their clients under a name other than commission. The governor of New York was prepared to sign the bill.[27]

But before it received the governor's signature it needed other approvals. It was drafted in such a way that the mayors of those first class cities each had a veto power over the measure; all had to sign it or it failed. New York Mayor McClellan signed it after a public hearing and a raucous debate in which evidence was introduced that some agents were charging acts as much as 12.5 percent in commission. But Mayor J. Adam of Buffalo vetoed the measure after being intensely lobbied by managers, and it died. There were then 138 theatrical agents in New York City, none in Buffalo.[28]

Around that time a movement developed in Chicago among the acts playing the small "split week" (an act appearing in two, or more, different houses in one week, usually three days per venue) time in and around that city to make a concerted demand for a salary increase. It was a demand to be made through the ANPU. Harry Ricardo, of the ANPU Chicago local, explained that the minimum scale for vaudeville acts in the movie houses (during the early days of the motion picture industry some managers tried to cover themselves by mixing vaudeville and films in the same house so as to be involved in all trends) was $20 a week for a single act and $40 for a double (two-person act). Players wanted that minimum scale increased to $25 and $50. Ricardo said that when those small circuits first came to his attention, acts were paid as low as $12 a week and sometimes played three different houses in a week. "By combining into a solid front we forced the $20–$40 scale and made it impossible to change bills more than twice a week — three and four day engagements," he said. Ricardo hoped to established a local at Cleveland where he had heard some picture houses were hiring vaudeville people for as little as $2 a night.[29]

Increasingly, the Rats become more militant. At a large mass meeting held June 26, 1909, in Chicago Mountford threatened a strike of more than 4,000 actors. Harry told the meeting the problem lay with the managers, and that the actors were not getting a "square deal." If conditions did not change in the near future, thundered Harry, a walkout of the entire WR organization would take place. Of course, the Rats had nothing close to 4,000 members, but one of Mountford's habits was a tendency to exaggerate, often wildly. That marked the first time the WR had taken such a militant position under Harry Mountford's direction.[30]

Many meetings had taken place between Albee, as the main representative of the managers, and Mountford, as the main WR negotiator, but nothing had been accomplished. Also, the attitude of Albee was to trivialize the whole affair and launch into personal attacks. Mountford and the Rats grew more and more frustrated as they made no headway toward winning an equitable contract form to be put into joint use, or even to have the Rats formally recognized by the Trust as the bargaining unit for the actors. Back in August 1908 Albee gave an interview to the *Mirror* in which he declared, "As far as the contracts are concerned, they are the things that really bother a performer or manager least of all.... When they [contracts] are brought into question, it is only when some outside agitator, having no interest to further except his livelihood, proceeds to stir up the dissatisfied ones and goad on those whose services are not sought for to the point of desperation."[31]

At the annual convention of the WR, held June 25, 1909, in Chicago, Timothy Cronin, president of the WR Political League, told the audience, "About twenty-five years ago Louis Aldrich, who has since passed away, went to Washington on behalf of the actors, and there met the political rulers, among them Congressmen who shook him by the hand and gave every promise of support. When he urged political recognition for actors a Congressman said he couldn't do anything for the actor because an actor does not vote." Speaking of the Voss bill, Cronin blamed the UBO for causing Buffalo's Mayor Adam to veto it. The New York State Governor was reportedly ready to sign the measure but first sent it to the mayors of Buffalo and New York City for their approvals. Buffalo's veto came 15 minutes after a hearing in that city. However, said Cronin, "We made the people who fought the Voss bill spend $25,000." Mountford gave the speech at that gathering that was described as the most impassioned, the most electric. "The vaudeville associations do not like me.... They say I am an agitator. They call us agitators." Allusions were made at the gathering to personal attacks on Mountford and to the hiring of private detectives by the managers to trail Harry to investigate him and to dig out any dirt that might have existed. As well, he was attacked for being born in England — that is, he was not a Native American.[32]

Later in 1909 an unnamed member of the WR told a reporter the UBO maintained a blacklist of WR members who played venues where the Rats had a financial stake during the group's short-lived and unsuccessful experiment of competing directly against the Trust.[33]

Meanwhile, in the fall of 1909, the ANPU was still trying to achieve a wage scale of $25 and $50 for the small-time vaudeville acts in Chicago.

One ANPU tactic was to place agents on an unfair list — those who booked acts at less than the target amount. At a meeting of players some questioned the wisdom of placing so many agents on the unfair list.[34]

By the middle of October 1909 rumors circulated to the effect that the WR and the ANPU had united in a general boycott of Chicago agent Frank Q. Doyle, who had just been placed on the unfair list of agents at a mass meeting of actors. A reporter surmised that while it may not have been true that the WR as an organization had taken action, "it is certain that many of the Rats, acting individually, have joined the concerted movement against the Chicago Vaudeville Managers' Exchange [the Doyle office]. The Chicago Vaudeville Managers' Association [offices in same building] has given him its moral support." According to the reporter, the result of the agitation for higher salaries had led to the cutting out of vaudeville at many nickel theaters. No acts were then to be seen at the nickel places for seven blocks along Milwaukee Avenue, where they were very numerous. Ed Stout, business agent of the ANPU, said his group had the support of the WR in that matter "as an organization."[35]

A week later the WR and the ANPU declared victory, with an agreement reached between the players and Doyle (with the latter removed from the unfair list). Doyle agreed in writing to accept the WR contract. But the agent did not submit to the desired $25 and $50 salary scale. Despite that, his action was taken as a victory by the leaders of the movement. Still, there were many in the two groups who hesitated to accept what had transpired as a victory, but at a mass meeting the settlement — Doyle agreeing to accept the WR contract form in exchange for being removed from the blacklist — was endorsed by the membership by a vote of 45 to 14.[36]

Just one week later, Local 4 of the ANPU placed agent Frank Doyle back on the unfair list. When his name had been removed from that list one week earlier there was much divided opinion. Many thought he should not be removed from the list just for agreeing to use the WR contract form while refusing all other demands, such as an increased minimum salary. While the members in that group had lost out a week earlier, they had somehow prevailed during the ensuing seven days.[37]

On January 12, 1910, a bill was introduced at Albany in the New York State Legislature to amend the state law governing theatrical agents. It was similar to the old Voss bill and was again backed by the ANPU. That earlier measure had been a "local options" bill requiring the approval of mayors in first-class cities. This new effort was not, requiring only the signature of the Governor, after passing both houses of the Legislature, to become law.

Even the UBO was said to favor the draft bill, with E. F. Albee conceding that the law as framed would be beneficial in restricting the unscrupulous agent, bringing all agents under stricter government supervision. For that reason, the UBO favored its passage. At this time the ANPU was said to have 2,500 members.[38]

Declining to support the Green-Wagner amended Employment Agency Bill sponsored by the ANPU, the WR caused to be introduced in the New York State Senate a bill that in effect repealed the existing law and substituted an entirely new one — it ran to 10,000 words. The Rats claimed that while the Green-Wagner bill was supported by the ANPU alone, the Rats' measure had the support of all the other artists' organizations. For its part, the ANPU declared its measure had the support of the city, state, and national organized labor bodies, as well as that of the city administration. New York State reportedly had 800 employment agencies, of which 240 were theatrical booking offices. Harry De Veaux, when he learned of the WR measure, said, "Any effort to introduce other legislation can only confuse the issue and result in the miscarriage of the whole movement, if indeed, it has not been done for that purpose."[39]

A few weeks later, in a surprise, it was announced that the WR and the ANPU had held a conference where they decided to withdraw the WR bill and make some additional amendments to the ANPU measure. As a result, the UBO, and other managers, withdrew their support and mounted stiff opposition. The UBO put together a 21-page booklet as to what was wrong with the new joint measure and why it was unconstitutional. With respect to the charge that the UBO "split" commissions with outside agents, the booklet admitted the fact, stating, "If it is right that the performer should pay us a commission, why isn't it just as equitable that the agent who makes his living through us should also pay something to us in return?" That booklet was signed "United Booking Offices of America, by F. F. Proctor, Vice-President."[40]

New York State Governor Hughes signed the new measure amending the employment agency law into effect on June 25, 1910. It, too, was similar to the Voss bill in what it hoped to accomplish. Among other things, it made it illegal to take more than 5 percent commission from an act, regardless of the number of agents involved. However, rumors that the law would be effectively evaded by agents calling themselves something else, such as "personal representatives," and/or having a player sign a rider to a contract waiving the new bill, were rampant. Passage of the bill during that session of the Legislature reportedly cost the White Rats $8,000 to $10,000. A year earlier, when the Voss bill failed to become a law, the White Rats filed a statement at Albany showing their expenses during that effort to have been $5,000. Managers simply ignored the law on commissions, treating it as no more than a joke.[41]

Tension between Doyle and the ANPU increased, and in March 1910 the union issued a notice of boycott upon theaters booked by him. That notice was mailed to all labor unions affiliated with the Chicago Federation of Labor. During the few weeks prior to the boycott notice being issued, it was reported that "stink balls" had been exploded in several houses booked by Doyle, driving the audiences out into the streets. Of course, the union denied all knowledge of those events.[42]

Finally, in June 1910, Doyle signed an agreement with the ANPU in which he agreed to book acts at a minimum pay scale of $25 and $50 a week, and that all acts booked through his agency after July 1 would be sanctioned by the ANPU. It was essentially the same agreement that Doyle had refused to sign when it was first presented to him many months earlier. Apparently Doyle's change of heart came about because of pressure brought to bear on him by firms that owned several of the houses that Doyle booked — the boycott campaign of organized labor had some effect. This final settlement with Doyle was arrived at almost a year after the dispute first surfaced.[43]

Over the summer of 1910 the ANPU and the WR clashed over the concept of having a closed shop in Chicago's vaudeville houses, and over how such a plan was to be implemented if it was ever attained. The ANPU envisioned itself as in charge of such a closed shop, but the WR could not see its members petitioning the ANPU for permits to work, as they would have to under the terms of an ANPU closed shop. Although the two unions held several discussions in Chicago over the issue, they could not resolve their differences over the working of a closed shop deal. Thus, the ANPU passed a resolution demanding that all of its members who were also members of the WR had to resign from one union or the other.[44]

As the two unions tussled in Chicago, between 260 and 270 vaudeville actors in Boston (constituting about 150 acts, mostly local) met in that city on a Sunday in August 1910 and, after three hours of discussion, agreed not to do any business with the National Theatrical Booking Association because, said a circular put out by some of the actors involved, National had been "unfair and unbusinesslike in methods of handling acts." National had just affiliated itself with the UBO. While broken contacts were said to be one problem, no details were given. The mass meeting was called by means of a few posters put up along Howard Street and in other vaudeville districts, and also by word of mouth. Only actors were at the meeting; some agents turned up and tried to get in but were turned away.[45]

No union was initially involved in Boston, but within one week the dissident actors had been organized as Boston Local 22 of the Actors International Union (AIU, as the ANPU had just changed its name). That local started out with 27 members.[46]

In September 1910 the Rats made application to the AFL to become affiliated with that body. The formal request was made in a letter from Mountford to Samuel Gompers, head of the AFL. Yet, as all involved knew, the constitution of the AFL made it impossible to grant the Rats a charter to organize actors, since such a charter was already held by the AIU. It was another test of strength between the two unions; it was another display of the discord and acrimony that existed, and grew larger, between the two groups. A reporter observed that the WR, which once had shunned the idea of affiliation with organized labor, had changed its mind. And that perhaps it was growing more and more worried about the strength of the AIU — that body had taken charge recently and organized a local in Boston; the Rats had not done so, or had been beaten to the punch. "The Rats for the past two years or more have taken a decided stand against becoming part of any organized labor organization, under the claim its members do not come under that heading," said a journalist. "During the same time there has been a pronounced feeling between the Rats and the New York local of the A.I.U."[47]

In the meantime, the AIU continued to organize and agitate for the closed shop outside of Chicago. Reportedly, it was a reality in Gary, Indiana, where, said an account, "Nobody can perform upon a Gary vaudeville stage unless he carries a membership card or permit from the Actors' Union."[48]

After Gompers received the application from the Rats, he decided to stop the troubles between the two unions before they got worse. To that end he called a meeting of the two groups, which he chaired. The outcome of that, said a reporter, was, "After years of factional fighting and arguments in the theatrical [trade journals] in which mud-slinging of no mean order was indulged in, the Actors' International Union and the White Rats have amalgamated." In future the one organization was to be known as the White Rats Actors' Union of America. It received its AFL charter in November 1910. However, it was not a merger as much as it was a swallowing of the AIU by the Rats; all of the union officials of the latter retained their positions in the new, larger union.[49]

At the time of the merger there were 450 members of AIU Local 4 (Chicago). One hundred and four of them were taken into the new WR. Many of the remainder were disgruntled and refused to join the Rats, trying instead to revive the old union. One reason for the animosity was that none of the various locals of the AIU had been asked if they wanted to merge or not. Only the executives of each of the unions had been involved in the decision. One of the AIU executives, Harry De Veaux, quickly became disgruntled as well, and was a frequent critic and thorn in the side of the WR over the following years.[50]

Within weeks of the merger of the Rats and the AIU, at the start of 1911, it was reported that four of the best-known artists in vaudeville had begun to form an "exclusive association," with a membership limit placed at 100. At least two of the originators were said to be WR, and, said a reporter, "The belief of the men who have started this movement is that 100 of the best vaudeville acts will comprise more real strength within its membership rolls in the attempt to effect remedies and benefits than any general organization could command."[51]

That new organization was to be called the American Vaudeville Artists (AVA), and its objects were to protect artists' material from pirates and "to obtain remedial measures by conciliatory tactics and the promotion of a better feeling between managers, agents and artists." It was intended that managers and agents should be admitted to membership, as laymen, without the right to active participation or to have a right to vote.[52]

Within a couple of months the AVA was said to be not "relished" by some of the actors' societies who feared the AVA was formed with the intent of disrupting the established groups. Membership was said to have reached 32 leading artists. However, nothing more thereafter was heard about the AVA. It may have been an early attempt by managers to try and set up a sham union — it was a tactic they would use, with mixed results over the coming decade — to undermine the real union with a company, or scab, union. Certainly when the Rats and the AIU merged it increased the fears of managers.[53]

During February 1911 the WR initiated two militant actions in Chicago and won both of them. Earl J. Cox, who booked the Ellis, Monroe and Century venues for manager A. Hamburger, was notified he must adopt a contract satisfactory to the Rats. When he declined to do so, the WR picketed the sidewalks and hallways leading to the building wherein Cox had his offices. Cox then prevailed upon Hamburger to accept the demands of the union — an action that prevented a threatened walkout of union actors from the three Hamburger houses that night. In the other action, a group of 25 Rats descended on the Hamlin theater, led by Joseph Callahan. A demand was made upon manager Howard that he immediately sign a closed shop agreement with the Rats, word having been sent to three acts on the bill not to give their performances until notified that Howard had surrendered. Finally, Howard signed an agreement with the Rats and the show proceeded.[54]

Managers were indeed in a state of fear early in 1911 after the merger and the newly found militancy displayed by the Rats. Also, Mountford was making noises about an actors' strike — nothing definite, just vague cautions. Thus, by April 1911 the UBO had restructured into the Vaudeville Managers' Protective Association (VMPA), which was simply the UBO expanded to include managers from other areas. The UBO remained in existence as the booking part of the VMPA. Within the ranks of the VMPA were vaudeville, burlesque and circus managers — the three entertainment divisions that employed the most vaudeville acts. Included, also, were a couple of men whose main interest was in the motion picture field. Catalyst for the formation of the VMPA was the Rats' new strength and a worry that perhaps the WR could bring off a strike, as threatened. When *Variety* sought a statement from the VMPA, a spokesman told the publication, "While we, the members of this body, are in no wise opposed to organization, we are opposed to such organization when it is declared to be for the purpose of curtailing our control of the business in which our own money is invested and is at stake." He added, "Unions are well enough in their way where the principles of unionism are applicable ... but our contention is that they are not applicable to the relations between the vaudeville managers and the vaudeville player. Each artist must, of necessity, be the individual to judge of the character and value of his artistic work and such a question cannot be left to any body of his associates."[55]

With respect to the right of a manager to hire whom he pleased, the VMPA declared, "The managers certainly will not consent that they be deprived of their full right to employ such an act because the artist has no Union card, or because some body of actors takes it upon itself to say that we must not exploit such an act nor offer it to our patrons." Managers declared themselves determined to do business with the "level-headed" artist who "is not influenced by those who, by harmful agitation, are endeavouring to upset the cordial relations that have existed between manager and player since the inception of the vaudeville business, relations that were disturbed but once, when the regrettable and unsuccessful White Rat strike threatened for a week or two to work serious and permanent harm to the cause of the artist." Then, again referring to the 1901 strike, the VMPA issued a warning and a threat to the actors.

> That unfortunate first break between manager and actor, like the first quarrel between close friends, left its mark, and many who before that time had been prominent as features and headliners of the vaudeville stage, have dropped out of sight, as they had made themselves undesirable. There is grave danger that should anything come of the present foolish agitation, the same fate will befall many who are now enjoying such prosperity as they never knew before.[56]

Additionally, the VMPA sent out a letter, dated April 1, 1911, to the managers of all houses affiliated with it, observing that a strike was possible in June but that no matter what, the VMPA would stand behind all its members whether in vaudeville, burlesque, the circus, or motion pictures, and work with them to keep their venues open during any disruption. On VMPA letterhead, 1493 Broadway was given as the address, and the officers were: Edward F. Albee, president; Marcus Loew, first vice-president; Percy G. Williams, treasurer; Martin Beck, chairman of the Board of Directors; John W. Considine, second vice-president; and Maurice Goodman, secretary. On the Board of Directors were: Edward F. Albee, Martin Beck, Charles E. Bray, Clark Brown, Chris O. Brown, George Castle, John W. Considine, Harry Davis, Herman Fehr, Harry Felber, William Fox, William Hammerstein, Benjamin F. Keith, Marcus Loew, Morris Meyerfeld, Jr., William Morris, John J. Murdock, Alexander Pantages, Sylvester Z. Poli, Frederick F. Proctor, John Ringling, Samuel Scribner, Gus Sun, Walter Vincent, and Percy G. Williams.[57]

A week later the VMPA spoke to the actor through the press by publishing its statements in the form of a paid advertisement. When *Variety* asked the VMPA what it hoped to accomplish through such a tactic, the managers' Trust said it had no special object in view, but, "The announcements are merely to enlighten the artist by bringing to his attention an unbiased view, as seen by the impartial observer...." Among those views that it addressed to the actors was:

> We do not consider you subjects of labor unionism. You are artists, and when joining a labor union movement, you must be content to lose your standing as artists and stand in the ranks of the mechanic, whether skilled or unskilled. Each of you, by reason of special talent, is in a class by yourself.... When, then, you join a labor union you lose the pride of your standing as artists and become, in the eyes of the public, just a mechanic.[58]

Players were reminded that joining a union could hurt their wallets because the present agitation would affect the artists' livelihood, for "when the managers' liberty to conduct his own business is curtailed the entire vaudeville business must suffer." Thus, the VMPA hoped the player would be wise enough not be a party to an attack on the business that provided his livelihood and "wisely conclude to lay aside petty imaginary personal grievances, close his ears to buncombe argument advanced by paid agitators or discontented incompetents and enjoy the growing prosperity of vaudeville." And, concluded the VMPA, "there were never such prosperous and equitable conditions in the world for any class than those existing for the vaudeville artist today."[59]

Six weeks later the VMPA issued another communication directly to the actors through an ad in the press. This time the managers' Trust strongly denied that salaries would be cut at all. With respect to the point that managers were organized — the VMPA always argued against the concept of organizing — it said, "but organization is nothing new among the managers. There has been a combination of managers for more than ten years and this combination of managers has done more to improve the condition of the artist than any artists' organization that was ever formed."[60]

A two-page ad in *Variety* in the July 8, 1911, issue mocked the WR over the fact that nothing had happened — a vague communiqué from the WR indicated something might occur in June. Mountford was attacked repeatedly but never by name, referred to only as "agitator." Wondering what all the clamor was about, the VMPA answered its question by stating:

> We will tell you what it is all about. The ambition of one man, who disrupted the business in Europe, who is trying to disrupt it here for his own selfish ends and nothing else. We don't want him to disrupt the business, since he cannot run it himself; neither can the actors run it.[61]

At a meeting of the VMPA Board of Directors late in August 1911 it was reported that a suggestion the managers meet a WR committee was talked down without even being put to a vote. It was decided any meeting held by the two sides would be an admission by the managers of the existence of the WR as a union — something the managers were determined not to do. After the meeting an unnamed manger told a reporter, "This was a case where we had to place ourselves on record, whether we intended recognizing the Rats as a union."[62]

Around the same time actors on the dramatic stage found themselves under further restrictions. A new clause in the Charles Frohman contracts had a proviso regarding motion picture work, with each actor being required to give the Frohman office a statement as to past performances before the film camera. That clause was inserted because films had proven to be an opposition to be reckoned with. Speculation was that players would be given the cold shoulder by the Frohman office if they had taken prominent roles in motion pictures. It was hinted that in the coming season the actors who did films in the summer and then took up dramatic stage engagements in the winter would have a harder time getting parts if other managers followed Frohman's lead. The catalyst for the move apparently stemmed from an incident in the past season wherein Henry E. Dixey played the Parsons theater at Hartford, Connecticut, in *Mary Jane's Pa*. Directly across the road was a cinema that displayed a larger banner with the following: "Why pay $2 to see Henry E. Dixey when you can see him for 5c?" Running at the nickelodeon was the Selig film *David Garrick,* for which Dixey had been paid $1,000 for acting the lead role.[63]

Those warnings against appearing in films were given again to actors at the beginning of 1912 when they were told that making films would make them ineligible for engagements with the big theatrical producers. The latest players of prominence lured into making films were said to be Nat C. Goodwin, May Buckley, and Mildred Holland.[64]

Suddenly, around the end of September 1911, Harry Mountford resigned from his WR post as International Secretary. His resignation, offered *Variety,* was evidence of an internal power struggle. Reportedly, the Rats were then having financial difficulties — partly from the upkeep of a lavish clubhouse for the membership and partly from the financial drain caused by the money-losing house organ, *The Player,* something instituted by Harry. His resignation was triggered when the WR reduced Mountford to the position he was given when he first joined the Rats, that of secretary to the Board. "From this minor job, Mountford rapidly assumed entire charge of the organization, with everything under his control," wrote the journalist. His reduction in position also "included the taking away of the official organ, known to have contained his name 47 times in one issue. That paper was commonly referred to as 'Mountford's press sheet.'"[65]

Several months later, at the end of 1911, *Variety* editor Sime Silverman offered his analysis of Harry's fall, admitting the details had never been made public and probably never would be. In July, when Harry ran the Rats "with the autocracy of a dictator," he left New York for Paris to attend the International Conference of Artists' Societies. When he returned to New York late in August he found himself "stripped of all power, shorn of even the lightest responsibilities, and placed in a position that forced his resignation within one month after." Silverman speculated that to hold his leadership required his presence, and while he was away the Rats assessed him in a colder light and saw his faults more clearly — because he was away he could not use his charm and charisma to quiet his critics. To his credit, argued the editor, was a large increase in membership during his tenure. To his discredit was his "monumental ego" (as in ventures such as *The Player*) and his inability to keep a promise (his insincerity).[66]

Harry was then about 38 years old. In his earlier years he was a page in the House of Lords, afterwards becoming a reporter on a provincial (English) paper. Later he became an actor, appearing with his wife Maude Walsh as Mountford and Walsh. That ouster from the WR, said Silverman, "washed Harry Mountford off the vaudeville map of America."[67]

Under his watch the actors' groups had solidified to the point where one union existed. Harry had increased membership and developed a more focused and more militant organization, one that was not afraid to openly see itself and present itself as a union. He had led a few actions and had some minor success. But he had no success with the big-time vaudeville managers. On the other hand, he had led the group for only some 3.5 years. Not that it mattered, for Mountford was gone, apparently forever. Most observers thought so, including astute ones like Silverman. Years of quiet and disarray and decline returned to the actors' union movement. But was Harry really gone forever?

6 | Years of Stagnation Return, 1912–1915

"Neither the White Rats nor the Comedy Club has helped the artist in his struggle with the big time situation.... There are so many abuses in vaudeville, the artist is forced to organize, whether he is an actor for glory or for money."

— *Variety*, 1913

For the remainder of 1911, after Mountford's departure, the WR remained active and militant. On October 24, the Rats sent a letter to the VMPA asking for a meeting between the two sides in order "to determine some plan whereby our mutual interests may be effectively and harmoniously strengthened." It was signed by the president of the Rats, Junie McCree.[1]

One week later the VMPA sent a letter to the Rats agreeing to a meeting, but only if others were invited, as many of the vaudeville artists were not members of the WR. The VMPA proposed that any meeting also include three members of the Vaudeville Comedy Club (who were not also WR members) and three vaudeville artists who were not members of any vaudeville artists' organization (one to be picked by the VMPA, one selected by the VCC, and one by the Rats). As well, the managers insisted that any meeting was pointless unless and until the Rats shed their labor connection, that is, until the WR surrendered its AFL charter. Needless to say, no meeting took place.[2]

At a November 1 meeting in Boston the WR in that city decided to ask for a minimum wage rate for all actors who played in Boston (amount not stated), and a closed shop for the vaudeville venues and the motion picture houses in which the Rats played. Around the same time, in Chicago, the WR were in negotiations with the management of the Alfred Hamburger circuit of popular (low priced) vaudeville houses, with a view to effecting an agreement that would set a minimum wage rate of $25 a week for a single act and $50 for a double.[3]

Within a week Hamburger (head of the Louise Amusement Company, which controlled a chain that included Chicago's President, Apollo, Monroe, and Ellis venues) signed a working agreement with the WR. Among its features was a closed shop, with all differences between the parties to be settled by binding arbitration, and a minimum wage scale of $25 and $50. Hamburger's attorney held out for the concession that the Rats would pledge themselves not to respond to a call for a sympathetic walkout in the event of a strike of the stagehands. But the union stood firm and refused to agree, and that clause was omitted from the agreement. When George H. Webster, the Fargo, North Dakota, booking agent, was in Chicago that same week, the WR got him to sign a contract with the union. In that agreement Webster promised to use only a contract form approved by the WR, to pay all transportation costs of acts that were in excess of $5 a jump, and to sign only acts that were members in good standing with the Rats.[4]

Formalizing its affiliation with organized labor still further, at the 1911 convention of the AFL held in Atlanta, a mutual aid and assistance pact (fathered by Gompers) was entered into between the WR, the American Federation of Musicians, and the International Alliance of Theatrical Stage Employees (IATSE).[5]

Whatever militancy remained in the Rats during the latter part of 1911 was gone by 1912. A good deal of energy that had been directed outward was redirected inward as old animosities continued to dog the Rats. So much of an irritant had Harry De Veaux become that he was expelled from the Rats. He complained all the more, to the extent of involving the AFL in an investigation of the situation.[6]

Late in 1912 the union held the dedication ceremony for the new WR clubhouse on West 46th Street in Manhattan. Six stories high, the newly built facility had a basement containing a billiard room, bowling alleys, bar, and a swimming pool. On the main floor were offices, reception rooms and a large assembly hall. The latter had a movable gymnasium. On the second floor were the offices of the executives and the directors. The top four floors contained 107 rooms, each with hot and cold water, while many had baths. They were rented to WR members at a daily or weekly rate.[7]

Also late in 1912, a follow-up was reported on the passage of the amendments to the agency law in New York State that had been passed into law two years earlier. Among its provisions was one that prohibited a licensed agent or agents "directly or indirectly" from receiving more than a 5 percent commission on an actor's salary. Immediately upon that bill's passage the UBO, through its attorney, informed all agents then booking through the UBO to turn in their licenses to the License Commissioner of New York City. At the same time, the UBO counsel informed them that henceforth, to evade the provisions of the agency law, they had to term themselves "representatives" or "managers" of vaudeville acts "and deny to the commissioner his law-given right to supervise their theatrical operations." According to this follow-up account, "These instructions were generally followed." The next order of business was for the UBO to figure out a loophole to allow it to collect more than 5 percent, bearing in mind that "indirect" collection was not allowed. Counsel for the UBO solved that by organizing a collection agency that would collect the commission due the outside agent (5 percent maximum) and from that gross amount deduct 50 percent as a service charge (the old 2.5 percent) for the collection agency. According to *Variety*, that UBO collection agency received about $200,000 annually from collecting half of the outside agent's 5 percent, but the collection agency office was comprised of just one room and just one bookkeeper employee. Sarcastically it wondered who was getting the other $198,000.[8]

For all intents and purposes the WR had disappeared from the scene by early 1913, resurfacing only occasionally with regard to their internal dissension and battles. *Variety* editor Sime Silverman saw fit in February 1913 to publish another series of editorials on the importance of organizing and why the actors should organize. They were very similar to the editorials he and Sargent had published for months back in 1906. His first editorial in this new series made no mention whatsoever of the Rats. It was as if the group did not exist. Either Silverman believed the group no longer effectively existed or, by omission, expressed a thinly veiled contempt for the Rats. "The actor will have to get together somehow to insure his future as an actor in vaudeville. Just now he has no chance," he declared. "A protective society of influential acts would soon put a stop to the indiscriminate routing of the big time offices," he was convinced. As an example, he cited an act playing Chicago that was booked for Cincinnati the following week. Then, on the Thursday of the Chicago stand the act was told its route had been shifted to Montreal instead of the Cincinnati date, with the Ohio city the week after. No offer to pay the excess transportation fees was made by management. Since a player had to pay all his own expenses he always factored in the transportation costs to determine if he could afford to accept the offered salary for a specific tour. In this case the act was forced to refuse the new routing. As a result the act lost a full week or two until it could find a new place. "There is a way to prevent that sort of work," said the editor. Silverman wrote of other abuses suffered by actors and other shady practices engaged in by agents and managers, as he had done seven years earlier. Apparently little had changed.[9]

In a subsequent piece Silverman warned the actors about salary cuts, and that the only way for the actor to improve his lot was to function collectively: "It really does look as though the big time actor must act for himself through concerted movements." This time, briefly, he mentioned the WR, but only in passing to say they had never protested a technical rule involving IATSE and the use of an extra stagehand when the Rats were allied with the AFL. He used the past tense when he made the mention, although the WR were still a part of the AFL.[10]

After giving more details of shady practices and the need to organize in his February 21 editorial, Silverman mused, "Is the big time actor going to protect himself against the big time manager?" Then he mentioned the Rats again. "And don't forget the union connections of the White Rats. The manager hasn't. The Rats had the softest thing in the world to beat the managers with and threw it away, or at least it seems so." However, he did not explain his last point.[11]

Around the time Silverman was fulminating, a couple of new organizations were announced. One was another of the type that barely surfaced before it disappeared. But the other was more significant. In 1913 Actors' Equity was formed (see Chapter Ten). It was the only actors' union that would truly last, and marked the first step to a lasting and continuing labor movement for the actor. As to the other, it was reported in May that a quiet movement was underway to organize what was to be called the Vaudeville Protective Association. Some 15 well-known vaudeville stars were said to be working on this new society. "The object and purpose of the Vaudeville Protective Association is covered by the title," said a reporter for *Variety*. He then echoed the sentiments of Silverman when he added, "That such an organization is an undisputed need among vaudeville artists is recognized and has been for a long while. Neither the White Rats nor the Comedy Club has helped the artist in his struggles with the big-time situation." A distinction was made between big-time or first-class vaudeville (such as found in the VMPA houses) and small-time (or popular, meaning lower-priced to the patron) vaudeville. Concluded the journalist, "There are so many abuses in vaudeville, the artist is forced to organize, whether he is an actor for glory or for money."[12]

After working covertly for months, a group of film actors gave up in despair, in July 1913, on their attempt to organize into a union the rank and file movie actors of New York and vicinity. "Everybody remembers a similar attempt at rounding up a union of movie actors, started more than a year ago, also suddenly came to naught. The plan abandoned yesterday was similar in scope to its predecessor," reported a journalist. Those trying to organize their fellow players hoped to have been able to come out into the open with a strike threat to the film producers unless certain problems in working conditions were addressed. But that never happened because "to be discovered agitating reforms meant a sweeping application of the blacklist, [therefore] each of the agitators was working under cover." At a final meeting of the organizers at the Hotel Astor it was decided to call everything off because they learned every move made by the organizers had been reported to the film producers by stool pigeons. With the collapse of the movement, said a reporter, "the movie actor falls back to his past and present condition of peonage." Earlier a group called the Screen Club had suffered the same fate as the Actors' Society. It began originally to address those problems, "But time reduced the club to a purely social body, where favors might be courted and exchanged between the directors who joined and the actors who belonged."13

The AFL announced late in 1913 that it intended to organize chorus girls and boys. P. F. Duffy, the AFL general organizer, explained he had called a mass meeting of choristers for November 23. At that time some 70 chorus members promised they would come to the meeting and testify to abuses of managers. Testimony would reveal 14 weeks of rehearsals were held for the production *Oh, I Say* before any salary was paid to the chorus people. As well, the Century Opera company kept its chorus members working every day from 10 A.M. until near midnight, demanding familiarity with all standard operas and paying salaries of just $12 to $16 per week. Producers Klaw and Erlanger never paid for any time devoted to rehearsals, while the Shubert brothers, producers, summarily dismissed 24 chorus girls after six weeks of unpaid rehearsals and two weeks of paid work. Duffy wanted to see chorus members receive half-salary for all rehearsals and planned to collect back salaries due to chorus members who had not been paid — if those managers were solvent.14

At the end of November it was reported that a union of chorus people was a fact — 25 paid the initiation fee on November 23, and 50 more were said to be prepared to do the same over the coming few days. Sixty-eight women and men attended the meeting. The Chorus People's Alliance was the name of the new organization. Monthly dues were 50 cents; the initiation fee was 50 cents. Other demands of the new union, besides half-pay for rehearsals, was full pay for extra performances over the standard number, and a two-weeks' notice clause. Among other abuses reported were that John Cort's *The Purple Road* closed abruptly in Brooklyn with three weeks' salary due the choristers. Cort and Gaites' *Enchantress* closed and stranded the company in Los Angeles, with two weeks' salary due the chorus people. Lee Morrison still owed choristers an unspecified amount for their services in *The Romance of Billy Goat Hill* after his company was stranded in San Antonio, Texas. The Century Opera company did not pay for the Sunday night shows in which their $14 and $16 a week chorus people were ordered to appear. One determination of the new union was to keep its members' names secret to prevent discrimination against them by the managers.[15]

Around that same time an arrangement was arrived at between *Variety* and the WR house organ, *The Player*, due to publish its last issue in late November 1913. In the future, the WR agreed to use *Variety* as its weekly news medium. That is, it purchased an unspecified number of pages weekly in the publication (probably an average of two pages per issue) in which it published its news, announcements, opinions, and so on. *Variety* assumed the money-losing organ's receivables, debts, and so on. Having come to this arrangement, *Variety*, which previously could rarely find a good word to say about the Rats, suddenly discovered a few. "In the White Rats Actors' Union of America, *Variety* recognized the only artists' organization that has the good and welfare of the actor as its motive."[16]

As of the end of 1913 the WR by-law concerned with membership went as follows: "Every white actor, performer or entertainer in the amusement world, male or female, of good moral character, and in mental and physical condition satisfactory to the lodge, irrespective of religion or nationality, who is now, and has been, a bona-fide actor and performer or entertainer in the amusement world for at least one year and pursues such as his principal means of livelihood, is eligible for membership...." Male applicants had to apply in writing and be endorsed by 11 male members of the Order who knew the applicant possessed the necessary qualifications. Female applicants had to apply in writing and be endorsed by two members — that is to become members of the Associated Actresses of America (set up on September 23, 1910), which was part of the WR, a sort of ladies auxiliary. Women members did not have a vote, nor could they bring forward business at a WR meeting, but were still classed as part of the Order, through this auxiliary. It was the Rats' way of dealing with the woman question. The initiation fee for male and female members was $25. A nomination for male membership had to be read at two consecutive meetings of the Order and thereafter called up for a ballot at any time. In the balloting, if a candidate received no more than two black balls he was admitted.[17]

Racism in unions, as in the above, was commonplace in the mainstream organized labor movement of the time. One had to go outside the mainstream to radical unions, such as the Knights of Labor and the Industrial Workers of the World, to find relatively non-racist unions at this time. In a speech at an AFL banquet in 1910, president Samuel Gompers said the supremacy of the Caucasian race in the unions should be maintained. Said Gompers, "There are 8,000,000 negroes in the United States, and to my mind they cannot all be expected to understand the philosophy of human rights."[18]

Ernest Hogan was a black variety artist who said, in 1906, that the total number of black acts on the variety stage then numbered over 50, giving employment to over 200 blacks. He wanted to see a labor organization started for black actors. According to Hogan, blacks first appeared in vaudeville around 1886 when Bob Kelley and Lottie Holmes (billed as Kelley and Holmes) appeared in the music halls in the East.[19]

A full-page ad from the Rats in *Variety* at the end of 1913 solicited members. Perhaps it was a sign of decline in the organization that it wanted to try and reverse. Or perhaps it was a sign the Rats were preparing to shed their recent dormancy for a spate of renewed activity.[20]

By September 1914 Frank Fogarty was president of the Rats and the author of many pieces in *The Player* section of *Variety* that touted the benefits of organizing. Editor Silverman commented that those pieces "breathed sincerity," and then went on to praise Fogarty and how the need to organize could be accomplished by joining the WR. It was a complete change of position. Concluded Silverman:

> The White Rats is for the actors, and "actors" cover any field where they act. Frank Fogarty is for the Rats and for the actors. He is doing some tall work single handed. Why let a man work along when he's not working for himself, and you can help him? Show the proper spirit. Now is the time. If you are a Rat be a good one, and if you are not a Rat, become a good one.[21]

Despite assurances from the UBO that vaudeville salaries would not be cut, that was precisely what the Theatrical Trust did in October 1914. A committee of managers appointed by the UBO got together, set new rates and then declared the general decrease would take effect two weeks later.

The delay in implementation was to allow any act refusing to accept a salary cut to cancel any existing contract under the two weeks' notice provision. Although no specified percentage was followed in imposing the salary reductions, it was estimated the decrease averaged around 15 percent. Acts paid $1,000 a week were cut $200 (down to $800), while acts paid $300 to $400 a week had decreases of from $25 to $75 per week. In a weak and ineffectual response, WR president Fogarty communicated with the UBO, requesting a statement be issued by them assuring acts that when better times prevailed either later that season or in future seasons, the former salary scale would be restored.[22]

Some eight months passed and the Rats offered no other activity with regard to the salary cuts. Not surprisingly, the union was subject to increasingly heavy criticism and for "permitting" the salary cuts. The annual report from the WR Board of Directors in June 1915 went off on a tangent by first arguing that if all the graft were eliminated that was siphoned off by corrupt agents and managers, enough money would remain that salary cuts would not have been needed at all. Then the report added, bizarrely, "It is up to the actor and actress to support the White Rats Actors' Union — not the White Rats Actors' Union to support the actor and actress." That is, the group did not have enough members putting enough money into the coffers. It then had perhaps 600 members.[23]

Just as suddenly as Mountford had left the Rats, so did he return, four years after his abrupt departure. A special meeting of the WR was held in mid–October 1915, attended by several hundred enthusiastic members of the Rats. It was announced that Harry had returned, at the request of the Board of Directors, to the position of International Organizer of the group. When that announcement was made, it was reported, Mountford received the "greatest demonstration ever recorded in the clubhouse" from the crowd — a standing ovation that lasted several minutes. When he spoke to the crowd he stressed the need for an urgent campaign to enlarge the membership. After that he wanted to go after an equitable contract and a closed shop. While he thought such things could be attained through conciliation or arbitration, he remarked, "In the event of a double failure, force will have to be utilized." Also emphasized by Harry was the need to address the salary cuts.[24]

In the same issue of *Variety* in which the return of Harry was announced, the subject was, of course, almost the only matter discussed in the WR pages of the publication. A special resolution passed at the meeting declared, "This special meeting of the White Rats Actors' Union hereby unanimously endorses and heartily approves of the action of the Board of Directors in re-engaging Harry Mountford, as International Organizer, and pledges to the Board of Directors and to him, their absolute support in any steps it may be necessary to take to re-establish the power and position of the Organization and to protect the actor in the exercise of his profession and obtain for him fair treatment and justice." Harry had a full page of his own wherein he urged old, lapsed members to return to the union, and for new ones to enroll.[25]

A brief item in the *New York Times* also announced the return of Mountford, and that he would lead the fight against the abuses actors were subjected to. It offered an entirely different reason for Harry's earlier departure, but provided no details. "Several years ago Mr. Mountford, who was then active in the economic affairs of the club, incurred the displeasure of the vaudeville heads, who finally succeeded in having him deposed."[26]

A worsening situation for vaudeville actors, emphasized and exacerbated by a stiff salary cut and an impotent response by the Rats, led to increasing dissatisfaction on the part of the actors and paved the way for the return of Mountford. Any qualms they may have harbored toward him from the past were lost in the urgency of the immediate situation. First the WR membership had to be increased, and then the VMPA had to be tackled. No longer could the Rats, and Harry, content themselves with a victory here and a victory there in small-time vaudeville. It was time for a direct battle with the Trust.

7 | Mountford Returns, a War of Words, 1916

"Will you ever know the great number of misled artists who gave up the last five dollars [semi-annual dues] they had in the world for hopeless and sinister agitation; that the agitator and his clique might ride in Pullman cars, smoke imported cigarettes and cigars and buy champagne for themselves and friends."
— Vaudeville Managers' Protective Association, 1916

"It is quite evident that dining car and first-class restaurant fare agrees with the Dictator of Ratdom [Mountford], for never was a rodent more hale and hearty of avoirdupois than this self-same 'Arry, who for several months has been regaling himself in luxury at the expense of the 'sheep.'"
— *Billboard*, 1916

One of Harry's first moves to try and increase membership was to announce a dramatic decrease in the initiation fee to $10 for the WR and the Associated Actresses of America, down from the previous $30 each had charged. Dues remained the same, at $5 for six months in each organization.[1]

Right at the beginning of 1916 the WR passed a resolution granting local autonomy to several branches of the organization. It meant each of those branches could elect local officers, and each branch would have complete charge of local issues, such as working conditions, minimum salaries, contracts, and so on. Also passed by the membership was a resolution admitting all members of the Associated Actresses of America to the meetings of the organization. Designed to give women "a voice in the government of the organization," it was another step toward equality of the sexes, perhaps designed to help recruit people in its membership drive.[2]

As Harry eased back into the leadership role at the WR and began to push them towards a more militant position, the Theatrical Trust carefully monitored the situation. In fact, they monitored everything far too closely for the union's liking. When an unnamed WR made an impassioned speech in favor of the Rats at a union meeting, he found that a prosperous vaudeville route he had contracted for was suddenly cancelled (with the invocation of the two weeks' notice clause found in all contracts used by the UBO). Inside vaudeville, wrote a journalist, "it is being said other cancellations may follow fiery appeals made before meetings of Rats, where the tenor of the speeches may not strike those booking men who have the placing of routes under their command as calculated to promote harmony between the manager and the artist." Blacklisting was a powerful weapon, and the stool pigeon was everywhere. "The cancer of all artists' meetings in the past is again evidencing its presence — managers know what occurs at Rats' meetings almost as soon as they are ended," explained the reporter. That same trouble had plagued the Rats in the past, but the union had never been able to put a stop to it.[3]

Blacklisting, or the fear of same, had played a part in *The Player* becoming a money loser and for its changed circumstances. Usually, the story was given that the decline of the house organ was all Harry's fault, one more example of his profligate ways, one more example of misdirected priorities and his general mismanagement and inability to lead. However, vaudeville historian Joe Laurie Jr. noted, many years later, that *The Player* started out with a lot of advertising, but soon the acts who had placed those ads, and even some of the commercial firms, started to withdraw their ads because of the fear of being blacklisted. According to Laurie, Albee used the blacklist freely:

> Albee had many spies in the White Rats, who reported everything that was said and done. He also had spies on bills who sent in reports on the acts as to how they felt toward the White Rats and the booking office; they were paid off with steady bookings. None of the White Rats would wear their buttons; that was a sure invitation for the blacklist. After four years the union had to give up *The Player* [and take the *Variety* space].[4]

The *New York Dramatic Mirror* and *Variety* had clearly established themselves in the past as anti–Rat and anti–Mountford. To that list could be added the third of the three most influential trade journals devoted to actors and their endeavors —*Billboard*. Early in 1916 it asked itself whether an actor who did not join the union was a parasite, as Harry had often described the non-union player in some of his pieces. "From our experiences and knowledge of the Rats and their methods we would say that a majority of them and not the non–Rats are the parasites in the true sense of the word," concluded the journal.[5]

At a meeting of the VMPA's Organizing Committee (as the union-fighting section was called) at the start of March 1916, it decided on a campaign of publicity from the manager's viewpoint to offset the WR's announced policy of trying to achieve a closed shop. Launching that campaign was a two-page ad in *Variety*, wherein much of the campaign would be waged over the coming months. The two sides engaged in a vigorous insult campaign through their paid advertisements.[6]

In the same issue of *Variety* there appeared a "news item" that ostensibly was written by vaudeville actor Charles Fletcher, who resigned from the WR and chose to reveal publicly his reasons for resigning. Fletcher pointed out the supposed autocratic rule of Mountford and the fact that no dissenting opinion was allowed. He warned his readers:

> Do not allow your mind to be distracted by the temporary excitement and hysterical enthusiasm of a mob of malcontents, who are led, or rather misled, by individuals whose sole purpose and business it is to stir up strife.... Who are the malcontents who shout the loudest when the agitator pours out his venomous eloquence? Look them over. You will see for yourself that this disgruntled army is largely composed of performers whose offerings have grown stale and threadbare with too long usage. They are men who lack the initiative and enterprise to keep up with the times.

While Fletcher may have resigned from the Rats, it was very unlikely he wrote this piece — simply lending his name to the item, perhaps for a price. The language, cadence and terminology had all the earmarks of a Sime Silverman editorial — the use of "agitator" as code for Harry, for example. Also, the idea that only performers with little or no talent joined the Rats, in the hope it would force managers to give them work, was regularly presented by Silverman, *Variety*, and the VMPA in much the same way as Fletcher supposedly wrote it. Presumably, when such ideas were presented from a former Rat they carried more clout than when rehashed for the umpteenth time by the trade journals.[7]

A few days later the VMPA reorganized its Rat-fighting committee to be comprised of William Fox, Marcus Loew, Sam Scribner, Edward F. Albee, B. S. Moss, Martin Beck, and John Ringling. They were charged with selecting and formulating plans to resist the Rats. It was the view of this committee that if the union persisted in its demands it would face a lockout and no WR would be booked at any vaudeville house in America. Adamantly opposed to the closed shop, the VMPA declared that to submit to it in any form would mean nothing less than "virtual conversion of their business interest to the hands of the actors' representatives in the union."[8]

Despite its open loathing for the Rats, *Billboard* somewhat perversely took credit in print for having brought about changes in the workings of its "clique," and that it had won local autonomy for the members, and that it had also won its fight to give the Associated Actresses of America the right to attend WR meetings and to vote therein. There was no truth in any of those claims. Also, *Billboard* still sided with, and aided, the so-called insurgents (the Harry De Veaux remnants, from the old ANPU, later AIU) in their long-running battle against the Rats, within and without the forum of the AFL. The whole matter ran on for years before finally dying out.[9]

A two-page tirade against Harry was placed by the VMPA in the March 10 issue of *Variety*, although his name was not used once — the code word "agitator" was used instead (many, many times). First, the players were called on to remember the past: "Must the artist be reminded of the agitation and threatened disruption of vaudeville, which practically bankrupted the organized actors. Were not the propaganda, the fancied grievances, the promises of the Agitator the same then as they are now?" Next the VMPA attacked the current spending of the WR as it campaigned for new members, took out ads, paid for trips so Harry and other Rat officers could attend meetings and rallies — train fares, hotel expenses, and so on. "Will you ever know the great number of misled artists who gave up the last five dollars [semiannual dues] they had in the world for hopeless and sinister agitation, that the Agitator and his clique might ride in Pullman cars, smoke imported cigarettes and cigars and buy champagne for themselves and friends?" (Mountford did not smoke cigars; he did not drink.) Then the VMPA harked back to the 1911 campaign of threats: "Do you realize the wasteful extravagance and the enormous amount of money dissipated in the last campaign of agitation and disruption? ... If any artist or organization of artists has derived any benefit which in the slightest degree equals any part of the expenditure of $200,000 of the artists' money, we would like to hear from him" [a nonsense number apparently pulled out of the air].[10]

After pounding Mountford for a while in this ad, the VMPA showed its soft and caring side — for a brief moment: "Why are the managers so solicitous? The answer is that the artist's welfare is our welfare and vice versa." Another point hammered home again and again by the VMPA was expressed in this ad in the following fashion: "Remember that the most efficient and capable bricklayer gets the same wages as the most incapable one"— that is, in a closed shop all were paid the same. Concluded the ad, "We are unalterably opposed to the White Rats as at present constituted," and, "There is no middle course; the artist is either with the agitator or against him.... If he is against the agitation he should likewise be man enough to assert his rights and get out of the organization and stay out until the organization is willing to stand for something good and practical in vaudeville." The battle of insults between the two sides was also a battle of typefaces and sizes. Each side was partial to peppering their text with a larger type face than used in the rest of *Variety* and to all-too-regularly make use of bold face, bold face capitals, and (less often) italics.[11]

A news story in *Billboard* in its March 11 issue was as biased and hostile and inaccurate a piece of reporting as you could find. After attacking Harry "the agitator" over his closed shop policies the piece noted that before acceding to such a "preposterous demand" the managers would institute a lockout "and shut every vaude house in America." Said the reporter, "Thus far the vaudeville managers have been on the defensive ... and while they are making no threats to precipitate a crisis, the managers are unanimous in their stand that at the first indication of insurrection on the part of the White Rats they will force a blockade unlike anything hitherto attempted in the vaudeville history of the United States." Managers in vaudeville were "not against organization in the vaudeville ranks, but they are strongly and unalterably opposed to unionism, so far as it affects the vaudeville actor and as planned by Mountford in his 'closed shop' policy, and it is Mountford and these policies that the managers are to fight," explained the account. In the view of the reporter there was only one solution: "the disposition of the disturber from their ranks." In any case, those managers contended unionism of vaudeville artists was "an impossibility in that vaudeville is an art, which can not be standardized, as can the stage hand, the carpenter and others." Finally, this reporter also explained the managers' soft, caring side: "The managers have always been willing to meet the actor in a social organization. They have always been willing to arbitrate any troubles that might arise and they are willing to meet the actor under proper conditions, but they will not for an instant tolerate the rantings of an agitator whose policies can only bring about ruin for the actor, as well as trouble for the vaudeville interests themselves."[12]

Billboard used a tactic similar to the one used by *Variety*, with respect to Fletcher, in its March 11 issue. It took the form of a letter to the editor from a former member of the WR, Major James Doyle, giving the "truth" about the WR. Unlike the usual letter to the editor, this one was not placed in the regular position of such items in the publication; rather, it was placed in the news section where it was given a full half-page of its own — as though it was a news item (although clearly identified as a letter to the editor) — and given a special border around it to set it off and make it stand out. Doyle's effort was the standard tirade and attack on Mountford and the closed shop, and on his supposed lavish spending of union money. "So tell your advisor, Mountford, to stop kidding about closed shops, as the only closed shops you will see will be the ones that are closed against you," he declared. With the WR semi-annual dues due on April 1, Doyle urged the Rats not to send in their money to Harry.[13]

As the Rats focused on the big-time vaudeville operators the group still occasionally scored a victory in the small-time circuits. As of March 1916 the Empress Theater in Des Moines, Iowa, became a Rat house after it signed an agreement with the union to play only acts that were in good standing as WR members. Last-minute non–Rat fill-in acts were allowed, but performers in such acts were expected to apply for membership in the union.[14]

After "resolving" the woman issue, the Rats turned to the Black issue. In recognition of the fact there was no provision for a black artist to carry a union card (according to a WR proclamation in March 1916), the organization announced it had just formed a Colored Branch of the White Rats Actors' Union of America for all black artists, male and female. The initiation fee, set at a special price good to mid–April, was $1, with the semiannual dues being $5, the same as for white men and women. Officially the new offshoot was styled White Rats Actors' Union, Colored Branch.[15]

Following a statement made by Mountford at an open WR meeting, a *Variety* reporter asked a VMPA official if what Harry said was true — that instructions had been sent out by the VMPA to all house managers to determine who were Rats among the acts on his bill. The VMPA spokesman admitted it was true and that the VMPA even had a special form printed up for the managers to fill in, declaring who were and who were not White Rats on his bill.[16]

A favorite point the VMPA loved to hammer at was the contention that the WR executives ran up huge expenses and were wasteful in their expenditures; it often demanded to see the WR books. Finally, Harry wrote them a letter wherein he agreed to show them the Rat books, but if and only if the VMPA allowed him to see the UBO books. An outraged reply letter said no, using the spurious argument that the UBO was not the VMPA (it basically was). At the end of its unsigned reply letter to Mountford the VMPA added a P.S.: "Having answered your first letter to this Association we do not wish to indulge in any further correspondence."[17]

Some 500 movie actors were said to have enrolled in the Screen Club by the summer of 1917. It was then strictly a social club, whatever it had started out to be. A year earlier the Rats had tried to interest individual members of the Screen Club, or the group as a whole, in joining or affiliating with the Rats, but had virtually no success. Only a couple of members of the Screen Club joined the Rats. Ever ready to attack Mountford, a *Billboard* article claimed that lack of success stemmed, for one reason, from the fact one of the Screen Club originators, a Mr. Knowles, knew Harry from way back and was opposed to him and his style, methods, and so on. No details were given.[18]

A large, enthusiastic mass meeting held in Chicago on March 24 was addressed by Mountford and many other labor people. In his address, Harry reiterated WR demands. As well, he referred to the numerous personal attacks on him in the media and claimed that a "Cincinnati theatrical publication" (*Billboard*) had offered him $50 a week to write two columns per week, and the management of the publication had written him to say that no one need know that he, Mountford, was to receive money for writing under his own name. If that seemed an unlikely offer from a journal that attacked him so severely, it was. Likely it was a lie from Mountford. Although the media made requests to see that letter, Harry could never produce it. Another rash statement he made at the meeting was that after May 26 next, all artists not Rats would be forced to join the union. Of course, it was all nonsense, as he had no ability to bring it about. Such foolish statements — and lies — came from Harry all too often; they were fuel for his critics, and caused discomfort among his supporters. He had perhaps made the statement about forced membership because dues were not coming in, and the resultant lack of money was crippling the union. A campaign by the VMPA urging Rats not to make the upcoming dues payments was perhaps successful enough to hurt the Rats. Said a reporter, "The managers are also making a stand on the dues of the White Rats. They were reported this week using their underground methods to inform acts the payment of Rats' dues hereafter would be considered an antagonistic step to the managements."[19]

Also at that meeting, various rumors surfaced. One had it that the organization of another union, "a friendly vaudeville association," was underway, but no details were then available. More stories about acts being cancelled because they were Rats also made the rounds. Booking agents were said to be compiling data on the attitudes acts they handled held toward the WR. A UBO executive remarked that some acts that played UBO time volunteered the information to managers that they were not in sympathy with the Rats' closed shop movement. To convince themselves such statements were genuine, the executive said, the VMPA managers had agreed upon a scheme of detection (no details given) and to take concerted action against those professing themselves in favor of managements and who attempted to promote the White Rat movement when not under managerial observation.[20]

Heralding an increase in the use of the blacklist by the VMPA, *Billboard*, in its April 1 issue, enthused in the article subheads: "Drastic embargo is being enforced on members of obnoxious organization," and, "Initial steps to crush the actors' union as at present constituted have been taken." Vaudeville managers all over America, according to the story, had launched a campaign to put the Rats out of business. To that end an embargo had been placed on WR acts, and "before the next two weeks have elapsed, few, if any, active White Rats will be found employed in any of the vaudeville theaters of the country. And, what is more, the managers are enforcing the embargo in a perfectly legitimate manner." Each vaudeville manager had been instructed to go to every act on Monday mornings (when the new bill for the coming week was required to check in) and personally ask every member on the bill whether or not he was a White Rat, "And upon the answers are dependent the booking such actors will here after receive." While there was likely some truth in the account, much of it was wild exaggeration.[21]

In the opinion of *Billboard*, many of the WR were having their eyes opened "and realize that the Rats are controlled by an army of unemployed whose attitude might best be likened to the bully of schoolboy days." Noting that Mountford had advised his members to deny membership in the union, in view of that embargo, the horrified trade journal declared, "This is but one of the many underhanded methods adopted by him." Rumors of another union started to become more fact than fancy. Managers believed the time was then ripe "for the conservative performers to affiliate in some new order" wherein they would "construct instead of wreck," and wherein they could "take advantage of the propositions that have been made to the heads of the White Rats" (none had ever been made). Those managers reportedly were willing and anxious to meet the actors on equal grounds, and debate and arbitrate all questions just as soon as they "eliminate the labor part from their organization." Confidently, *Billboard* declared that the WR was tottering, and, with the help of the embargo, within a short period of time it would be "practically a nonentity, with Harry Mountford deposed and ruin in its wake."[22]

One week later *Billboard* announced that because of the embargo actively pursued by the VMPA, "hundreds" of WR acts had already been cancelled or were slated to be so treated during the coming week. Also reported was that resignations from the union were pouring into the WR headquarters from actors all over the country, with many of those actors going to the extent of sending carbon copies of their resignations to various vaudeville managers in order to have the documents placed on record as evidence they had severed ties with the union. Boasted of by *Billboard* was that what it had reported was all inside information obtained from the WR head office.[23]

Numbers were downgraded a week later in *Billboard* in a similar story about mass cancellations of acts and mass resignations from the union. Within the fine print was the following: "It is conservatively estimated that fully thirty-five or forty acts playing the U.B.O. time have been cancelled in the last two weeks," not "hundreds" as had previously been stated. All of those 35 were "prominently identified" either with the agitation for a closed shop or as one who had "signified his or her acquiescence with existing conditions by paying dues for the ensuing term."[24]

Results of a WR election in April 1916 were a cause of great consternation to *Billboard*. Harry had been acclaimed as International Organizer — the fact that no one chose to run against him was considered testament to his popularity and his support among the rank and file. Two slates of candidates ran for the other positions, such as president, treasurer, board of directors, and so on. The slate considered to be the most in line with Harry won every position contested — except that of president; James William Fitzpatrick won that post. "By sanctioning the past performances of the officers and board members, a majority of the Rats have gone on record as being heartily in accord with the policies which have put them in disfavor with organized vaudeville, and which now, more than ever, will result in a relentless fight on the part of the vaudeville managers to wipe the White Rats out of existence," moaned *Billboard*. Completely unable and unwilling to accept the election result, the publication added, "The Rats have no one to blame but themselves. The *Billboard* has from time to time pointed out to them the folly of sticking to the sinking ship, but, like the sheep that many of them are, they have allowed themselves to be led to the inevitable slaughter." The clique was still in charge. As a final thought, the piece warned all WR and potential Rats to think twice about even attending any of the union's meetings because "there will be representatives from the Vaudeville Manager's Protective Association on hand to check up the enthusiasts" at all such gatherings.[25]

Did such spies exist, and did they attend all meetings? *Variety* offered evidence that indeed they did. As part of their boast about knowing every-thing that went on at Rat meetings, the VMPA declared it knew all that had transpired at a secret WR meeting held in Boson on April 14, despite the fact that all at that meeting were obliged to take an oath of silence with respect to that meeting. Then a full account of that meeting was forwarded to the VMPA headquarters in New York the next day. A *Variety* reporter went to the New York office and asked if the story was true. A VMPA executive told him, "Our sources of information are such that we do not believe any vaudeville organization can keep secret what we wish to know." And, "If it is of any general interest, you may say that we have a complete record of the Rats to date, taking in those who have paid their dues and those who have not, we securing that, as well as reports of their meetings, to protect our-selves against those who might wish to deceive us in personal conversations." The cynical reporter, who felt the whole thing might be a bluff, asked the VMPA executive for proof of his statements. Within 10 minutes he pro-duced a typed copy of the doings at the Boston meeting and read from it in detail—all determined to be accurate.[26]

Throughout this period, Harry Mountford's style, whether in giving speeches or in writing items for the WR pages in *Variety*, was as strident and over-the-top as was that of the VMPA and its media supporters. He con-tinually hectored and badgered actors who were not then members of the union. In an April 21 item in *Variety* designed to win new converts to the union and to regain lapsed old members, Harry headed the piece, "To the cowards and cry-babies. To the weepers and the weak-kneed." As far as Mountford was concerned, all those who did not join the Rats and show sol-idarity were cowards, traitors, parasites, and so on.[27]

Billboard continued to run articles about Rat acts being cancelled due to the embargo, and that "hundreds" of letters of resignation from the union continued to pour into the WR office. As of late April it gloated that not one of the recently elected officers of the WR, and only two of the 21 mem-bers of the Board of Directors, were then working in vaudeville, and boasted that when that pair each finished his current week they would not work again "for some weeks to come." Concluded the report, "There are still a number of White Rats working in vaudeville, but the managers are hot on their trail. They are being weeded out as rapidly as is possible and with as much speed as is consistent in the matter of proceeding without completely disrupting bookings, and it will not be many weeks before the ranks of organized vaude-ville are entirely freed of the agitating members of the organization."[28]

A week later *Billboard* delivered an attack on WR membership numbers in an illogical and mathematically challenged way. Reportedly, only 30 percent of the members who were in good standing on April 1 (nearly one month earlier) had paid their dues for the coming six months. Paid-up membership totalled 5,500 to 6,000 on April 1, and thus was no more than 2,500 then. Bizarrely, it added that the WR union had been paying a per capita tax to the AFL (all affiliated unions paid the Federation an annual amount, to run the AFL body, based on a tax on each member) on an alleged total membership of 11,000. "The *Billboard* is in a position to state, and without fear of contradiction, that at no time in the history of the White Rats Actors' Union of America has the total membership been more than 6,800. This highest membership was in the heyday of the organization right at the time it became affiliated with the Federation of Labor." After saying again that Harry and the WR Board of Directors deliberately misquoted their membership numbers and paid a per capita tax "grossly in excess of the actual paid up membership," it went on to state that shortly before Harry's return to the union the WR was paying a per capita tax based on 11,000 members. That is, it did not just happen on Harry's watch. However, it added, the pre–Harry Rats then reduced the number reported to the AFL down to 8,000, at a time when there were only about 2,500 paid-up members. As soon as Harry returned, he advised AFL officials that the WR had 1,400, while at the same time instructing his bookkeeping department to increase the number each month so AFL officials might believe it was Mountford who was rehabilitating the WR. In December 1915, continued *Billboard*, Harry paid a per capita tax on 4,000 members when it was actually 3,500 at most. To confound the issue even more, at the recent WR election — when there were 6,000 paid-up members at most, 18,727 votes were said to have been cast — the yes and no total on a referendum question. Of course, none of those figures were accurate; nor did they make any sense. Unexplained was why Harry, and the WR before his return, would pay the AFL far more than necessary. Undoubtedly, the Federation wanted to be paid an accurate per capita amount, but it had no interest in receiving padded numbers. The Rats and Harry gained nothing. Moreover, the Rats never officially released membership numbers, probably because they were low. It may have made sense for the Rats to lie about membership numbers and present an inflated number to the VMPA, but they never did so. When such blatant lies were printed about the Rats and Harry they were never refuted in the media — for the simple reason they were boycotted by that media. A charge against the VMPA usually brought a responding interview from that organization — their side — but it did not happen with the Rats. Charges and slanders against the union were left hanging, with "their side" afforded no opportunity to respond. The only way the Rats could get a message out was through their paid-for pages in *Variety*.[29]

Hostility turned into taunting at the end of April when *Billboard* editorially challenged Harry to make good on his vague statements that perhaps the Rats would have to strike if union demands were not met:

> Prove to us that we are in error as to your sincerity and we will apologize. Call a strike — no matter how effective it may be. Call any kind of a strike — and see where you and your henchmen land.... Mr. Mountford, it looks very much as though you will bring about a CLOSED SHOP in vaudeville, but it will be a closed shop against White Rats. The *Billboard* warns you, Mr. Mountford, to call your threatened strike in a hurry, for soon there will not be any "active" White Rats left in vaudeville for you to call out.[30]

On May 1 the National Vaudeville Artists, Inc. (NVA) filed articles of incorporation with the Secretary of State of New York. That oft-rumored other union had officially arrived. Of course, it was a company union, a scab union, formed and controlled by the VMPA, but such was never publicly admitted, as lip service was paid, sort of, to the idea it was a real union, a true alternative to the Rats. Principal objects were said to be the promotion of the general welfare of actors, artists, and vaudeville performers, and to encourage and promote closer and more harmonious business and social relations between the actors and theatrical managers. It had been formed, said a reporter, by actors who had become "disgusted with the internal conditions" of the Rats, and who had determined that an organization for social and beneficial results "is far more preferable than one identified with organized labor, and having labor principles as its policies."[31]

According to the account, the fledgling organization had already received over 7,500 letters, telegrams, and cards of support, and the NVA would start out with a "bona fide membership of between 2,000 and 3,000." In order to avoid going into debt, the new society would lease a modest clubhouse instead of an expensive one (an indirect dig at the Rats, their expensive home, and "profligate" ways), and spend the money saved on benefits for the members. Admitted was that the VMPA had signified a willingness and desire to back the new organization, and that it would go out of its way to foster and promote it. Also, the VMPA promised the NVA an equitable contract and that a Grievance Committee would be empowered to deal with the managers. And if that was not satisfactory, the aggrieved NVA members "will have the right and privilege of negotiating with the managers direct." The ten incorporators of the society — to act as a Board of Directors, pending the first election, slated for June — were: Eddie Leonard, George McKay, Hugh Herbert, Henry Chesterfield, Oscar Larraine, Bert Fitzgibbon, Bob Albright, Harry Carroll, Al Lydell, and Hale Norcross.[32]

A full-page ad for the NVA appeared in the May 13 issue of *Billboard*, an unsigned ad. As the new group was barely in existence and likely had no money in the bank, it was probably reasonable to assume that the VMPA paid for the ad. Its attack on the WR contained old, familiar themes: "The average White Rats do not possess acts that are saleable, and many of them have been so long out of bookings that they have practically ceased to be recognized as performers, and yet they are the ones in the White Rat organization who sit in the New York clubhouse and vote on the rules and regulations that are to govern the performers who are out working." Addressing the idea that it was actually the managers who had formed the NVA, the ad declared, "It was not the managers who conceived the idea, but a number of high-class vaudeville performers, who first approached the managers to ascertain whether they would lend assistance to a new organization based on sane principles, and receiving that assurance went away with their plans of organization."[33]

Also addressed by the ad was the question of bookings. "Inasmuch as the managers are lending their moral support to this organization, it is only natural that members of the new order will receive preference in the matter of booking in the future. Every circuit will be supplied with a complete list of the membership so that the managers will know who are and who are not affiliated," explained the ad. What it all came down to, though, was, "the main feature of this great new organization is the harmony that it will promote between the managers and the artists. It will forever do away with strife between these two factions that are so necessary to each other's welfare."[34]

Back in New York early in May, after an eight-week organizing trip through the West, Mountford got a big reception at the Rats' clubhouse. Many people made speeches. Scotch comedian Harry Lauder praised the WR and Harry, and urged actors to join. Lauder pointed out Mountford as the man who organized the English artists without receiving any pay for it. WR vice president Eddie Clark identified himself as one of the victims of the UBO blacklist. In his remarks Harry alluded to the NVA as an inspiration of the UBO executives, and read from several newspaper clippings in reference to that order that he explained were public relations material issued by the UBO.[35]

As time passed the attacks on Harry and the Rats by *Billboard* became increasingly strident and personal, almost reaching the point of hysteria. An editorial addressed to AFL president Samuel Gompers by the journal stated the publication and the dissidents:

> have proven to you that White Rat Affairs are rotten.... You have been shown that the membership has been padded. You have been shown that funds have been diverted. You have been shown that the agitator is insincere and is for himself only. You know that as a union the White Rats are a joke. You know that they don't live up to the first principles of union labor.... WHAT ABOUT IT? DO SOMETHING.[36]

In its May 20 issue *Billboard* complained that the WR pages in *Variety* cost the union $5,000 a year, another example of waste on the part of Harry. Then it issued another challenge to Mountford. Noting that the NVA would soon publish its list of members, the piece challenged Harry to print the list of WR members side by side with the other list, to see who was really in which organization. Of course, the Rats ignored such nonsense. It would have been foolish for the Rats to publish their members' names — as they had once done some 15 years earlier — making it all the easier for the managers to blacklist them.[37]

The same issue of the publication gave an account of Mountford's return from that two-month Western organization trip mentioned above:

> Harry Mountford, fresh from his two months' invasion of the Far West, where he went in search of more shekels for the Rat Trap in Forty-sixth street, returned to Broadway and White Rat circles this week, rotund, aye fat, to an almost abnormal degree. It is quite evident that dining car and first-class restaurant fare agrees with the dictator of Ratdom, for never was a rodent more hale and hearty of avoirdupois than this self-same 'Arry, who for several months has been regaling himself in luxury at the expense of the "sheep."[38]

A full-page NVA ad in *Variety* on May 26 set out the principles of the new group and included an application form for people to fill out and mail in. Dues were $5 for six months, the same as those of the WR. That application blank asked for name, address, age, and marital status, and then asked three other questions of its prospective members: "Are you a member of any other theatrical organization, if so state names thereof"; "Are you in good standing in said organization?"; and "If not in good standing state reasons briefly."[39]

In an NVA two-page ad early in June it was declared that over 1,200 applications for membership had already been received from vaudeville artists. Much of that ad space was given over to printing the names of 186 of those 1,200 artists. Among the prominent ones were: Weber and Fields, McIntyre and Heath, Adelaide and Hughes, Bessie Clayton, Eddie Foy, Eddie Leonard, Cecil Lean, Willard Mack, and Lew Dockstader.[40]

Declaring it had been privileged to look over the list of members of the NVA, *Billboard* observed, "it was astounded to learn who were identified. Many of the members were former rabid White Rats, who have become disgusted with the workings of Harry Mountford and the clique in the Rodent outfit and who have joined the new order, feeling satisfied that it is to become the big vaudeville organization. The performers who are joining the N.V.A. are those who have no ax to grind but who have something marketable to sell."[41]

In its June 10 issue *Billboard* reported on some action that Gompers and the AFL were supposedly going to take in respect to the WR. Hugh Frayne, of the AFL, described in the report as Gompers' "right-hand-man," was given as the source (as in, "Mr Frayne told The Billboard....")[42]

However, none of it was true. Frayne, general organizer of the AFL, sent a letter to the journal, which was published in the news item pages (taking up about the same amount of space as the above report had occupied), denying he made any statement at all to the journal. He demanded they print his denial and give it the same prominence and space as they had given the original lie. *Billboard* did so; they probably complied to avoid any possible lawsuit.[43]

Around mid–June a mutually agreed upon "equitable" contract was published by the NVA, after being endorsed by the VMPA. It contained some of the items the WR were after, such as paying the difference in the jump expense if a route was changed after a contract was signed and the route change involved an increased transportation expense. Reportedly, the contract would only be issued to NVA members. As part of its account, *Variety* said NVA membership was 3,000.[44]

If *Variety* reported the NVA contract in a straightforward, matter-of-fact way, *Billboard* positively gushed over it in its own account, declaring it was "an equitable contract which is considerably better than the contract requested by the N.V.A., in that while it embraces every point made by the artists it also includes clauses which the artists had never dreamt of asking for and which are most desirable in that through their insertion the artists will reap inestimable benefits." According to the story, the contract was agreed upon after just two meetings between NVA and VMPA committees. But then the VMPA took it back and, after receiving permission from the NVA to insert some clauses on its own initiative, added clauses it felt the artists could not possible object to. "In fact, the additions made by the managers are all for the good of the performers, especially the clause with reference to maximum jump, which is a big reduction over what the artists had anticipated."[45]

Meanwhile, after many conferences between WR representatives and Ackerman and Harris (they controlled the Western States Vaudeville Association, an agency based in San Francisco), the latter signed the WR contract in mid–July, agreeing to employ only union artists and acts in their theaters. Following that agreement, other San Francisco showmen signed similar agreements. Bert Levey was a vaudeville manager and agent in that city who signed on; the other was the Graumans, who ran the local Empress venue. The WR had signs printed for distribution in houses where the closed shop was in force. Those signs notified artists that only union players were employed by the house.[46]

Apparently made furious by the San Francisco agreement, *Billboard* attacked the deal with scorn, pointing out that only a small number of houses were involved, perhaps 10 to 12 in all. Not to mention that, "Practically all of the theaters lined up in the White Rat agreement are in or about San Francisco, a notoriously strong union district, where such action on the part of the theater manager was only to be expected."[47]

Toward the end of July vaudeville agents doing business with members of the VMPA were requested to forward to those managers lists of all the acts they handled, indicating upon the lists which acts belonged to the NVA. One manager said that was done so that a preference could be given to NVA members, and that the contract agreed upon by the NVA and the VMPA could be issued to such members. Of course, that was all unnecessary, as the NVA was the VMPA's own creation, and it knew who all the members were. Perhaps it was done to reinforce the false notion that the NVA was independent from the VMPA, or simply as part of the ongoing campaign of harassment against the WR.[48]

A report in *Billboard* about the recent election of NVA officers listed many prominent members of the organization, including Irene Franklin, then a huge star in vaudeville. However, that was not true. Franklin took out a large ad in *Variety* to state otherwise — that she was not a member of the NVA; that her name had been used without her knowledge or consent; and that she was a member in good standing of the WR.[49]

In a July 1 editorial in *Billboard* the publication expressed jubilation over all the supposed desertions from the WR, and over the embargo imposed by the managers and the blacklisting of WR members from vaudeville. It claimed the NVA "now finds itself without doubt the strongest and most safely entrenched organization in the theatrical world." As usual, the editorial (in the World War I era) contained an attack on Harry, the German soldiers are not original in their peculiar methods of warfare. We know of some "gas bums" in the good old U.S.A. The green, vomiting vulture of Forty-sixth street has taught many of the parrots to say "Uncle." ... Watch the lion change into a lamb. Soon. Very soon. The new organization will put an end to the vaudevillifications. [The adjective "green" referred to Mountford's alliance with *Variety*. For many years the publication had a distinctive green cover and was often referred to in the industry as the "green sheet."][50]

Then the White Rats went out on strike in the somewhat unexpected location of Oklahoma.

8 | Rats Strike Oklahoma, 1916

"We are satisfied from the evidence placed before us that actors have been grossly imposed upon by managers in cities of this state...."

— Oklahoma State Board of Arbitration, 1916

"For that is what the White Rats membership really is — a list which, if regularly and systematically worked, will yield easy money for the support of a bunch of New York grafters that have never worked and never will as long as they can help it."

— *Billboard*, 1916

"Any actor who deliberately walks out of a theater or refuses on any pretext to play out his contracts will be handled as an individual enemy."

— VMPA, 1916

"The menace of Mountford is so apparent, so dangerous to the vaudeville artist...."

— Sime Silverman, *Variety*, 1916

An unfair order was placed by WR traveling representative Francis J. Gilmore (then in St. Louis) against all theaters in Oklahoma City, Oklahoma, toward the end of July, excepting the Metropolitan opera house there. All union stagehands, musicians, operators (film projectionists), and White Rats walked out of the Liberty, Unique and Lyric theaters, among others. On the Saturday the Lyric ran with non-union personnel, including some vaudeville acts that were not Rats. The Liberty was dark, however, while the Unique (a cinema that mixed in vaudeville acts with films) ran just films.

Oklahoma City's combined unions rented the Metropolitan, giving a show there on Saturday night that consisted solely of Rat acts. They vowed to continue to operate it as long as the other local venues remained unfair. Instructions were issued by Gilmore from St. Louis that all acts playing any house in Oklahoma City excepting the Metropolitan would thereafter be known as strike breakers.[1]

A week later the strike continued, with the forces preparing for a long battle. The Lyric continued to run a non-union show, while the Rats continued to give shows at the Metropolitan. According to a report, the Oklahoma City theatrical managers' association was backing up the houses against the strikers. John Sinopoulo, an oil magnate, had offered to buy the Metropolitan for the sole purpose of evicting the Rats. At that house the Rats had a bill of 10 acts giving four shows a day, with some 60 musicians generating an outside ballyhoo on the streets each evening. Orders were issued by the managers to secure the names of all acts playing the Metropolitan. At the Empress Theatre in Kansas City, Kansas, an act refused to appear on the same bill with E. E. Clive and Co., alleging the latter had appeared at the Liberty in Oklahoma City as a strikebreaker. When Clive withdrew, another act was substituted in his place.[2]

When another week had passed it was observed that the Metropolitan was playing to big business, and since picketing around the non-union houses had commenced nearly a week earlier, their business had fallen to the point where they drew "very low" crowds. Managers had vainly appealed to civic authorities, which said they would not be partial, and that if the strikers complied with the law there would be no arrests for picketing or other activity in front of the venues. Reportedly, the Rats had made several recruits in Oklahoma City since the strike started. Two acts — Ford and O'Neil, and the Toki Japs — arrived on a Monday to open at the Lyric, but when apprised of the strike situation they left the Lyric and opened at the Metropolitan instead.[3]

Local opinion had it that the managers were responsible for the strike, according to reporter Carl Shannon. On July 14 the stagehands requested a meeting with the theatrical managers to explain why they wanted an increase in salary. But they were ignored, and they finally told the managers that if they continued to be ignored they would strike. After being told by the managers to go ahead and strike, they did. At the same time, the film projectionists approached the managers to ask that a meeting be given to the stagehands. They were told to mind their own business. Other efforts by the projectionists were equally unavailing, so they went on strike in solidarity with the stagehands. Following that, the musicians tried to intercede but were equally unsuccessful. By this time the Rats had become interested, and when the musicians decided to strike the WR went out with them. It was a controversy that carried over to the pages of the local newspapers. In one of the managers' ads was a quote from *Billboard*, referring to the WR, which said, "It died because it was a rank fake and not a labor union." Responding to that dig, the Metropolitan's quarter-page ad in the Oklahoma City papers said, "The *Billboard* is a non-union newspaper, printed by non-union printers. It had always opposed organized labor. It is a paper for carnivals, crooks and balloon acts, and is not considered seriously by decent theatrical people." That ad was signed by John Campbell, president, Stage Employees' Union. The Liberty was then playing movies, while the Lyric operated with a five act, non-union bill, but lost some of those acts most weeks as some players shifted over to the Metropolitan when they learned of the strike situation.[4]

Still another week later W. M. Smith, manager of the Empress Theatre in Tulsa, Oklahoma, gave a contradictory account of business being done in Oklahoma City. He said business in the non-union houses was then about normal. Out of 40 acts booked in the Lyric since the strike, at least 20 had been Rats, and only about six of those acts had walked out, meaning that 14 White Rat acts had ignored their union's strike call. Smith said the one thing that hurt business more than anything was the fact that the venues had no musicians and "consequently the shows did not go over good." Explaining the origin of the strike, he remarked, "During the negotiations with the managers, the stage hands signed up with the White Rats, then the managers refused to meet with them."[5]

As the strike reached the end of its third week it was extended to Tulsa, Oklahoma, with all but one house there, the Wonderland, being declared unfair and boycotted by the unions. Employees of six Tulsa venues left their work after receiving the call and began picketing in front of the theaters. The determination to extend the strike to Tulsa was made almost at the same time as it was announced that John Sinopoulo (who owned the Lyric in Oklahoma City) had purchased Tulsa's Broadway Theater. Sinopoulo and other members of the Managers' Association of Oklahoma City issued what they said was to be a final statement — that it was their intention to grant none of the strikers' demands.[6]

Management went to great lengths to keep the struck houses going, and were aided by managers in other parts of the country. Journalist Carl Shannon observed that high-priced acts and expensive orchestras (that would not have performed in Oklahoma City under normal circumstances) had been brought to the Lyric and Liberty houses from Chicago, and, notwithstanding efforts by strikers to dissuade them, the shows went on as scheduled. At the request of the managers, policemen were at the train stations when the new acts arrived, with instructions to prevent all disorders, but nothing happened. Management determination to keep their houses open during the dispute prompted the strikers to double the number of pickets at the venues. "These pickets, men and women, wear large white satin ribbons extending from their shoulders to waistlines, bearing the name of the theater they are picketing and calling attention that the house is unfair," wrote Shannon. "In addition, the pickets orally convey to prospective patrons the object of their activity, and so orderly has this work been done that no objection by other than the managers themselves has been made." Meanwhile, managers continued to bring some of the highest priced vaudeville in America to Oklahoma City with an assurance to patrons there would be no increase in admission prices.[7]

As the strike reached the one-month mark, several arrests of strikers were made during that fourth week as a result of charges preferred by the managers or their employees that some pickets were armed with guns. All were quickly exonerated; the charges were false. Union people argued that the business at the Liberty and Lyric houses was less than half the normal amount, while the managers insisted it was good. The Metropolitan had played to capacity since it became the exclusive union vaudeville venue of the city. Regular admission rates were charged, with a percentage of the proceeds going to the strike fund. Pickets continued to march before all the Tulsa houses except the Wonderland, which was a union house, and theater business there was said to have suffered considerably during the previous two weeks. Some of the pickets in front of the Empress in Tulsa were arrested on a complaint by management, which declared they were creating a disturbance by verbally telling passers-by the house was unfair to organized labor. At a court hearing the following day all the pickets were quickly released, with the charges quashed. To that date, striking WR members had not asked the WR headquarters for any money; they had financed the strike locally, from their own resources. The Chicago Federation of Labor entered the fray when it sent a communication to the theatrical agents in Chicago that if they booked any acts to work the Oklahoma houses labelled as unfair, the Federation would urge the Rats, and others, to boycott the agents. Charles Hodkins, a Chicago agent, took a six-act show to Oklahoma City a week earlier, but out of the six, only two acts refused to join the ranks of the strikers once they reached Oklahoma.[8]

Billboard gave very little coverage to the Oklahoma strikes. A brief summary late in August argued that business was normal in the picketed Oklahoma City venues, and that picketing in Tulsa had occurred "without appreciable result," as the Broadway and Empress venues played to "full houses." Managers were cited as saying, "Unfair and underhand tactics on the part of the striking organizations have disgusted the public, which has apparently grown tired of the entire affair and is evincing very little interest either here or in Tulsa."[9]

As September 1 neared, and with the strike about six weeks old, the Lyric opened with a four-act bill that was all single entertainers (normal would have been eight to 10 acts, many of which would not have been singles, or one-person acts), while the Liberty began its second week of running a musical stage production (that is, it was not running any vaudeville at all). Also unable to secure any vaudeville of any kind, the Folly venue had returned to running films, with a greatly reduced patronage. At the Metropolitan the Rats continued to present a strong bill of mostly double acts. Tulsa remained relatively quiet, with little change. When the Oklahoma Federation of Labor held its annual convention in Tulsa a week earlier, it adopted a resolution condemning the action of all city officials identified with the fining of two strikers who, while on picket duty in front of a venue, were arrested on complaint of the management on charges of disturbing the peace. Managers in Tulsa were said to be having difficulties in securing acts, as the strikers had experienced success in pulling out several acts billed into the Broadway and Empress and taking them to the Wonderland. "Many non-union acts which have reached Tulsa during the past ten days have joined the Rats upon being apprised of conditions," concluded the account.[10]

A meeting of the VMPA was held in New York early in September to discuss the Oklahoma situation. Members of that group represented over 700 vaudeville and burlesque houses across America. At the meeting a motion was passed that prohibited the members of the VMPA from employing any acts that had played, or would play, the Metropolitan in Oklahoma City. Further, the members of the VMPA agreed not to engage any actor who was a member of the WR after October 31. The time delay was said to be so the VMPA could compile a list of Rat members and distribute it to the venues. Also resolved was to thereafter play no act that appeared in a union house in Oklahoma City, or any act that broke a contract to appear in an "unfair" house in that city.[11]

On September 13 in Oklahoma City the strike of White Rats, union musicians, projectionists and 100 stagehands went to a hearing before the

Oklahoma State Board of Arbitration, with W. G. Ashton, State Commissioner of Labor, presiding. It went to a hearing despite the fact that D. I. Johnston, counsel for the managers, emphatically declared that notwithstanding the findings of the Board, the managers would under no circumstances grant the demands of the quadruple alliance for a closed shop. That stand caused a furor because the law empowered the Board to offer the best means of adjusting the dispute, with a penalty for the side that ignored the recommendation. Meanwhile, things remained quiet in Tulsa. While the strike was still on, there the pickets had been withdrawn from the Empress and Broadway venues; no reason for that action was given.[12]

Over two days the Board of Arbitration heard the strikers' side of the situation, and then set a date 10 days in the future, hoping that by then it could convince the managers to voluntarily present their side of the story. But on those two scheduled days the mangers, through their counsel, refused to discuss the situation at all. Commissioner Ashton lashed out at the managers and their counsel, Johnston, telling him that he resented their attitude toward the Board, feeling they were determined to make a joke of the whole process.[13]

Among those who testified before the Board was Harry Mountford. In the opinion of *Billboard*, Mountford showed up to give evidence "with proper pomp and ceremony" and bearing proof of the "existence of a gigantic theatrical trust which controlled the vaudeville world and like a giant octopus stretched its tentacles from Coast to Coast and sucked the life blood from the actor and manager alike." Of course, the publication was being sarcastic, but that is just about what the Board eventually did conclude in its report.[14]

Just before he testified before the Board, Harry offered to call off the strike for the time being if the managers would consent to putting all their former stagehands, operators, and musicians back to work, and to be bound by the final decision of the Arbitration Board. It was an offer the managers rejected, explaining they were willing to treat with their former employees but would have nothing to do with the White Rats or Mountford. When he testified, Mountford produced a transcript of what had taken place in the office of agents in Chicago recently. That information came from a Dictaphone record of what had been said at the meeting, although Harry did not explain how he came to have it. From that transcript it was revealed the managers and agents wanted to keep the strike going in Oklahoma as long as possible so as to forestall any similar activity planned by the Rats for elsewhere. Many actors playing in Oklahoma during the time of the hearing were subpoenaed to testify, and all admitted they were paying high commissions to the agents and managers — ranging from five percent to 20 percent. As well, it was revealed, "The majority had been cancelled by the managers without notification."[15]

Another witness was John Sinopoulo, owner of the Lyric, who said he had not cancelled an act from his house in over a year. But when cross-examined, he admitted, "There might have been one or two cancellations of the kind" (that is, without notice). He said he didn't know if the acts booked by him were WR or not, and did not care. Also, he claimed he was unaware of the existence of any booking trust, and equally unaware of any other combination of theatrical interests outside of Oklahoma City. Asked if he had received a check for $10,000 from the Chicago headquarters of the trust (the UBO and VMPA had their Western headquarters in that city) with which to continue to strike, Sinopoulo refused to answer. Manager McCall of the Liberty testified he did not know much at all about the booking business. So vague was his memory on the matter that his usual answer to questions was, "I don't recall." No one from the managers' side voluntarily testified before the board, as all stuck to their original plan of boycotting the procedure; but a few were subpoenaed to appear.[16]

When the Oklahoma State Board of Arbitration released its report on September 26 it recommended the reinstatement at a wage increase of all the stagehands that went out on strike. No recommendation was made by the Board with respect to the WR's demand for a closed shop. Instead, it sidestepped the issue, declaring it did not feel qualified to pass judgment "on this important issue, by reason of the fact that Oklahoma City is only one of a chain of cites on circuits, which are booked by foreign concerns or booking agencies and we, therefore, doubt the feasibility of imposing upon managers in Oklahoma City this duty." Also urged by the report was the use of an "equitable" contract to be employed by the managers, with one feature of that contract to be that it be a play or pay contract. That is, if the actor was not allowed to play he should be paid — no dismissals for arbitrary reasons or on the basis of no reason at all. One conclusion of the board was, "We are satisfied from the evidence placed before us that the actors have been grossly imposed upon by managers in cities of this state and that managers have been imposed upon by certain booking agents in other cities [a veiled reference to the UBO]." Further, the Board declared, "The contract in universal use in this country is unjust, both to the actor and to the management." And, "We further find from the evidence the existence of a combination which controls managers and actors throughout the United

States and we recommend to the United States Congress that proper laws be enacted to regulate the booking agents...."[17]

So how did *Billboard* report the Board of Arbitration's decision? After dismissing Harry as being ineffective in his testimony, it then dismissed the Board because it was "in the very nature of things an organization biased in favour of organized labor." Then it declared that the Board recommended "a dissolution of the famous quadruple alliance and the elimination of the White Rats from consideration in the local controversy" (which was untrue). On the other hand, it did report the recommendation that the stagehands be reinstated with a raise, and that the use of an "equitable" contract be implemented. For its final remarks, the publication observed, "Inasmuch as there has been so much bitterness injected into the disagreement here, principally inspired by the Rat representatives, the managers seem to feel that there is no need for haste in settlement, and they have not hesitated to state that as long as there is a White Rat representative participating in the councils of the strikers and advising them they, the managers, will not consider a settlement of the strike under any circumstances."[18]

Early in October the Western Vaudeville Managers' Association (based in Chicago and a member of the VMPA) notified all outside booking agents that contracts would not be issued to any vaudeville act that refused to appear in an Association-booked theater at Oklahoma City. Acts refusing to play Oklahoma City were termed by the Association as "undesirable," and a notice to that effect was sent to all managements. Some of the acts already cancelled by the Western Association included the Six Castrillions, and Dunbar and Turner. Also, Pearl Brothers and Burns refused to work at Tulsa, and as a result the UBO cancelled the remainder of their contract. The same thing happened to Chauncey Munroe and Co. after it passed up a Tulsa date. Meanwhile, in St. Louis at the start of October, John Williams and Fred Butler were arrested on the complaint of Harry Wallace, manager of the Grand opera house, who alleged the men passed out hand bills in front of his venue which declared the acts performing there to be unfair to union labor. Those acts had formerly appeared at one of the unfair houses in Oklahoma City.[19]

On October 11, the City Commissioners of Oklahoma City passed an ordinance prohibiting the picketing of theaters by union strikers. The measure took effect immediately, and heavy penalties were provided for those who violated the provision.[20]

By then the strike was about 11 weeks old. On October 8 the Metropolitan was handed by the strikers back to its original lessees, the Tucker

Brothers, bringing to an end the union vaudeville shows. Management pointed to that as meaning the strike was almost over. Bravely, the strikers said it did not mean that at all, offering the lame explanation that their shows were ended so the personnel involved could be freed up for more picket duty. The attention of the strikers was then focused on three houses exclusively — the Empress, Lyric, and Liberty. All were said to be playing to large matinee audiences and to capacity at night. Managers happily noted that a few members of the musicians' union had broken ranks and voluntarily returned to work, and that more were expected to follow. Then Oklahoma City banned picketing.[21]

Picketing of unfair Oklahoma City venues by strikers resumed about a week later, following a hearing in the Criminal Court of Appeals on the writ of habeas corpus of Eva Sweitzer, a picket in front of the Lyric who was arrested on October 10 and charged with violation of the city's ordinance prohibiting picketing. Attorneys for the strikers argued that the action of the mayor and city commissioners was unconstitutional. The Court then gave the city attorney 15 days to file a brief showing the city had a right to pass such a law. After the hearing the mayor issued a statement that no more pickets would be arrested (until the court rendered a decision), but their names would be taken and arrests would follow immediately if the ordinance was held to be constitutional. Picketing then involved five venues, the three listed above, and the Folly and the Overholser.[22]

One month after that the situation was little changed. The strike and picketing were still ongoing — the court had not yet rendered a decision. Pickets orally conveyed the message to passers-by that the venues were unfair to organized labor. "Please remember friends," they said, "this theater is unfair to the working man, unfair to the wage earner, and your patronage means the taking of bread from the mouths of the hungry." But things were not going well for the Rats. According to a reporter, few acts had been pulled from the unfair houses in recent weeks, "and the majority of acts now playing the unfair houses are admittedly Rat acts."[23]

Manager B. H. Powell of the Folly Theatre in Oklahoma City announced that starting November 25 his house would recognize union musicians, stagehands and operators, and that only members of those unions would be employed by him. The White Rats were not a party to that agreement. The Folly played vaudeville acts and films. As a consequence of renewed picketing at the Lyric, owner John Sinopoulo caused the arrest of P. Walker, L. E. Irwin, Eva Sweitzer, Sid Pollard, and W. A. Salter, all pickets whom he alleged had disturbed the peace by talking on the street in front

of his venue. Sinopoulo swore out warrants for the arrests of those patrol-
men who declined to make arrests under the anti-picketing law (still in legal
limbo). In police court a day later Walker was fined $10, Sweitzer and Irwin
$5 each, Pollard $1, and the charge against Salter was dismissed.[24]

By the end of 1916 the strike was still officially on, but to all intents and
purposes it was over. Virtually no picketing had taken place in December,
with a few sporadic exceptions that had no effect. In March 1917 the Court
of Appeals upheld picketing, in spite of the city ordinance, but by then the
matter was moot. No houses in Oklahoma had any trouble getting acts to
perform; all were functioning normally, with normal business. No WR acts
avoided any of these once-unfair venues. Officially, that strike was never
called off; it just faded away, and, of course, represented a defeat for the
Rats. Things remained busy in other ways during that part of 1916 occupied
by the Oklahoma strike, as the Rats and the VMPA continued their war of
words in the media and battled over recognition of the union and the advent
of an equitable contract. Oklahoma was just a sidebar for them both.[25]

Movie actors made another move of their own to try and organize in
August 1916 — at least the screen extras did. At a mass meeting of the extras,
plans were formulated for the formation of an organization for mutual protection and affiliation with the American Federation of Labor. The catalyst
for that move was reported to be the behavior on the part of some agents
who had been receiving orders from film producers for extras and, instead
of taking a nominal fee for their services, had been paying the extras only
about 40 percent of the money they received from the filmmakers. Another
complaint was that those agents would advertise in newspapers for extras and,
after tentatively engaging them, would keep them calling at their offices daily
for several days, or longer, prior to telling them of the location for the film
shoot or that the order for extras had been cancelled by the film producer.[26]

Around five weeks earlier, agent William A. Sheer advertised in one of
the papers for experienced horsemen as extras in a film. Over 500 men called
at the Sheer office and left their names and were tentatively engaged at a
salary of $1.75 a day to begin work on a picture to be shot at Whitestone,
Long Island. All were told to call at Sheer's office a few days later; at that
time they were told to call again the next day. And then they were told to
call again in a few more days. That stalling continued for about 10 days until
Sheer's brother George told them they would receive a post card in the mail
when they were needed. Many of those extras complained about expenses,
such as carfare back and forth to the Sheer office and a loss of time when
they could have been looking for work. Also, three weeks earlier Sheer sent

one of his employees to Tenth Avenue to recruit from the street a number of men of the "tough guy" type to be used as screen extras. Twenty men were recruited, taken to Sheer's office and then sent to the film studio. Only six were accepted by the film producer; the remainder insisted Sheer should either put them to work or pay them for their time. When he refused, an argument broke out that ended only after one of Sheer's employees called the police and had the men arrested for disorderly conduct. All were fined the next day in court.[27]

With respect to the horsemen, Sheer explained to a *Variety* reporter that a film director told him to engage that number and hold them in readiness for a movie that would start to shoot most any day. It was cases such as these, said a reporter, which caused extras to agitate to form a union. What they wanted was a wage scale that paid extras $3 a day (if less than 100 were used in a film) or $2 a day (if over 100 were used) or $5 a day for full dress or fancy dress, and $7.50 a day for hazardous work, and time and a half for night work, beginning after 6 P.M. Most importantly, they wanted no commissions to be deducted from those amounts. Several film producers had been approached on the subject and, reportedly, indicated a willingness to employ their extras direct from the proposed new union instead of from the agencies.[28]

Hugh Frayne, general organizer of the AFL, and Harry Mountford held several meetings with the leaders of the extras and arranged for the granting of a charter to any group that might be formed, and that it would be known as the Motion Picture Extra People's Association of Greater New York, Local 30, White Rats Actors' Union of America. During the time of those meetings, agents and contractors that recruited extras were greatly perturbed over the steps the extras were taking, and word was conveyed to them from those people that any of the extras that joined the fledgling union need expect no work from them. A representative of the William Sheer office told the extras there was no possibility of any organization being formed, and that they should stay away from the union agitators or they would be blacklisted. B. A. Rolfe, president of Rolfe Picture Corp, told *Variety* that he hired all his extras through the agent Ben Weiss because it saved a lot of time and trouble. As to the fee that Weiss exacted from the extras, Rolfe said he understood that the agent got 50 cents from each $2.50 a day he received for extras — that is, the screen player got $2 a day.[29]

Billboard continued to publish editorial tirades against Harry. One, in the August 26 issue, lashed out at *Variety*, as it had done in the past, for printing White Rat News in its pages, taking the money and therefore, in its view, not attacking Harry because of it. After noting that vaudeville artists feared ridicule and panning more than anything in the world, the editor said, referring to *Variety*, "The Green Slut depends upon ridicule almost entirely to maintain its position — call it ascendancy if you will — in the vaudeville field. It uses it to compel advertising. And it uses it successfully, for many a frightened and wretched artist, terrified and desperate at its impending derision, is prompted to offer a propitiatory advertisement in the hope it will at least temper the severity of the panning he is in for." *Billboard* also argued, "There is little doubt that Mr. Mountford uses this blackguardly sheet for his White Rat propaganda, hoping that its menace and the horror of it will scare vaudeartists into signing his sucker list. For that is what the White Rat membership really is — a list which, if regularly and systematically worked, will yield easy money for the support of a bunch of New York grafters that have never worked and never will as long as they can help it."[30]

The number of WR pages in the September 22 issue of *Variety* was expanded to five and styled as an open letter, signed by Rat president James William Fitzpatrick, to the VMPA that asked for a conference to see if an amicable adjustment of prevailing vaudeville conditions could be made. In the letter to E. F. Albee, Fitzpatrick listed the four men appointed to the committee that stood ready to meet with the VMPA — Edward Clark, Theodore Babcock, Fred Niblo, and himself. Explaining his reasons for the members appointed to that committee, Fitzpatrick noted (in the *Variety* piece, not the letter), "Care was taken, in selecting the men to confer with the Vaudeville Managers' Protective Association, that no one should be a member of it whose personality would be a reason for refusing to receive that committee [a reference, of course, to Harry]." When that letter reached Albee he did not respond for a time before sending a reply that the letter should have gone to the secretary of the VMPA and not to him. Fitzpatrick then sent the letter to that individual. When no reply was received, Fitzpatrick decided to make the matter public.[31]

One week after going public with the request for a meeting, the VMPA issued a public reply, also in the pages of *Variety*, wherein it rejected the call for a meeting, declining to discuss professional matters or organization troubles while the WR was affiliated with organized labor. As far as the VMPA was concerned, the matter was then closed. An unnamed executive of the VMPA reiterated that the group would not deal with the Rats on an arbitration basis as long as that body was officially classified as a labor union, nor would they confer with any of its representatives while such an affiliation remained. He also said that a rumor that the managers would meet a representative committee of WR as long as Mountford was not among them (which apparently prompted the Fitzpatrick committee picks) was without foundation.[32]

At a WR meeting early in October it was resolved the organization would refuse to accept resignations from any of its members from that date until May 2, 1917. No reason was given for the action, but it likely meant the union was being hurt by the VMPA campaign urging members to resign from the Rats. As well, semi-annual dues were payable as of October 1. Refusing to accept resignations allowed the Rats to keep the members not paying their dues on the books. It was a desperate move on the part of the union.[33]

Around the same time, the Rats pointed out that at the S. Z. Poli theater in Waterbury, Connecticut (he ran a chain of vaudeville houses and was a member of the VMPA), acts were forced to perform there on Sundays and were paid only $1.60 each. Notice was given to the manager that a sum equal to one-sixth of the act's weekly salary should be paid for the Sunday shows. Poli paid no attention to the WR notice. Said WR president Fitzpatrick, "These Sunday shows in Poli's Waterbury have from 18 to 20 acts, brought in from the Poli theaters out of town that do not play Sunday performances. The acts are given only their transportation, and often must miss other engagements through not being able to get out of Waterbury late Sunday night.... It is an injustice to the actor." According to a reporter, "Poli has been trying a practice of playing six-day acts on the seventh day at Waterbury that was given up by one or two big-time managers some years ago when their notice was attracted to the unreasonableness of it. The difference in the one-sixth salary for the Sunday Poli performance might amount to $75 or $100 in all for Poli."[34]

Because the notice delivered to Poli had no effect, Fitzpatrick complained to the police, who ordered Poli to stop his Sunday vaudeville, as it was in violation of the Sunday laws. Poli, like others off and on, had tried to get around the law, or simply ignore it. Instead, the venue ran film shows on Sundays. At the Poli booking office in New York, P. Alonzo, booking manager for the circuit, said acts were never forced to play Waterbury on a Sunday unless they had no other booking a Sunday performance would interfere with. Yet, the Poli contract had a clause that said, "The artist agrees, if requested, to play a Sunday night concert at Waterbury, Connecticut, instead of the place above specified [meaning the Monday to Saturday contracted for city], in which event the manager will pay as additional salary a sum equal to any additional transportation charges so incurred." Explained Alonzo, "Owing to the composition of the Sunday show in Waterbury we are not able to give the regular week-day bill. Only singing and talking acts can be played, so we must draft the Sunday bill from other cities."[35]

Discussing the WR victory at the Poli house, the editor of *Billboard* said, in print, to Mountford, "You hurt the artists here. It cuts down their weekly stipend. Mr. Poli is going to play pictures, and pay the performers on a six-day basis instead of seven." (Of course, that conclusion chose to turn a blind eye to the fact the acts appearing on Sunday never got paid any salary, at best being compensated for their extra travel costs.)[36]

In a full-page ad in October the VMPA declared it would not employ any Rats at its venues: "Watch the bills. You will see White Rats' names disappear from them shortly." Also contained in the ad was the following warning: "Don't deceive yourself into thinking we don't know who are and who are not White Rats, and we will know who pays their dues." Further, the advertisement advised the reader not to forget that the VMPA had a "friendly" agreement with the NVA, "which has enough members at present to keep every known vaudeville house in America open, and we propose to give the members of that organization the preference in booking. When you can show a N.V.A. card it will mean something."[37]

Blacklisting continued to be a threat and a reality wielded by the theatrical trust over the heads of the players. Jimmy Dun quit the act he performed with Florence Lorraine on VMPA time in the middle of October. It was alleged that pressure was brought to bear on Dun to leave the Rats, and when he refused to resign, it was made clear to him that he would no longer play Association time. Lorraine continued the act, but with another man substituted for Dun.[38]

In a full-page ad in *Variety* on October 20 the VMPA declared, bizarrely, in its headline: "Vaudeville Managers Are Not Against Organized Labor." Despite the headline, the text of the ad went on to state that the VMPA members "will not engage any artist who is a member of the White Rats...." As proof they were not against organized labor, the managers' group pointed to the "friendly relations" between itself and the NVA.[39]

Joseph M. Schenck, general booking manager for the Loew circuit, explained his position by saying, "I will not be able to play a member of the White Rats, if I know it, or unless such a member resigns." His agency also booked for the Pantages circuit, among others. Vaudeville artists the Wilson Brothers stated they were Rats and refused to resign from the order. For that admission, Schenck cancelled them for the remainder of their Loew time and for the Pantages circuit, where they had been slated to appear the following week. Later, though, the Wilson Brothers submitted an affidavit to Schenck and to Walter Keefe (who booked the Pantages circuit out of the Loew office) saying they had resigned from the Rats. Thus, the contract cancellations were revoked.[40]

Other acts cancelled around the same time were Dorothy Jardon, Stella Mayhew and Billie Taylor, Eddie Foyer, and Adams and Guhl. Immediately after she was informed of her cancellation, Jardon repudiated the Rats and insisted she had resigned from the union. Her time on the Keith circuit was then restored. Adams and Guhl made affidavits that they had resigned from the WR, and had their time on the Loew circuit restored. Foyer pursued the same course, with a similar outcome. The signing of affidavits was said to have been made necessary to counteract the WR strategy recently adopted to not accept any resignations from members through May 2, 1917.[41]

At a mid–November meeting of the VMPA a committee was appointed to pass upon the application of all Rats (cancelled by any member of the VMPA) for restoration to their former standing on the booking sheets of the circuit cancelling it. Heretofore when an act was cancelled because of its membership in the Rats, the circuit or manager cancelling it had the discretionary power to restore the act upon its books when satisfied the act had complied with all necessary requirements to achieve that reinstatement. Supposedly this new method was implemented to achieve "equal treatment" in all cases. Some acts believing their time had been restored had since learned differently. Among them were Mayhew and Taylor, Jardon, Dugan and Raymond, and Willie Solar. All had been cancelled for having failed to resign their Rat memberships. Solar lost 35 weeks of vaudeville; Mayhew and Taylor lost around 20 weeks at $1,000 a week; Jardon lost nine weeks at $700 per week. Other acts cancelled within the previous few days for supposedly not cancelling union cards were the Headliners (Henry B. Toomer); Tallman, the pool expert; Bowman Brothers; and Apdale's Animals. Upon receipt of his notice of cancellation, Toomer was said to have wired a resignation to the union.[42]

Applauding all the cancellations and the many resignation from the organization was *Billboard*, which gleefully said, "The Rats are scampering around to the managers' headquarters with their affidavits, disclaiming all connection with the obnoxious club." Most recent cancellations included Mercedes, Patsy Doyle, Hunting and Francis, and Derkin's Dogs.[43]

Meanwhile, some of the internal problems came to a head at the AFL convention in Baltimore in November. Two resolutions were presented. One was designed to separate actors in the theatrical field into distinct bodies, each holding a charter, and limiting the charter held by the WR to the variety field only. Especially interested in that resolution were the recently formed Actors' Equity and the old dissidents from the AIU, merged years earlier into the WR. That second resolution left the Rats with the sole charter in the theatrical field — that is, the status quo. Any actors' group, no matter what field they were in, if it wanted to affiliate with the AFL, had to do so through the WR, not with a direct charter from the Federation. At the convention the AFL unanimously adopted the latter resolution, the status quo.[44]

Not surprisingly, *Billboard* put its own false spin on the situation when it reported, grudgingly, that the AFL had given its "moral support" to the Rats by allowing them to keep their charter. (There was never any question of the Rats losing their charter, as the editorial implied, only if it was to be a wide charter or a narrow one.) Then, with no evidence or facts, it declared, "There is every indication that the Rats as an organization, will be completely wiped out in a very short time, and it is doubtful if this could be postponed much longer, even if the Rats had the real support of the American Federation of Labor, instead of the moral support which the A.F. of L. tenders them."[45]

December 1916 saw an increase in the level and intensity of activity on the part of the Rats and the VMPA as a showdown loomed. Harry and Fitzpatrick made the rounds of the principal vaudeville circuit offices in New York (other Rat representatives did the same in various other parts of the country) as the Rats sought, for the final time they said, to arrange a meeting with the managers, with the object being to peacefully adjust the differences between the sides. Their demands remained the same: a maximum commission extracted from acts of five percent, no matter how many agents were involved; a closed shop; pro rata payment for extra shows; no more than three shows daily; no act to be farmed out on Sundays to a different venue (if an act performed on a Sunday then it was only to be in the same house where it performed on the Saturday); no public rehearsal (one circuit manager had instituted the custom of opening rehearsals to the public and charging a small admission). By declaring this to be their final effort to arrange a meeting, the WR was painting itself into a corner.[46]

But no meeting was arranged, and the VMPA stiffened. It announced that any act that walked out of a VMPA house in response to a WR strike call would be blacklisted for all time. That would be followed by a legal suit against the performer for damages based on a contractual violation. Said a VMPA member:

Any actor who deliberately walks out of a theater or refuses on any pretext to play out his contracts will be handled as an individual enemy, and once he becomes carded as a striker subservient to the orders of Mountford, he can look to Mountford for future engagements ... any actor who obeys Mountford cannot be looked upon as friendly to the interests that supply him with his livelihood and we propose to handle those particular individuals in our own way. Our legal department will see that we collect on every single judgment.[47]

A widely believed story, but never an official one, was that the Rats would strike several cities in the East, including New York, on December 11. However, nothing happened on that date. On the following two days both Fitzpatrick and Harry were in Chicago to address upcoming meetings. One reason given for no strike call was that the WR had found they could not enlist the support of the stagehands' and musicians' unions. Representatives from each union stated in New York that no stagehand or musician would be ordered out in sympathy without giving two weeks' notice, as required in each of their contracts. Reportedly, Mountford had spent eight weeks in vain trying to get pledges of support from those two unions. On Sunday, December 10, New York vaudeville managers prepared for trouble by dispatching a large number of stand-by acts to major points covering Eastern cities in order that no bill in any venue could be disturbed for any length of time. If those stand-by acts were required to perform they would have received full salary, and if not, a portion, rumoured to be one-third of their normal salary, would be paid to them. Even though there was no strike many of the stand-by acts performed anyway, lengthening existing bills — done to demonstrate that the managers took good care of people that stood by them. Those emergency acts were generally kept on stand-by beyond the week of December 11, as a worry remained that a strike would be called sooner or later. It was a wide-ranging, and very expensive, program instituted by the managers.[48]

Silent for some time with respect to the Rats and Harry (except for more or less factual accounts of developments), Sime Silverman delivered a much longer editorial than he usually issued, in the December 15 issue of *Variety*, just on the topic of the WR possible strike. Said Silverman:

> We are not in sympathy with this proposed strike or the strike movement so individually engineered by Harry Mountford, who has entrenched himself as the sole arbiter of the White Rats and who alleges the White Rats as headed by him is the representative of the vaudeville actor at large. Whether the White Rats is or is not, it is the actor at large who has made Mountford in his present position possible, and it is now the actor at work who sees what power wrongly invested can mean to his future and himself.... What are they striking for.... We don't know. Who does? [Such a statement was disingenuous in the extreme because Silverman and his reporters had often published stories of the abuses actors were subjected to, and the WR demands featured regularly in the WR pages in Silverman's own publication.][49]

One thing explained by this editorial was why *Variety* had been silent for years. They had once attacked Harry with as much vigor as did *Billboard,* but had not done so for some time. The rival publication had once made a brief reference to the silence and guessed correctly as to the cause. Explained Silverman:

> This paper holds a contract with the White Rats. It provides for the Rats to secure a certain advertising space at a certain price. The contract also provides that *Variety* shall not publish a news story attacking the Rats without first giving the Rats an opportunity to answer it in the same issue. But the Rats' contract with *Variety* has no bearing whatsoever upon *Variety*'s editorial policy. [That is, if *Variety* attacked the Rats in a news story — as opposed to just reporting events — the WR was not obliged to "waste" any of the space it had contracted for and paid for to answer charges. *Variety* was obligated to furnish for free the extra space, equivalent in size and placement to that of the original attack.][50]

Apparently, Sime was relieved to get that out in the open and off his chest. He then declared, "we don't wish to make this a personal attack upon Mr. Mountford," in this editorial, but then proceeded to do just that. And he demonstrated clearly that his journal did not take a back seat to *Billboard* when it came to blasting Harry. Silverman savaged the union leader for being concerned only about his "bloated salary," being an autocrat, a dictator, an egomaniac, and of being power hungry and insincere ("His insincerity is but another form of his mania for power, using the actors and the White Rats as his pawns"). Joining a growing group, Sime declared that he, like *Billboard* and the VMPA, was not against organized labor, but his journal "is unalterably opposed to a strike at this time and Harry Mountford's single-handed rule over the White Rats. The menace of Mountford is so apparent, so dangerous to the vaudeville artist and so selfishly set forth for himself that we once more warn" the players not to strike.[51]

An editorial from the New York Sunday *Telegraph* of December 10 was given a full-page reprint in *Variety* in its December 15 edition. No hint was given as to who paid to reprint it. If it wasn't placed by *Variety* itself, then the VMPA was the most likely guess. Totally against any strike, the *Telegraph* thundered, "The White Rats are actors, nearly all of them engaged in vaudeville, and the idea of their forming a labor union and allying themselves with a central labor organization is ridiculous on the face of it.... There is nothing of union labor about this sort of thing." For several years, said the editor, agitation had been going on over alleged grievances "which could have been settled — if they existed — by a visit to the offices of the United

Booking chiefs." Not observed was that Rats had been trying to do just that — arrange a meeting — for some time. With regard to Harry, this newspaper attacked him, for one thing, on not being an American. "We know little about this person, except that he seems to be an actor who never acts — at least in this country. He is trying to lead Americans in a movement which appears was to be against their interests — and he is not an American — we have not heard of his showing any naturalization papers."[52]

As of December 19 nothing had happened; chaos and uncertainty reigned. Harry's every move was watched and speculated about. When he traveled to Detroit, rumors circulated that the auto magnate Henry Ford had promised him money. Fuelling that speculation were other rumors that the Rats were in serious financial difficulties. Still, managers maintained a strict preparedness, with duplicate shows held at the ready on stand-by, a position they were expected to maintain at least into January.[53]

E. F. Albee was given a full-page of op ed space in *Variety* in its December 22 edition, a piece that was full of the troubles and woes of a vaudeville manager, and the need for him to have unfettered control. As well, he related how much the manager had done for the vaudeville artist over the years, how much better things were then, and that while he believed actors should have an association, it should be one based on business principles. Its objectives should be to take care of the sick, bury the dead, establish a fund to take care of the needy, and so on — an organization containing "a spirit of the friendliest relations existing between the manager and the artist." Modestly, he did not mention the NVA by name. "The Actor's Fund of America, of which I am a director, has done much good for its unfortunate members. I can find no record in the vaudeville actors' association of any such results." Actually, the Rats did perform some charitable-style work. They regularly bailed out stranded actors (mostly loans, but some were forgiven), but such things were rarely mentioned in the media. Albee apparently saw no connection between charity being needed to bury indigent expired players, to look after the old and sick players, and actors determining that a union was necessary. Then Albee heaped scorn on a particular concern of female players when he pretended that sexual harassment — also a very real problem but rarely mentioned in the press — did not exist. "Much has been said by the agitators of the treatment the women of vaudeville receive from those they are obliged to do business with. I have been in vaudeville for thirty years, and in all that time I have found no actual cases of this alleged despicable practice."[54]

Silverman delivered himself of another extra-long editorial tirade against the Rats, sarcastically headlined, "Merry Christmas," also in the December 22 issue. Mostly it was a rehash and repeat of early attacks, but this one contained a suggestion the Rats affiliate with the NVA. Said Sime, "Without a union charter, without a Mountford for a leader and without force, coercion, spleen, libel or threats, the National Vaudeville Artists obtained all the White Rats wanted, through the managers recognizing it as a friendly organization."[55]

In another part of that issue a recap of the year 1916 was fairly accurately presented, and done so in an unbiased way. Mountford had returned to power in the WR in October 1915 when the organization was on the verge of bankruptcy. Harry deliberated for some time before accepting what then seemed to him to be an almost impossible task — rebuild the Rats, who were saddled then with a heavy indebtedness. He was given a salary of $60 a week when he returned, along with the promise of $150 a week when the WR could afford it. Through his aggressive campaigns for new members, Harry caused a turnaround in the union's fortunes; it was enough of a turnaround that managers got worried and decided to retaliate through their own aggressive campaign of publicity, threats, intimidation, blacklisting, and so on. Thereafter the WR and the VMPA used one to two pages weekly in *Variety* to attack each other — such pieces appeared almost nowhere else. That was because the managers knew that the articles by Mountford had to be read in *Variety*— no other publication would allow him access to their pages — and thus it would be a waste of time for the VMPA to publish its material elsewhere. According to this report, it was estimated that from October 15 to December 1, 1916, nearly 200 vaudeville acts were cancelled on the alleged grounds that they were White Rats. Most resigned from the Rats, and/or used affidavits in order to appease the VMPA, and in the end, remarked a reporter, "Nearly all were re-engaged."[56]

Rejoicing over the apparent disarray in the Rats as December moved to a close was *Billboard*. Again the editor argued that trade unionism was not likely feasible among the artists. Even if it were it would not have worked with the current WR clique because that group was self-serving and selfish. And even if unionism was feasible and the clique was unselfish it still would not have worked because the WR leadership lacked ability. Throughout the piece the WR was spoken of as a group that no longer existed.[57]

Evidence that the Rats were in financial difficulty came December 19 when the WR executed a chattel mortgage for $5,000 to Jacob J. Lubell, mortgaging all the furnishings in the WR clubhouse in New York City. That mortgage was due and payable on March 19, 1917, three months from its issue date. Everything in the clubhouse was itemized in the mortgage, including beds, mattresses, typewriters, barber chairs, pool and billiard tables, pool racks, pool cues, office fixtures, liquor, wine, and so forth. The clubhouse was built by the Rats on leased land, with a bank holding a bond loan that was also due in 1917. Rumors that Henry Ford was to supply the union with money circulated again and were persistent enough that Ford, through a spokesman, issued a formal denial, adding he had never been approached by the WR and, in fact, had never even heard of the union.[58]

When Silverman went public with the WR deal the union promptly broke its contract with *Variety*. It revived *The Player* as an independent publication and published its first edition in its new incarnation on or about December 23 — as a four-page sheet with the price set at five cents, although that first issue was distributed for free. Revealed at that time was that under that deal the Rats had paid *Variety* $37.50 per page while, in the past, the VMPA had criticized the union for paying $150 a page. Apparently that latter figure was the standard price, the one paid by the VMPA. James Fitzpatrick explained the Rats had found it impossible to publish the material they wanted to in the trade press — hence the *Variety* deal — but referred to the journal's editorial stand against the union as "*Variety* at last tearing off its mask," this being the reason for breaking its contract with the publication.[59]

As 1916 closed, the Rats appeared to be in a weak position; they had suffered losses in membership numbers due to the harassment, intimidation and blacklisting against them by the VMPA. As well, they had financial problems. A failure to strike on December 10, widely expected but never officially announced, left the Rats looking like they were adrift, without any sort of plan or strategy. Lost was their house organ from the pages of *Variety*; now it had to stand on its own, causing perhaps more financial drain, as it had in the past. Yet *The Player* was crucial to the actors, more than a house organ to most other unions. A stable residential address allowed unions to mail information as needed to members, but that was impossible for actors, with so many of them always on the road. A house organ a Rat member could obtain easily, no matter what city he was in, was crucial. But that was then under threat. Militant action seemed less likely at that time for the Rats than ever before. But on January 1, 1917, the Rats issued a strike call.

9 | Rats Strike Again, Then Fade Away, 1917–1919

"The whole thing is a joke when only these few acts walk out....
I have no sympathy whatever for the outlaws, and so long as I
am in show business none of them will ever work for me, you
can depend on that."

— Marcus Loew, 1917

"If you disobey [a strike call] you are a traitor to your class, you
are guilty of the one universal crime. You are a tool of the employers, being used to defeat your brothers and sisters."

— Harry Mountford, 1919

On the afternoon of January 1, 1917, George L. Whalen, a WR deputy
organizer in Boston, got the go-ahead to start the strike in Boston when he
received a telegram from James Fitzpatrick that declared, "Start the Boston
Tea Party at six o'clock." But it was apparent that John L. Shea, president
of the New England Vaudeville Managers' Association, was aware of the
union president's wire and its contents as soon as Whalen was because the
preparedness program went into action that same afternoon. Stand-by acts
had been waiting in Boston all day and were assigned to every vaudeville
house in the city and its suburbs. Most of those emergency acts were seated
in the audience at those venues. Sixty-three acts were working on the various bills in Greater Boston houses that day, and exactly that number of
stand-by acts were on hand, each house having a complete substitute bill
under its roof and sitting in its audience waiting to perform if need be. That
strike was a complete failure, with, reportedly, not a single act walking out

on any bill in the city. Booking agents, who handled the working acts, were said to have also been brought in to be on hand to "see there were no defections." Reports were made by house managers to Shea at the Boston UBO office every hour on that Monday, January 1, with instructions to report more often at the first sign of trouble. On the previous Saturday and Sunday 150 stand-by acts had been marshalled in Boston (the other 87 were for venues outside Greater Boston in case any action spread). While all substitute acts were sent to Boston on a half-salary basis as long as they were on stand-by, in the event of not being used, they were given to understand they would soon get regular bookings in the area.[1]

Nothing more happened in Boston over the following couple of weeks. It remained unclear why no act had heeded the strike call. Certainly there would have been a high level of harassment by managers, all of whom seemed to know the action was coming. As well, outside agents were on hand to some extent and probably joined in the intimidation and harassment. No high-ranking Rat official bothered to journey to Boston, leaving the strike call and implementation to local WR representatives only. Regardless of the reason, *Variety* now also began to speak of the end of the WR and the end of Harry — *Billboard* had often spoken of them in the past tense over the previous few months. Mountford, said *Variety*, "for the second time has directed the destinies of the order to a point where its existence is seriously threatened ... from this point it looks as though the Rats, under Mountford leadership is permanently through...." Also reported was that a blacklist of about 300 acts had been produced for the information of vaudeville managers. Acts on the list were said to be mainly those remaining members of the WR, players attending recent meetings during the strike trouble, or those "making their unfavourable managerial attitude pronounced in circles through which it was reported back to the managers."[2]

Undeterred by the failure, the WR once again called a strike in the Boston area, to a limited extent, for Monday, February 5, 1917, when Rat officials served written notice on all acts (Rat and non–Rat) appearing at the theaters owned by Nathan Gordon and Dr. Lothrop not to play the Monday night shows. Houses affected were the Scollay Square, Olympia, and Bowdoin Square (all in Boston), and the Olympia (Lynn, Massachusetts). Lothrop owned the Bowdoin, with the others owned by Gordon. All four were booked through the Sheedy agency in New York, and it "seems significant," said a journalist, that the Gordon houses in Chelsea and Gloucester, Massachusetts (booked through the UBO Boston office), were not included in the strike order. On that Monday, WR officials hunted down every act and handed them long, official looking documents that read as follows: "All members are hereby forbidden to enter the Olympia, Boston, or appear upon the stage of the Olympia, Boston, until further notice." The order bore the typewritten names of Harry Mountford and James Fitzpatrick, and the handwritten signature of Whalen.[3]

Acts who obeyed the strike order and refused to perform that day were: Bubbles, Trout and Mermaid (a tank act); the University Four (songs); Henry Horton and Company (sketches), who left the Olympia; Nelusco and Hurley (songs); Penn City Trio (songs); Corcoran and Mack (comedy); Dayton Family (acrobatic troupe, 11 people), who left the Scollay; Mott and Maxfield (comedy, man and woman); Brinkman and Steele Sisters (singing); Selbini and Grovini (cycle act, man and woman) out at the Bowdoin; Charles McDonald and Company (sketches); Frank King (comic); Lane and Lane (acrobats); Revers and Earl (song and dance) out at Lynn, Massachusetts. None of those 14 acts were said to be well-known.[4]

When the VMPA headquarters in New York was apprised of the situation, it told the Boston VMPA office to take charge of the strike. Acts were sent to the affected theaters from all Boston vaudeville houses to play one show in order to allow the Trust the time to transport sufficient talent to New England from outside areas to prevent any house going dark. And indeed, on February 5 every one of the four houses played with a complete bill. On Tuesday morning, February 6, Pat Casey (the VMPA executive in charge of the Trust's response) arrived in Boston with about 60 acts and to supervise the situation. During Tuesday afternoon all houses played to big audiences, despite the efforts of four strikers who picketed in front of the doors of each house telling passers-by, "This theater is unfair to organized labor." Those pickets were not interfered with except at the Bowdoin, where two pickets, Lew Moore and Arthur Leroy, were arrested by the police and charged with "loitering and sauntering." Gordon declared that from that point on his venues would be supplied with acts by the VMPA. A day later Moore and Leroy were fined $10 each by Judge Dowd in the City Court. Dowd ruled that although peaceful picketing was permissible by law in Massachusetts, since the accused were picketing in a manner to cause the assembly of a crowd and to cause the obstruction of the sidewalks they were guilty of an infraction of the law prohibiting sauntering and loitering.[5]

Managers declared they would hold all the property of the strikers until the end of the week (most acts dropped their props and equipment at the venue they were playing on the Monday morning when they checked in and left them there all week). Included in the seized equipment was the trained seal belonging to Bubbles, Trout and Mermaid. However, the WR attorney went to court and got an order issued to have the property released after he successfully argued the property was essential to aid the owners in making a living. Unknown was why the Rats had chosen the theaters they did to call a strike against, except perhaps, mused a reporter, that for some reason they saw them as a weak point. Also, that reporter classed the strike as "a dismal failure" because it did not close a single house. He also could not understand why any acts had walked out and likely ruined their futures, because, "It was universally accepted that the acts walking out had become marked with V.M.P.A. managers and booking agencies connected with that organization."[6]

On the day after the strike, the WR announced, after a meeting, a special assessment of 5 percent to be levied upon the salaries of all working members of the union. It was an assessment against all working Rats, whether they were in vaudeville, burlesque, cabaret or legitimate, to help finance the strike. When the VMPA learned of the levy it notified all managers to be aware of it and to watch for any acts obeying the direction and remitting money to the union. "Immediate cancellation was to be the penalty with no reinstatement under any circumstances to follow for any act obeying the assessment order," went the VMPA directive. The managers' order for penalizing assessment payers was said to be more stringent than that issued for the punishment of acts paying dues to the WR or remaining members of the order.[7]

Little happened over the week after the strike call was issued. On February 13 Judge Duff found six more pickets, all arrested in the previous few days, guilty of loitering and sauntering, and fined each of them $5. All four affected venues were still picketed, although the Rats had issued instructions that pickets were to work in five-minute relays in hopes of preventing further arrests. Fitzpatrick was still trying, through the Central Labor Union federation in Boston, to get other unions involved in the walkout, but received nothing except "moral support." Despite continued efforts by the Rats to pull more acts out, only two performers added themselves to the list of strikers over the course of the week — Walter Percival, and Fred "Broomstick" Elliot, who both refused to work at the Olympia in Lynn.[8]

Meanwhile, the managers maintained a state of preparedness by having double shows waiting in the wings of every house in the "danger zone," including the big-time houses, where the duplicate shows continued to report daily and to be paid half salary. Attendance at all houses was reported to be normal or very close to it. The majority of the outside agents who had arrived for the start of the strike on the first Monday had returned to New York by this time, with the remainder slated to leave over the following three days. That was taken as a sign that the managers were becoming less fearful about the situation. Strike activity had little effect on the wider community, according to one reporter, who wrote, "The local people seem to display little interest in the affair and it is doubtful if their support will be forthcoming unless a general strike is called, including all theater help. The papers have passed up the strike entirely and beyond the continual picketing there is nothing to show a strike is in progress."[9]

Then a fifth house, the Central Square Theatre in Lynn (owned by the R. Bailey Amusement Company), had a strike notice served on it. Rats managed to keep that house dark for three shows until Pat Casey arrived with substitute acts and the house resumed running full bills. According to *Billboard* 240 NVA members made up the emergency stand-by players overall, and to that date 18 WR pickets had been arrested.[10]

On Sunday, February 18, the Central Labor Union of Boston held its regular meeting, with resolutions, debates and then a vote by the assembled delegates to place every theater controlled by the VMPA (not just those picketed) on the labor list of "unfair" organizations. But a measure of dissent was apparent because the delegates from the unions most directly involved — stagehands, musicians, and operators — all refused to take part in the voting. A *Variety* reporter tried to add more dissension to the mix when he reported, without evidence of any kind, "There seems to be a strong undercurrent of suspicion against Mountford in labor circles about here ... it would not be surprising if a break was announced in the immediate future, with Mountford and Fitzpatrick going their separate ways." On Tuesday afternoon, February 10, two more theaters were added to the picketed list — Keith's Boston Theatre and the Franklin Park house (also in Boston). Rat officials tried to pull the acts out of both venues, but not a single performer walked out with, said an account, "the strike there being confined to the regulation picketing, each picket taking seven minutes before the front entrance of the house."[11]

Following that came a small strike on Wednesday, February 21, in St. Louis where George W. Seargjeant, WR deputy organizer for the area, called a strike on Joe Erber's vaudeville house. Erber was given until 10 A.M. the next day to declare his venue a WR closed shop, but he refused. No acts walked out, and there was no interruption of Erber's shows. So George started to picket. To swell the ranks he got his wife and adult son to picket with him. Passers-by were given flyers in front of the house informing patrons the place was "unfair to organized labor." Then the family were attacked by four men and roughed up. All received medical treatment, but none picketed after that. George insisted his family was attacked by four VMPA "thugs," but officially the perpetrators were classed as "person or persons unknown." And that ended the St. Louis strike. It was not clear from accounts whether the strike call in St. Louis came from WR headquarters or if it was something George decided to do locally, on his own initiative.[12]

All the acts that refused to walk out of the three Gordon venues back on February 5 when the strike call was issued were rewarded two weeks later by the VMPA when the managers' group placed them on a special list for a route that gave them steady work for the remainder of the season — which ran through the end of June.[13]

Another week passed and little changed in the strike situation. No new houses were added to the strike list, and the Boston newspapers continued to "virtually ignore" the strike. At the Bowdoin venue in Boston the noisy calliope band Lothrop had installed to drown out the cries of the picketers was silenced that week by the local authorities when they declared it to be a nuisance. According to an account, "A canvas of a number of members of the local musicians, stage hands and picture operators today revealed a pronounced hostility toward any sympathetic strike in support of the Rats." But there remained a possibility the Central Labor Union might somehow be able to get some of the other local unions to go out in support of the WR.[14]

As the strike dragged on, so did the blacklisting and personal attacks on the union. Near the end of February the VMPA distributed its list of those who paid the 5 percent special assessment to the WR. With the list that went to all affiliated managers were included instructions to see that the listed acts were not booked, and to cancel them if they happened to be currently playing. Twelve of the acts were reportedly then playing with one of them having a contract in big-time vaudeville through June. All were immediately cancelled. According to the VMPA, since the Rats had initiated the special assessment two to three weeks earlier the union had received about $130 gross, made up mostly of small sums ranging from $3.50 downward.[15]

Billboard chided the Rats, declaring its special 5 percent levy had fallen flat, with hardly anybody sending money in, and then went on to attack the union for extravagant spending and for wasting money in the past. It then declared, "The White Rats' leaders have already burned up $400,000 of their hard-earned money in riotous living." No supporting data was presented, but the figure was nonsense. Mountford had returned a little less than 18 months earlier when the union was broke or nearly so. If 3,000 actors had paid $10 a year in dues the gross Rat income would have been $45,000 over that time.[16]

Early in March more strike orders were issued by the WR, "to be placed on the long list of unsuccessful attempts to tie up vaudeville made by the White Rats organization under the leadership of Harry Mountford since last summer, starting with Oklahoma City at that time," observed a jaded reporter. On Friday, March 9, a strike was called against five Chicago houses controlled by the Western Vaudeville Managers' Association: Kedzie, Academy, Lincoln Hippodrome, Avenue, and Windsor. No acts walked out. A strike was called the same day against the Marcus Loew theaters in Greater New York, New Jersey, and Boston. No acts walked out in Boston. Picketing was begun in Chicago and at the new Boston venues, "with several arrests following." In the 17 Loew houses in New York and New Jersey there were only 15 acts "who, for one reason or another, forgot to appear at their appointed time." Monday, March 12, saw the Rats serve strike notice on the Poli vaudeville circuit. Of 80 acts then playing the circuit, seven walked out, affecting four of the 12 houses. Acts striking the Poli circuit were: Charlie Mack and Company; Tilyou and Ward (both at Poli's Waterbury, Connecticut); Collins and Lloyd; Williams and Held (Poli's Hartford); Stagpoole and Spire; Johnson, Howard and Lizette (Palace, Hartford); May Marvin (Poli's Bridgeport). No show in any house a strike was ordered against was interrupted, nor were any of the struck venues closed at all. Handbills and banners carried by pickets in Chicago read "Unfair to the White Rats Actors' Union," but were said to have had no effect on business at any of the houses. With the exception of the arrests of some picketers, there was no disruption.[17]

Eight minutes after the strike had been ordered at the Poli chain, notification of it had been received by the UBO office, which booked the Poli circuit. Later that same Monday a list of over 1,000 available acts was presented to P. Alonzo — the Poli booking manager — for any selection he might care to make. The Loew circuit was supplied with a list of 600 available acts it could call upon. As usual, the Rats were shut out of the media. "The New York, Chicago and Boston papers paid no attention to the Rats matter.... The White Rats through its press department made extravagant and misrepresented claims, but they could not get them into print," remarked an account. Marcus Loew ordered that any act walking out of any of his houses would never again be booked on his circuit. When the involved parties issued statements about the number of acts that had walked out of the 14 Loew houses in New York and New Jersey they were very far apart and both wildly off the mark. Harry estimated that 62.5 percent of the acts walked out; a Loew spokesmen insisted only three acts had walked out.[18]

When some arrested picketers were arraigned in Police Court in Boston on March 8, the presiding judge asked the strikers, "What are you trying to picket, actors or audiences?" He then told them, "Actors don't go in at the front door; they enter at the stage door, and that is where you must picket if you do so hereafter."[19]

Variety printed a list of the names of the acts placed on the managerial blacklist as a result of the WR strike ordered against the Loew theaters on March 8 — 28 acts from 14 houses in New York and New Jersey. Also on the list were the seven acts named above who had struck the Poli circuit. A second part of the list held the names of those blacklisted for either failing to report at the theaters assigned during the strike or for doing WR picket duty; an additional 39 acts were listed, but with no theater name attached.[20]

In a full-page editorial on March 16, Sime Silverman declared, "The White Rats in its dying days is making a slow but certain exit. Before that grossly misdirected organization shall have passed away it will have cost the vaudeville managers many thousands of dollars and much annoyance." Followers of Mountford were all without talent, he added, and "would follow Mountford anywhere, if he could get them money or work. They couldn't get it for themselves, and as Mountford couldn't get it for himself either all were in the same boat." According to Sime, 85 percent of vaudeville artists were not in sympathy with the WR movement, although he did not cite any evidence in support of that figure. As well, he bemoaned the fact there was no law against using "deception and false representation" that took away a person's livelihood, as did the action of the union and Harry, knowing any who heeded the strike calls would be going on a blacklist "that never sleeps." Sime believed "the law should intervene if it could, to stop this merciless sacrifice of the innocent."[21]

As he continued his tirade, Silverman targeted the interaction of women, vaudeville, and the Rats. Like Albee did a little earlier, the editor chose to pretend sexual harassment did not exist at all in his industry. "The use of women as pickets and the general play made for the women who are thus involved in this fruitless struggle of the Rats explains by its very nature the weakness of the organization," he wrote. Not only had the Rats put many artists out of vaudeville, "but it has reviled the women of it. That Rats monolog about women and what they must go through to secure engagements would be an awful indictment if true. It's not true, but it's enough to work upon the sympathies of those artists already red fired against the manager...." When a Rat had recently mentioned sexual harassment during a speech a listener asked the speaker if the women subjected to such treatment ever rebelled. The reply from the Rat, said Silverman, was, "she does, once in a while, with the result she is outcasted from vaudeville, to earn a living as she may thereafter, usually winding up on the streets." Such a reply was proof to the editor just how fanciful the WR were: "That will show to what a degree these talkers go with their misstatements (that not alone refer to women) in their attempts to deceive hearers."[22]

When the VMPA placed an ad that covered two full pages in the March 16 issue of *Variety* about the strike situation it led off with the subhead "Indisputable Facts." One of those was: "The so-called White Rats Strike and lock out in the City of Boston has been in existence for over three weeks and nothing has been accomplished for the actor but dissolution and failure." After giving the matter much thought and deliberation, continued the VMPA, it had decided that after March 19 it would engage "only the 'worthy artists' who are and are known to be real, honest members of the National Vaudeville Artists, Inc." Then the VMPA declared that while the NVA existed, "no vaudeville artist who walks out or has walked out of any theater operated by a member of this association or pickets any such theater on an order issued or instigated by the White Rats will secure an engagement in any theater or from any manager that is a member of the Vaudeville Managers Protective Association." Still, the VMPA insisted, "This is not a warning or a threat." Dismissive of the actors picketing, the VMPA remarked they were all "low talent, small time" performers and were "not vaudeville artists or recognized performers. The few that have been once have long outlived their usefulness in the Vaudeville business." Outside of those low talent actors who picketed, "The remainder of the pickets are made up of waitresses and hangers on around the Boston pool rooms."[23]

Marcus Loew told a *Billboard* reporter, with respect to the strike against his chain:

> The whole thing is a joke when only these few acts walk out.... I have no sympathy whatever for the outlaws, and so long as I am in show business none of them will every work for me, you can depend upon that. There is absolutely no excuse for their action, no extenuating circumstances, and they will never be given work over our circuit. [24]

Another step was taken a week later by the VMPA when it pointed out another way an agent could get in trouble with respect to acts on its blacklist. That was by way of an agent booking an act or a player who was on the list, under an assumed name. The VMPA made it incumbent on the agent hereafter, before accepting an act he was not entirely familiar with for book-ings, to investigate the previous engagements of all members of the act and to ascertain beyond a doubt that no member of a turn was on the blacklist. "The rule to disenfranchise outside agents placing or attempting to place acts containing a blacklisted person has been made without reserve and the expulsion will follow immediately the attempt is discovered," explained the directive.[25]

In its March 23 issue, *Variety* reported that nothing had happened in the strike situation since March 12 and all was "unseemly quiet." Labor lead-ers went to Boston at the behest of Gompers, but in the end it was announced that stagehands, musicians, and operators would not walk out in sympathy with the WR. Judge Jesse Baldwin, in Chicago, issued an injunction against all forms of picketing there. Twelve picketers who had resumed the distri-bution of flyers in front of the Grand Opera House in St. Louis were arrested in that city, making a total of 60 strikers arrested since the strikes were called. A bond of $200 was required from each picket arrested before he was released after being booked, and since bondsmen charged $5.45 per person per bond, it was just one more expense for the severely cash-strapped union.[26]

According to an article subhead in the March 24 issue of *Billboard,* the Rats tried to break up vaudeville performances by attacking and slugging "peaceful artists and otherwise place themselves on a par with anarchists and thugs." The tone of the piece was that there was chaos and violence every-where in the strike cities of Boston, Chicago, New York and St. Louis. Yet the period referred to was precisely the same week that *Variety* characterized as "unseemly quiet." Also according to this piece, the NVA, then a little over 10 months old, had 6,100 members, with new applications coming in at a rate of almost 100 a day.[27]

Another article in the same issue of *Billboard* brought up the "well defined rumor" that Mountford and Fitzpatrick had come to a parting of the ways, as they differed as to strike strategy, and after Fitzpatrick's admis-sion in Boston that WR membership was only 700. Once again, it was an example of a mainstream press boycott of the WR executives. In the face of such a rumor it was usual to contact one or both for comment. Yet it did not happen. No WR reached print unless he had something negative to say about the union, or was prepared to let his name be signed to such stories. When slanders or unfounded rumors were printed about the Rats — there was no serious discord between Fitzpatrick and Mountford — the principals were never contacted; the rumor was allowed to stand.[28]

Silverman reported on the editorial page at the end of March that there was less activity at all the strike cities that week; even picketing was falling off. According to the editor, the Rats' strike calls went as follows: "The procedure is for the White Rats to order a strike, but no one strikes other than those who have been planted in the theaters the order is aimed against, or one or two other acts who are influenced, usually by timid women in the turns who listen to the intimidation threats made by the Rats." After the strike was ordered, it gave "the opportunity for the Rats leaders to send out undiluted misstatements, and also gave them a chance to beg more money from actors to keep up the fight (that is, no fight), the Rats then declare picketing." Once picketing was declared, concluded Sime, the Rats went to local labor unions and asked for aid, but "While the sort of aid the Rats want from local unions is money, what they get is sympathy, and it's doubtful if they would even receive that if the local unions fully understood the situation."[29]

On Tuesday, April 10, at a WR closed meeting Harry Mountford declared all strikes by the WR against vaudeville theaters to be off. All picketing, and other activity, was ordered stopped. To save face, the strike activity was not ended, just suspended. Harry explained it was the WR patriotic duty, with the nation at war, to refrain from striking as proof of their loyalty and patriotism. Therefore, the strike was suspended until America was again at peace. *The Player* was suspended after sustaining another financial loss during this, its second, run (during its first run it reportedly sustained a total loss of $60,000). At the meeting there was an angry sentiment among WR members that other trade unions and organized labor as a whole (the AFL) had let the Rats down and betrayed the order. Harry told the meeting the union had liabilities of $250,000 when he returned to lead the organization; that thousands of members had failed to pay their union dues in the past year, and that receipts at the clubhouse had dropped from $2,000 per week down to $700. Mountford also said the union faced bankruptcy, and it would be forced out of its clubhouse because of foreclosure proceedings within a month. In fact, the Rats were ousted from their clubhouse before the end of April.[30]

With the Rats all but finished, the VMPA had no thought of easing up. Early in May it sent out a notification that urged, in part, houses to "Play loyal acts." Also contained in that memo was an injunction to strictly observe the blacklist until advised otherwise by the VMPA. Managers were reminded the onus was on each theater to ascertain that all acts upon its bill were carrying paid-up membership cards in the NVA — that the six-month dues payment for the period starting April 1 had been made.[31]

Billboard also reported that, despite the strike being over, the VMPA would not be quick to forget:

There will be no letup on the part of the members of that body until every White Rat, every supporter of the order, every agent who booked outlawed Rats, and every theater which played White Rat acts during the recent strike fiasco will have been severely disciplined.... It will be a long time before members of the now defunct White Rat order will ever again be permitted to play in the theaters identified with the Vaudeville Managers' Protective Association. It will take more than a "now I'll be good" to restore erstwhile Rats back into the good graces of the V.M.P.A. And this also will apply, and with especial severity, to those managers and agents who declined to affiliate or co-operate with the V.M.P.A. in its campaign against the Rats, and who, on the contrary, lent whatever assistance they could to the outlawed organization.[32]

The company union, the NVA, celebrated its first birthday early in May, when *Variety* stated it had 3,500 members. In an article full of lavish praise for the group, the reporter had nothing but good things to say about an organization he described as having "a policy of promoting benefits for its members in their theatrical engagements through a foundation of friendliness in thought and action toward the theatrical managers who may engage them." An editorial equally lavish in its praise of the NVA and of its bright future appeared in the same issue of the journal.[33]

Pat Casey, the VMPA executive involved in handling the strike on a day-to-day basis, had still another article in that issue, under his own byline. In his self-serving piece he argued that the VMPA had only been formed as a defensive response after being attacked by the Rats:

At the beginning this organization stood on a line of defense, defending their interest against the machinations of a rather self-conscious individual, whose specialty was agitation. As the profession knows, he found it rather simple to impress some of the acting profession with the time-worn arguments of capital and labor. The managers pictured in all views as a schemer, arch-villain and grafters, and finally, after a period which carried threat after promise and promise after threat, this individual threw the profession into a state of turmoil that will go down in theatrical history as the most ridiculous move ever made by the artist.[34]

Speaking of the Oklahoma City strike, Casey praised the managers there as "honest, upright conscientious and fearless men" who "stood firm together, one helping the other, asking no outside help from anyone, until finally they emerged victorious...." Apparently Casey had forgotten that very early on the VMPA had shunted the local men aside, and it was Casey himself who took over and ran that show. He ended his piece with a plea to those outside the VMPA to join his group, since one never knew when trouble would strike. Therefore, "Arm yourself with the preventive, and, in the vaudeville manager's instance, the V.M.P.A. is the preventive." Then Casey delivered to those outsiders a warning: "If you persist in remaining outside, that's your own business, but remember the Vaudeville Manager's Protective Association is continually working, and perhaps when you wish to join, the friendly hand of welcome that now awaits you may be pictured in the guise of the mailed fist."[35]

Devoting an equal degree of lavish praise to the NVA on its first birthday on May 9, 1917, but spread over several more pages, was *Billboard*, which continued to claim the group had over 6,000 members. According to reporter J. E. Edwards, the NVA was formed by artists in response to the fact that thousands of artists were opposed to the WR, their tactics, and so on. But then he was a little more honest and added, "The heads of organized vaudeville themselves not only favored such a new organization, but actually brought about its formation."[36]

Journalist A. P. Knutt authored one of the many *Billboard* articles in praise of the NVA. Knutt went a little further in explaining the origins of the company union when he wrote.

> The N.V.A. is the godchild (figuratively speaking) of that masterful tactician in the art of organization and systematizing of important affairs, Edward F. Albee, who is its sponsor. Mr. Albee is also the head of the Vaudeville Managers' Protective Association, so it can readily be seen that the welding of the two will form an alliance through which all future menace between performer and manager will be forever eliminated.[37]

A large entertainment benefit was held June 3 at New York's Hippodrome theater by and for the NVA. As well, it was used to provide a check for the VMPA to see who was in sympathy with the NVA and who was not. In a letter sent to each of its managers, the VMPA asked them to send it a list each week of all the acts that bought tickets for that benefit, and how many tickets each act bought. Also requested was a list of acts that refused to buy benefit tickets and whether they were members of the NVA, "as we are very desirous of knowing who is and who is not interested in the welfare of the N.V.A. There may be a few performers who joined the N.V.A. feeling it might assist them in getting work, and who may still have White Rat sympathies. This we want to know." Marcus Loew remarked, "Why should not every manager expect every member of the N.V.A. to do its duty?" Said E. F. Albee, "We expect every member of that order to do their share in helping to carry out the policy of the founders of the organization."[38]

B. S. Moss (of the Moss circuit) observed, "Any performer who is a member of the N.V.A. and who fails to do their duty in carrying out the policies of the N.V.A. certainly is not entitled to any consideration from the managers." J. J. Murdock (an executive with the UBO) declared, "I believe every artist should not hesitate to buy from $10 to $200 worth of tickets, according to their salary. However, the members of the Managers' Association are certainly interested to know just how the interest of the artist lies, and there is no better way for them to show it than by the interest they take in this benefit." Adding to the pressure was Pat Casey, who said:

I believe every actor should take from ten to 25 percent of a week's salary in tickets. It has been claimed by White Rats that some of their members joined the N.V.A. thinking it would aid them in securing time, and I don't know of any better way to find out whether there are any members in the N.V.A. who sympathize with the Rats than through this benefit, for certainly no member will fail to do his duty except those with White Rat sympathies at heart.[39]

At the beginning of June the VMPA officially discussed the blacklist, for the first time, at one of their meetings, wherein it was decided WR acts would be engaged after all others had been placed. Acts were to be put into one of three categories and booked in that order: acts that had not struck at the affected houses; acts that took no sides in the dispute; Rat acts. Before adjourning the meeting, the managers' group appointed a representative who was charged with the task of investigating and then preparing a report for the VMPA listing the names of artists and acts that had changed their names and material to avoid detection as a blacklisted act.[40]

Near the end of June the WR held their last meeting. Fitzpatrick and Mountford each had good words to say about the other, with the former lashing out at organized labor, the AFL, and various local unions that he believed had failed to support the strikes. Harry reported that over the previous two years the receipts from dues amounted to $36,000, with an additional $12,000 derived from assessments, or total receipts of about $48,000. The strike against vaudeville, he reported, had cost the Rats $23,000 to conduct. Since his return to the union, added Mountford, he had received no salary.[41]

Later in the summer, at the end of August, the VMPA announced it had decided to pare down considerably, but not eliminate, its "Undesirable List," or blacklist of Rat acts. To that end a VMPA committee removed the names of 164 acts from the blacklist. Over time more names would be removed. However, destined to remain on the blacklist were the acts described as "hard-core" WR supporters, "the anarchists," those who had contributed money to them, and so on. Names on the blacklist carried stars that denoted the degree of severity of their transgressions — one star denoted the most serious offense; four stars indicated the lightest offense. Prior to the pruning of names the blacklist was believed to have held several hundred names of vaudeville actors and acts.[42]

The Cora Youngblood Corson Sextet did not appear at the Family theater in Rochester in mid–October nor at the Lyric in Buffalo the next week, even though a contract was held for each house. Managers of each venue were informed by the VMPA they could not play the act — the VMPA became aware of the booking through an outside agent. Both houses were given the option of not allowing the act to appear in their venue and remaining members of the VMPA, or of playing the act and losing their membership in that group. Even though the Cora Sextet threatened to sue, both houses barred the act, which was described as one of the most "aggressive" of the Rat acts in the strike. That act was one of the 100 or more names that continued to remain on the blacklist.[43]

Almost two years later, in July 1919, the Rats placed an ad in *Billboard* that covered two full pages. One page was signed by James Fitzpatrick and explained that he still stuck by Harry and restated his belief in Harry's good character. It was also an attack on *Variety* for trying to drive a wedge between them, and for its relentless and false attacks on Mountford and the WR. As well, Fitzpatrick, on his page, called for people to come forward again and join the Rats. The other page was signed by Harry and was devoted fully to an attack on *Variety* and its editor Sime Silverman, referring to the publication as "The Serpent." Mountford mentioned nothing at all about the WR or about rejoining it, leaving it all to Fitzpatrick. Curiously, not a word was said against or about *Billboard*, even though it was more relentless and hysterical in its attacks on the union and on Harry. Perhaps that was the price for getting the ad published at all? In any event, of course, there was no revival in the Rats; there was no resurrection of the union. It remained all but officially dead.[44]

One month later Harry took out a 1.5 page ad in *Billboard* in which he praised and supported Actors' Equity — then two or three days into its own strike — and chastised his former people for what they did not accomplish in 1917 and for what Equity accomplished in 1919. To those old Rats he said:

> It was the legitimate actors who won, it was you who lost it. Take your hats off to the legitimate actors of the United States. But the damage is not irreparable. It can yet be undone. No cause is lost until its leaders admit it. We have never admitted or conceded for one moment that we were defeated or that we were

out or that we were defunct or that we were dead. You will still have a chance to prove that you're as brave, as gallant and as obedient and loyal as the Actors' Equity Association.

Urging non-union actors to join a union, and pointing out those who worked in the face of a strike call were scabs, he concluded, "If you disobey you are a traitor to your class, you are guilty of the one universal crime. You are a tool of the employers, being used to defeat your brothers and sisters."[45]

With no explanation, and for no apparent reason, *Billboard* suddenly reversed itself completely and sang the praises of Harry Mountford in an article in its December 20, 1919, issue. (Of course, he was completely harmless by then, being a threat to no one):

> Nine out of ten of the artists and performers of the country who have never met him, picture him as a big, burly, beef-eating, reckless, leather-lunged agitator. This false impression of the man is deepened in many instances by the propaganda sedulously coined by a malign opposition among actors and eagerly circulated by a subsidized trade press. As a matter of fact, the real Mountford is the direct antithesis of the widely entertained idea of him.

This was disingenuous in the extreme, as *Billboard* was one of the main creators of that false impression. Continuing on, the piece said of Harry, "No one could be less radical in disposition. He is not only eminently safe and sane, but very conservative. He combines great courage with rare perseverance, intense application and an honesty that's entirely above all suspicions." Shortcomings of the man were said to be an artistic temperament, an uncompromising disposition, impatience, and a lack of tact, but those handicaps "are more than counter-balanced by his deep sincerity, sterling integrity and likeableness."[46]

Commenting on the 1917 strikes, performer and vaudeville historian Joe Laurie noted in 1953 that, with respect to Harry, the theatrical establishment "started pounding the guy in the trade papers, charging him with everything in the book, burglary, rape, bigamy, and mayhem."[47]

Historian Douglas Gilbert also wrote about the 1917 strikes and said, with regard to Harry:

> Both *Variety* and *Billboard* published cartoons of him in a brothel with a girl on each knee, and a $1,000 bill in his hand, the caption reading: 'What does it matter? White Rats Money.' Another depicted him staggering from a saloon with a cigar tilted in his mouth with the same caption: 'What does it matter? White Rats Money.' Mountford did not drink nor did he smoke cigars.

Sometime after the strike was over Pat Casey appeared before the Federal Trade Commission, where he admitted the strike cost the managers $2,000,000.[48]

The White Rats continued to exist, technically, for a time, being supplanted in July 1919 when the Associated Actors and Artists of America was formed at a joint meeting between the WR and Equity. Most of all it was a housekeeping move by the AFL to allow Equity to receive its charter directly from the Federation and not through the Rats. Also, the Rats agreed to get rid of their name, becoming the vaudeville branch of the 4As. It was a group that played no role or had any effect on actors' lives; it existed more on paper than in reality. In every meaningful way the Rats expired late in 1917. On June 4, 1950, Harry Mountford died at the age of 79 at his New York City home, living out the last three decades of his life in obscurity and near poverty.[49]

As the White Rats withered and died at this time, another actors' union began, grew, and strengthened.

10 | Actors' Equity Association, the Beginnings, 1913–1919

"The only classes of workers that haven't organized for self-protection long ago are actors and washerwomen...."
— Francis Wilson, 1913

"And even such contract as he [the actor] has is a most unequal instrument. The manager holds the handle while he holds the blade.... As the system works out, his contract is binding on one party and not the other."
— Hiram Moderwell, *New Republic*, 1916

Early in March 1913 an editor with the *Christian Science Monitor* noted that people in profession after profession had sought mutual protection for themselves through the formation of some type of union. Last among them seemed to be the acting profession, where word had just come that something called the Actors' Equity Association was forming. Commenting on the difficulty of an actor making a first contract and the harsh conditions players often faced, the editor said, "Custom and managerial decree even now compel an amount of unremunerated service in rehearsals. Extra performances do not imply extra pay." He wasn't sure if a group such as Actors Equity would have formed up at all were it not for the continuing combination of managerial forces into the Trust in the theatrical field, but he had no doubt that managerial combining had at least sped up such a development.[1]

Back in December 1912, eight actors held an organization meeting to discuss the formation of an actors' union powerful enough to obtain a fair contract from the managers. Based upon the preliminary plans from that meeting, 112 actors met at the Pabst Grand Circle Hotel in New York in May 1913 and formed Actors' Equity Association (AEA). One initial reaction came from producer Lee Shubert, who said, "No person who delivers as little as the actor is paid so much."[2]

Francis Wilson became the first president of Equity, and he remarked at the end of 1913, "The only classes of workers that haven't organized for self-protection long ago are actors and washerwomen, and now even we are beginning to get together." A general interest publication of the time, *The Outlook*, commented:

> In America, with the centralization of capital and the crystallization of class feeling have come strikes with increasing frequency in widely divergent trades and industries. We have had miners' strikes, textile workers' strikes, and strikes of railway men, of course, and more recently we have seen waiters and even barbers at war with their employers. But does any one remember a widespread strike of actors? ... Never, that we remember....[3]

Agreeing that the abuses Equity was fighting were many and of long-standing duration, the editor of *The Outlook* was nevertheless surprised a union had been formed at all, because, "An incapacity for co-operation seems to be one of the traits of the artistic temperament. At any rate, all past attempts of players on the legitimate stage to organize have failed. In view of this fact, the success of the present movement is all the more notable." Initial demands made by Equity were to have transportation expenses to and from all points on the road paid; no actor to be forced to give more than three weeks of rehearsals without compensation; two weeks' notice of dismissal to be given; extra pay for extra performances; full salary for all weeks played (that is, an end to weeks where half salary was paid because such weeks had traditionally had low business); and that actresses should not be forced to bear the expense of supplying an unlimited stage wardrobe. As of the end of 1913 it was said Equity had over 1,000 members. In conclusion, the editor declared, "*The Outlook* believes in the right of all labor to organize; and even though the artist has certain rewards which the factory laborer, for instance, does not have, there is no reason why artists should not unite for common protection, if in so doing they do not degrade their calling."[4]

When Equity celebrated its first year of existence it reportedly had a membership of over 1,500 players, of whom 800 had pledged themselves to sign only the type of contract that AEA deemed to be equitable. Membership was said to contain many of the leading players (George Arliss for one), with the standard needed to join being that a player needed three years of professional experience before being eligible for membership, although generous exceptions were made for newcomers to the field. Equity's own draft contract indicated a change to some extent in the union's demands; it called for not more than four weeks of rehearsal of a dramatic production and not more than five weeks of rehearsals for a musical production without pay. At the time, rehearsals still often ran to six, eight, or even 12 weeks without pay. AEA agreed to play extra holiday matinees and Sunday evening performances in cities where they were customary, as well as the regular two matinees and six evening shows in a usual week, but expected extra pay for all added performances over and above the more or less usual eight. Another clause in AEA's draft contract — it hoped to get producers to use it — provided for "run of the play"; to correct the practice of engaging famous players to create a part, and generate media attention and reviews, and then replace them with much cheaper and unknown players, hoping the play's early reputation based on the now-absent star power would carry it along.[5]

For a time after its founding in 1913, Equity admitted only male players, with that policy coming from a belief, according to historian Benjamin McArthur, that actresses ought to be spared the expected backlash of hostility and aggression from managers towards a player joining a union. But the membership campaign went so well that the bar only lasted a few months, and around July 1913 the bylaws were changed to allow actresses to become members. By 1918 three women players had reached the point where they were elected to AEA's council: Helen Ware, Katherine Emmet, and Florence Reed.[6]

Supposedly, Equity was not a racist organization. Grant Stewart, an AEA official, made it emphatic (in 1919) that there were no race or color distinctions drawn in his union, and that any actor was eligible for membership who came within the regulations with respect to the length of experience necessary. Stewart acknowledged that as of 1919 no request to join the union had ever been made by a black artist. "We have members who are of various races and nationalities, and the Negro actor is at all time welcome," added Stewart.[7]

During 1914 Equity got involved in negotiations and discussions over a standard contract. It submitted drafts to the combination that controlled legitimate theater, the United Managers' Protective Association (UMPA), which contained most of the important producers of legitimate productions. The UMPA was the legitimate theater industry's equivalent to the VMPA in the vaudeville industry.[8]

Before contract negotiations got really serious, AEA was sidetracked for a time in 1916 when the question of affiliation with the organized labor movement arose, generating heated emotions on both sides. At a meeting held early in March 1916, AEA, with a membership then estimated to be 2,500 legitimate players, discussed the issue at meetings held simultaneously in various cities. Because only one charter was issued by the AFL to any line of trade, such a move (affiliation) would have to be through the White Rats, which then held the AFL charter for the theatrical profession. The final outcome of the meetings was to place the matter of the proposed alliance before AEA members for a full vote at the end of May.[9]

At the meeting in New York that March some 800 Equity members were in attendance and reportedly voted unanimously in favor of affiliation with the AFL. Similar results came from the 200 members who met in Chicago, the 65 who got together in Boston, and smaller meetings held in Philadelphia and Los Angeles. Since near unanimous votes in favor of affiliation had been obtained everywhere, observers were led to believe the results of the vote slated for May were a foregone conclusion.[10]

At the New York meeting one of the speakers said organized labor had spread from less than 200,000 members in 1881 to two million in 1916. Equity president Francis Wilson remarked at the meeting, "Hitherto actors have refused to organize for their own protection, giving as an excuse that theirs was an artistic profession, and that it was beneath the dignity of an artist even in his own protection to employ the methods of a mechanic." While he thought that was alright at a time when few classes of people were organizing and there was little need for protection of acting as a profession, Wilson added, "but at this particular time and period, when all classes, that is artists and artisans and professors, are organizing for protection, even the actor at last, thank God, has his protective association. So that there is no need to hide our dignity, our artistic dignity, which has given way to necessity."[11]

As Equity waited for the May affiliation vote, Hiram Moderwell published a piece in the *New Republic* about actors and unions:

[An actors' labor union] sounds strange.... The mere idea of it has long kept the actors from organizing. Though they are working under modern industrial conditions they have stubbornly refused to admit that they are members of a trade. "Are artists to place themselves on a level with hod-carriers?" they asked. And while they hugged their romantic pride, the managers gave them the short end of every contract.[12]

Moderwell believed it was important for actors to overcome any such fears about unionization because there were a lot of bad aspects within the acting industry; he then mentioned most of the obvious ones, such as no pay for rehearsals; the half-salary weeks; the requirement for the actor to usually provide his own costumes; and so on:

> Whenever his play fails, his contract automatically becomes void. And even such contract as he has is a most unequal instrument. The manager holds the handle while he holds the blade. He must give two weeks' notice of his intention to leave, but he can be dismissed, if his employer chooses, on no notice at all. Even if he fulfills the conditions of his contract he can often be coerced to remain by means of an insidious blacklist in the hands of an unscrupulous manager. If he believes himself injured he has no practical recourse. As the system works out, his contract is binding on one party and not the other.[13]

As far as Moderwell was concerned, the actor's economic position could not be secured until he recognized himself as a wage earner, a member of a trade. As an economic unit he was exactly in the position of the hod-carrier. And the fact that actors had formed their own union — Equity — meant they were finally realizing that fact and acting on it. Nearly all the first-class theaters in America, explained Moderwell, were controlled by two large firms, "And production itself is largely in the hands of a score of managers. These entrepreneurs are organized to meet the prevailing conditions." Underlying this seemingly extremely strong desire to affiliate with the AFL, thought Moderwell, was that AEA to that point had only enjoyed indifferent success. It had been meeting off and on for three years with the managers' Trust in order to achieve a first contract but had not gotten very far.[14]

As expected, when the AEA held its annual meeting on May 29 it voted overwhelmingly in favor of affiliating with the AFL. Present at the meeting were 518 members who voted 517 to 1 in favor of the proposal; 800 votes were mailed in by actors on the road, 781 to 19 in favor. Equity then had 2,719 members and over $12,000 in the bank.[15]

What was left open at that meeting was the actual way affiliation would take place. That was a matter left to the discretion of the AEA council. The most obvious way to join would have been to apply to the White Rats for a charter, to be swallowed by that union and to become a part of it, or to be taken in by the Rats as a distinct branch in its own right. On the other hand, Equity could have ignored the rules, applied directly to the AFL for a charter and forced president Gompers of the federation to deal with an awkward situation. But nothing was said one way or another at the meeting; it was left to the council and was postponed for some time to come.[16]

Nevertheless, when *Billboard* reported on the vote it let its venom for the Rats show through, because it, said "The Equity Association will in no wise become subservient to the White Rats' organization." That, despite the fact nothing at all was said at that meeting about the WR or against the Rats.[17]

According to the *New York Dramatic Mirror,* most managers did not display open hostility to Equity's AFL vote, except producer/manager Lee Shubert, who was reported to have said his "firm would run their business to suit themselves" and would "submit to no dictation" from the players. Already at that time it was said that three managers were using the AEA so-called equitable contract — Oliver Morosco, A. H. Woods, and Corey, Williams and Ritter, Inc.[18]

Howard Kyle, AEA secretary, said that a fashionable woman had remarked to producer Daniel Frohman, on hearing of the contemplated AFL affiliation by the actors, "Why Mr. Frohman, you don't mean to tell me that actors will march down the street on Labor Day with a lot of ordinary mechanics. It will take all the glamour away from you." And Frohman replied, according to Kyle, "You need have no fear, Madame: actors will never stick together."[19]

The AFL situation was not resolved until July 18, 1919, when, in a surprise move, the Associated Actors and Artists of America was formed at a joint meeting between AEA officials and WR representatives; it came to be referred to as the 4As, designed to cover the entire acting profession but broken down into four parts. After the AFL recognized the new group, the WR AFL charter, which had covered the entire acting field, passed out of existence, superseded by the 4As. Thus, it became the 4As that granted charters to other branches of the profession not already organized. Theoretically, each actors' union would be under the leadership of the 4As, but in fact each individual unit — such as Equity — would be autonomous in its own field. As part of the agreement, the WR agreed to drop its old name and rename the vaudeville branch of the 4As something else. In that way the name "White Rats," which had so many negative connotations attached to it, disappeared, and Equity could affiliate with the AFL but not have to go through the Rats to do it. Meanwhile, the AFL had managed to sidestep a dicey situation, which, of course, was the reason for the formation of the 4As. At that meeting Francis Wilson was announced as first president of the new 4As, Fitzpatrick as vice president, Mountford as executive secretary, and Frank Gilmore as treasurer. All four of those men kept their respective positions as executives with Equity or the renamed Rats. At the time of its formation the 4As consisted of: Actors' Equity Association, the Chorus Workers' Union, the Hebrew Actors' Union, and the Vaudeville Actors' Union (the renamed Rats, but still dead in all meaningful ways).[20]

Late in 1917 it was reported that men and women players in motion pictures were being admitted to membership in Equity, but under the condition that an applicant from the film world had to have at least two years' experience in individual acting on the stage in the spoken drama. AEA was never successful in recruiting film actors into its folds, although it tried a few times. The White Rats had also tried to recruit film players at least a few times but also had no success. For that matter, the Rats had never been able to recruit players from the legitimate stage, nor could Equity ever recruit members from variety. Of course, there were a handful of crossovers in all cases, but nothing to speak of. Each union that was organized was only able to recruit from its own area, no matter how hard it tried to recruit from outside. Motion picture actors were not successfully organized until their own union formed up — SAG (Screen Actors' Guild) — in 1934. After 1919 vaudeville artists had no union to speak of, even though the old Rats continued to exist under another name. But by then vaudeville was on the way out. It declined rapidly in the 1920s and could barely be called alive in the 1930s — mainly a victim of first films and then radio.[21]

After four years of tough, back-and-forth negotiations an announcement was made early in June 1917 that the United Managers' Protective Association (UMPA — Marc Klaw was its manager) and AEA had agreed upon an "equitable" contract, and once a few minor details were fixed it would be put into effect. It was the first ever such contract for the players; it eliminated the half-salary weeks (usually around Easter and Christmas), and limited the amount of unpaid rehearsals to four weeks for a drama and six weeks for a musical. Rehearsals in excess of those periods were to be paid for at the rate of half the player's usual salary. As well, the contract imposed a two weeks' notice clause — for dismissal or resignation — on each party to the contract.[22]

Formal approval of that contract came on October 2, 1917, when it was ratified by both Equity and UMPA and became binding on both. It was to go into effect immediately, just as soon as the document could be printed. One other feature of the contract was that it provided for a Board of Arbitration to settle any disputes.[23]

Some managers within the UMPA were reported to be unhappy with the new contract, as of March 1918. One item they did not like was the proviso that called for a pro rata extra salary for all performances over eight per week (the usual week of six evening shows and two matinees), and nine per week in the West (Chicago was defined as part of the West). Another clause the dissidents did not like was the one that guaranteed an actor his place if he was ill, so long as the illness did not last over 10 days. Because of the bar in the contract against half-salary weeks, some managers were said to have cancelled the pre–Easter week altogether, arguing they had never made money that week but played a production then only to help out the actor by ensuring he got at least some money that week.[24]

Two months later it was reported that several of the UMPA managers had started to sidestep or ignore the AEA-UMPA contract, even though it was legally binding on both sides. They did not like it, so, in some cases, they did not use it at all; in other cases they used it but ignored any clauses they did not agree with.[25]

Later that month, at its annual meeting, AEA revealed it had made an appeal to U.S. President Woodrow Wilson that he consider the matter of aiding the actor in bringing about the universal use of the standard contract. In a brief note of reply to Equity, President Wilson told Equity head Francis Wilson that he saw the importance of the matter and that he would talk it over with his advisors. As well, Equity had taken other steps to try to stem the tide of managers either not using the contract or using it and ignoring it. To that end, two forms of pledges and agreements were being promulgated among its members. One stipulated that members pledge they would not accept or sign any contract with a manager other than the UMPA-AEA standard form. Or if they did, they were not to accept or sign any contract in which the conditions were not as advantageous to the actor as set forth in the standard form. If an actor who signed such a pledge violated it, the right to damages arose, with AEA entitled to recover $1,000 from the actor as liquidating damages. A second pledge was aimed at managements that did not pay debts to actors or who had not paid since January 1, 1915. It stipulated that whenever the council of the AEA determined any manager to be in that "prohibited" class, the signers of the pledge agreed not to work for him until such time as the manager was removed from the list. As in the other pledge, should any signer default on this one he became liable for $1,000 in liquidating damages. Such an action was deemed necessary because of the number of non-paying or slow-paying managers in the industry. With most productions being incorporated, the actor had little chance of recovering unpaid salary. A manager could mount production after production, incorporating each one separately, and then not pay and move on to incorporate the next one, leaving the actor to sue the old corporation, which, of course, no longer existed and/or had no assets.[26]

Also in the month of May 1919 the UMPA reshuffled itself to a minor extent and renamed itself the Producing Managers' Association (PMA), but it was virtually the same organization. However, that shift allowed the PMA to make the bogus argument that it was an entirely new organization, and since the UMPA no longer existed, the two parties had no agreement and no contract. Negotiations commenced anew. One snag came up immediately when the PMA rejected eight performances as being a normal number per week in the East (with more money for extra shows) and instead held out for nine — it anticipated the arrival of Sunday amusement in New York, then barred. Another contentious point was Equity's demand for a closed shop. Many AEA members complained that non-member players got the benefits won by AEA without being members of the union and without paying any dues.[27]

As the summer of 1919 moved along, no agreement was reached between Equity and the PMA, nor was there likely to be one. While Equity was willing to submit most, if not all, of the points at issue to arbitration, the PMA was adamantly against arbitration and against having a proviso for an arbitration board in any contract it was to be a party to. With respect to the Equity pledge about not accepting any other form of contract except the old AEA–UMPA one, by mid–July about 1,400 Equity members had signed that pledge, approximately one-third of the union's membership.[28]

Things came to a head in July when news of Equity's affiliation with the AFL broke, and the way it had been done by the shuffling of groups and names. And the spectre of Harry again reared its head. A few days after the July 18 announcement of AFL affiliation, Equity held a meeting with the PMA and requested that a committee be appointed by each side to get together in conference and settle the differences. L. Lawrence Weber, PMA secretary, issued a statement that refused such a meeting, with one reason being "the recent action of your Association in bringing into your councils men who have proved in the past neither friends to the actor nor to the managers [Mountford and Fitzpatrick], men who have only thrived in the fostering of bitterness and discord where it did not previously exist, your Association has made impossible any serious conference between it and the Producing Managers' Association."[29]

Contract talks had thus come to a standstill by late July. Even though Mountford, Fitzpatrick, and the old WR organization had nothing at all to do with Equity (they had no impact, they were not consulted, and so on), the PMA used that as an excuse to shun Equity. Underneath it all, of course, was the real reason: the PMA was furious over Equity's affiliation with the organized labor movement, with the AFL. Negotiations had then been underway for six full years, off and on, since AEA was formed, and all the players had achieved was a "binding" contract that was little used and often ignored by the Theatrical Trust, almost before the proverbial ink had dried. Managers insisted on an open shop, no arbitration board (actors had to be "free" to treat individually with the employer), more than eight performances per week as the standard, and so on. Gilmore explained over and over that Mountford had nothing to do with Equity, but his words went unheard. As a reporter noted, "Neither the managers nor the actors are willing to admit that the mere act of becoming affiliated with the American Federation of Labor has been the real reason for the breaking off of negotiations between the two organizations." By this time the pledge to not sign a contract that had not been approved by Equity had been signed by 2,300 of the 4,000 union members.[30]

On July 22, 1919, the PMA held a meeting after the breakdown of talks with AEA. Those in attendance, besides Sam Harris in the chair, were the Shubert Brothers, A. L. Erlanger, Edgar Selwyn, L. Lawrence Weber, George M. Cohan, Al Woods, and William Harris. Also present, at the request of the legitimate managers, was E. F. Albee of vaudeville. Albee was asked to explain his strategy in successfully fighting the actors' strike against vaudeville managers in 1917. He told how he took actors from one house and put them in another in which there was a strike. Legitimate managers explained it could not be done in dramatic houses because star parts could not be replaced overnight, whereas in vaudeville one act might easily replace another, as all parts were independent (everything was a dependent part of the whole on the dramatic stage). Following that exchange, said a reporter, "Mr Albee then enlarged on the fact that it was impossible for the managers to win in a struggle with the actors unless they destroyed the actors' organization." By way of advice, continued the journalist, "He [Albee] suggested various methods by which this might be done, such as attacking the leaders of the organization, making a fuss over actors and gaining their friendship temporarily, starting a new organization and offering temptations to actors in the form of contracts and increased salaries. He recommended getting two or three prominent actors to be heads of a new actors' organization and under no circumstances to recognize the A.E.A."[31]

Legitimate managers would follow Albee's recommendation to the letter, at least for a time. And they would start following them very soon, because Equity was about to strike.

11 | Actors' Equity Association Strike, 1919

"I am with the Equity Association and will go back to the cloak-and-suit trade if they lose their fight against the managers."
— Eddie Cantor, 1919

"Before I will ever do business with the Actors' Equity Association I will lose every dollar I have even if I have to run an elevator to make a living."
— George M. Cohan, 1919

Frustrated by six years of fruitless negotiations, Equity decided it had little choice but to act. Some years after the strike, journalist Paul Gemmill revealed (in 1926) that with respect to the old 1917 contract the UMPA put into use, an investigation disclosed that the contract was used by only 20 percent of the producing companies controlled by members of the UMPA, despite the fact that the binding contract had been agreed to and ratified by the UMPA.[1]

And conditions for the player on the legitimate stage had not improved at all during all the time of the negotiations. John McCabe, who wrote a biography of George M. Cohan, the legendary showman and producer, commented on those conditions in his 1973 biography:

In the American theater of 1919, working conditions for actors were abominable: there was rarely a limit to the hours of rehearsal, actors were frequently not paid for the rehearsals, contracts could be broken at will (the producer's will), and instant dismissal of an actor without cause was also a managerial option.... Frequently, actors who had worked hard and long in preparation for a production were casually dismissed after a successful opening night because they were no longer needed once the good press notices were garnered, and less

154

expensive actors could be substituted. Or an actor after such a successful open-ing could have his salary reduced under threat of such a replacement. Actors furnished their own wardrobe.

As to the reason for those conditions, McCabe declared, "In 1919, the source of these inequities was the greed of most Broadway producers. Of their num-ber, the Shuberts and Klaw and Erlanger were archetypal."[2]

The opening skirmish in the long–threatened war between Equity and the PMA took place on Tuesday, July 29, 1919, and was won by the man-agers that afternoon when nine out of 10 Equity members rehearsing with the Comstock and Gest New York production *Chu Chin Chow* refused to walk out in obedience to orders from AEA after Morris Gest had refused to meet the demands from Equity that its members be given the UMPA-AEA standard contracts. Only one Equity member tendered his resignation before the Tuesday 2 P.M. deadline. Frank Gilmore, Equity secretary served notice on Gest on Monday evening that unless the standard contracts were forth-coming before the Tuesday rehearsal time, the Equity members would quit the production. Gilmore then issued an order to the union members to walk out of the show if they did not receive those contracts. Gest made no response until shortly before the Tuesday rehearsal was set to start, at which time he addressed the assembled company and stated he did not intend to issue the contract, and any player who desired to walk out was free to do so. Also in that speech, Gest attacked Harry Mountford as "a labor agitator from England," Francis Wilson as a millionaire, and Gilmore as an English actor who had not worked at his profession for the previous six years. (The influ-ence of Albee's advice was obvious in those false attacks.) On Tuesday eve-ning those nine Equity members who did not heed the call appeared at Equity headquarters, in response to a summons from Gilmore. According to Gilmore, all signed a pledge that evening placing themselves on record as committed to refusing to rehearse on Wednesday afternoon unless produc-ers Comstock and Gest issued the standard contracts. Nevertheless, when *Chu Chin Chow* started to rehearse at 2 P.M. Wednesday only two players were missing. Speaking for the PMA, Sam Harris, its president, declared that under no circumstances would his firm or any of those in the managers' organization issue any contracts other than the PMA contract — that is, the one the PMA had drafted itself unilaterally.[3]

The producing firm of F. Ray Comstock and Morris Gest (one of 28 members of the PMA) was singled out to receive the first strike call, thought a reporter, because not only did it not issue the AEA contract, but as far as possible it did not issue written contracts at all. "The verbal contract has been its policy for years," he explained. "Hence in the dispute over contract forms its attitude was deemed especially unreasonable and offensive. Firms that refused to issue the Equity agreement were deemed bad enough, but a firm that would give none at all was especially and peculiarly obnoxious."[4]

Producer Sam Harris (of Cohan and Harris), in a more general interview, discussed the topic of actors and unions. "We are friendly disposed toward the actor and desire to continue so. We are not fighting the actor, but we are strenuously opposed to the methods of the people at the head of the Actors' Equity Association," he explained. As far as any alleged unfair treatment of the players was concerned, the actors could rest easy because, "Should differences arise, or should an actor receive unfair treatment at the hands of a manager, the Managers' Association will make it its business to see that the actor does get fair treatment." Harris added, "I feel certain that an association of actors, headed by the best man in that profession, would find the Managers' Association willing and glad to do business with them. I think everybody should have an organization." Then Harris launched an attack, "In my opinion the high-class actor doesn't like this affiliation with labor. Mountford and Fitzpatrick killed the Rats' organization, now they are going to kill the Actors' Association." As far as he was concerned, "We can't do business with the Actors' Equity Association while they have leaders in whom we have no confidence." Mark Klaw (a producer and one of the more dominant individuals in the PMA) added his opinion that "Wilson and Mountford are leading the actors upon the rocks, and they [actors] are so color blind that they cannot see the danger signals.... Mr. Wilson, being a failure as author, actor and manager, he is a success as an agitator."[5]

Following those two days of activity around the *Chu Chin Chow* show things quieted down, but everyone knew a more general strike was only weeks or days away. A meeting was held in which representatives of the PMA, VMPA, Columbia Amusement Company (burlesque interests) and the National Association of the Motion Picture Industry were in attendance. Those four industry cartels covered all the theatrical fields of the era and upon the formal resolution of William A. Brady, formed an affiliation: "If trouble should come, this affiliation will resolve itself into an offensive and defensive alliance." An emergency committee was appointed by the PMA to meet daily in the event a strike took place. Members were: W. Brady, Lee Shubert, John Golden, Henry W. Savage, Morris Gest, George M. Cohan, Mark Klaw, Arthur Hopkins, and Arthur Hammerstein. As well, Albee was to continue to cooperate and offer advice.[6]

A reporter commented that in preparing to meet a strike situation, "the managers are proceeding along the lines followed by the Vaudeville Managers' Protective Assn. preceding and during the White Rats strike in 1917." Harris continued to state the PMA would never do business with any group with which Mountford, Fitzpatrick, or Francis Wilson was connected. Even at this early stage the managers had floated the idea of a company union. However, with respect to that attempt, and with respect to the personal attacks on individuals, the PMA's efforts were so crude as to be easily seen for what they were by observers. Said the journalist, "The managers' association seemed to be trying an extensive campaign of propaganda following the *Chu Chin Chow* affair, but the propaganda portion [attacks on Mountford, Wilson, and so on] was so apparent it carried no weight. The managers also appeared to be in difficulty on how to start the proposed Co-operative Actors' Association, stamping that proposal so clearly as a managerial move that little attention was given it."[7]

On Thursday, August 7, 1919, Equity struck in New York City. That strike call went into effect at 7 P.M. on August 7, and as a result of actor walkouts, the following houses were dark that night: Shubert Playhouse, Forty-Fourth Street, Lyric, Republic, Astor, Gaiety, Princess, Broadhurst, Selwyn, Knickerbocker, and the Cohan and Harris. Equity's strike resolution read:

> We severally agree, each with the other, that until the Actors Equity Association is recognized as the representative of the actors, and until a satisfactory arrangement is made with it covering the working conditions of the actor, we will not perform any service for any manager who is a member of the Producing Managers Association or who refuses to recognize our association or issue its contract, either in plays now being presented or in plays which are now or may hereafter be rehearsed.[8]

At one theater, the Booth, where *The Better 'Ole* was running, a second company that had been rehearsing the play for a tour supplied the places of five men and one woman who walked out. Most of the important venues in New York, though, were dark. Also shut down were a number of plays that were not then running but were in the rehearsal stage. In a statement released to explain its position, AEA said:

> In this conflict there is but one important issue: Shall the actor have the right to collective protection? When the manager and actor dealt with each other as individuals, a situation existed which had no duplicate in any other field of activity. The actor, while free as an artist, was economically a slave. He often rehearsed the better part of a season, but worked and was paid a salary for only a few weeks. The contract, which a majority of the managers forced the actor

to sign, was so trickily drawn that legally there was not even one square meal for the actor in it. The women of the stage were inadequately protected.

Furthermore, explained Equity, the contract it did negotiate back in 1917 was not lived up to by the majority of the managers. Still, Equity followed a policy of avoiding conflict, but "This policy, however, proved ineffective, for when the Producing Managers Association was formed, it forthwith insisted that the actor give up some of the rights which had been grudgingly granted [under the old UMPA contract]."[9]

In its page 1 article on the strike, the *New York Times* started off by declaring, "On notice varying from five to thirty minutes a hundred or more actors and actresses last night closed twelve attractions in New York's first class theaters and precipitated one of the most remarkable situations ever known in the history of the American stage." According to this report, the managers in most cases were "utterly unprepared," and while attempts were made in at least a couple of cases to mount a show with the understudies, only in one case was that successful. Patrons stood in long lines up to 10 P.M. to get refunds from the box offices of the 12 dark houses. An estimated $25,000 was refunded that night. Extra problems occurred with some of the patrons who had bought their seats from scalpers; those customers wanted the price they paid to be refunded, but the box office only gave back the listed price.[10]

One of the more dramatic events that night took place at the Cohan and Harris Theatre, which was playing *The Royal Vagabond*, and which was managed by George M. Cohan and Sam Harris (PMA president). Here audiences were kept uninformed and in their seats until 9 P.M. before a statement was made. Then the curtain was raised to disclose the 35 or so members of the play's chorus — men and women — grouped on the stage in their street clothes. At the head of that group was Sam Forrest (general manager of the Cohan and Harris firm), with Harris at his side. Forrest told the audience, "In calling this strike the actors did not take into consideration these boys and girls of the chorus, nor did they consider the inconvenience of the public. The striking actors are all players receiving two or three hundred dollars a week. They have no grievance against this management. We have played fair." Turning to the chorus he asked if they had any grievances. Shouts of "No!" came back. He then asked them if they had always been treated fairly by the management — and cries of "Yes!" answered him.[11]

Much of August 8 was spent by the managers, said a journalist, "in frantic efforts to recruit actors and actresses who would sign ironbound nonstrike contracts. Many a mediocre player who had met with scant courtesy in managerial offices hitherto suddenly found himself or herself cordially urged over the telephone to come around and talk to them. The more optimistic of the producers predicted that much unexpected talent might be uncovered as a result of the strike." Nine of the 12 venues remained dark on that second night. The Cohan and Harris venue used substitutes in *The Royal Vagabond*, as did *The Challenge* when it reopened at the Selwyn. At the Forty-Fourth Street Theatre, where *Gaieties of 1919* had been the attraction, a variety program was substituted instead. As part of its offensive, the PMA threatened to sue actors who, it said, had walked out on valid contracts, thereby making themselves liable for damages.[12]

August 8 was also a hectic day for the union because Equity announced that 1,200 actors had joined the organization on that single day, bringing the membership total in the union to 5,400.[13]

On Tuesday, August 12, chorus members packed a theater and organized an auxiliary of the AEA, to be known as the Chorus Equity Association, with famed and beloved actor Marie Dressler chosen as its president. Much earlier in her career she had got her start in the profession in the chorus. Perhaps stung by the accurate assessment that Equity had forgotten the chorus people (heretofore they had not been eligible to join Equity, and were, of course, the lowest paid people in the industry), it acted quickly to remedy that situation. Equity would not settle the strike without seeing that the demands of both actors and chorus people were met. Apparently the strike was called on August 7 following a mass meeting at the Hotel Astor where a secret vote on the strike resolution was called. (Note it was not a membership-wide vote, but limited to those who were able to attend the meeting.) Before 5 P.M. that day Equity was on record as issuing a strike call to hit all PMA shows no later than 7 P.M. Another bulletin issued by Equity declared that Al Jolson, then in Atlantic City, would stand by the strikers. In a huff, George M. Cohan suddenly announced his withdrawal from both the Friars and Lambs clubs (each was a social, fraternal association for actors — Cohan was a performer as well as a manager/producer). Explaining his withdrawal, Cohan declared to a reporter:

> I am not going to associate as a fellow club member with actors who give me the raspberry on the street and insult me and my family. I am an actor and have always been a friend of the actor. The stage is my very life, but I repeat that I value my manhood above everything else. I am through with the Lambs and Friars, and that is final.[14]

Billboard's account of the first two or three days of the strike seemed to be sympathetic, as the publication remarked:

The press of the entire country is taking a keen interest in the struggle and is carrying detailed stories. While, as was expected, the ad-gyp trade press and kept dailies are arrayed against the actors, many more of the reputable papers are giving the actors credit than was expected.... Enthusiastically, but calmly, the actors are pushing their fight and the Equity Association is growing in membership by leaps and bounds, while subscriptions are pouring in at a tremendous rate. Developments of today indicate that the solidarity of the producers is cracking.... Confidently, but carefully — not recklessly — the actors are fighting their battle and every indication points toward a tremendous success.[15]

On the day of the meeting, wrote *Billboard*, an emissary of the managers, and an actor, E. Sothern, received permission from the chair to address the meeting. Sothern stated the managers had told him that they were willing to debate their case against actors in a theater at a public meeting. But, he added, neither any member of the AEA council nor Equity president Francis Wilson would be allowed to be present, "as they were objectionable to the managers." At that point Sothern was soundly booed and, his proposition voted down, and he left the meeting. Also on August 7, Florenz Ziegfeld (producer) assured Equity he was not a member of the PMA; that he was ready to issue Equity contracts, and that he was for the actor in the fight. Under those conditions Ziegfeld's production of the *Follies* at the New Amsterdam venue was not put on the strike list. Eddie Cantor, a member of the *Follies* cast and a member of the Executive Council of AEA, said he was ready to obey all orders of the union. Cantor was among those who briefly walked out on August 7 but went back in and put on the show as scheduled after Equity officials accepted Ziegfeld as not being a member of the PMA.[16]

However, pressure from other producers caused Ziegfeld to join the PMA within one week, but at the same time Flo tried to secure an injunction to prevent the *Follies* cast from striking. Cantor arrived at the New Amsterdam on Wednesday night, August 13, met with Flo, went to the box office and drew out $230 — the amount due him, on a per show basis, for the current week to date — walked out on strike and gave the money to the AEA strike fund. Fellow cast members Johnny Dooley and Rae Dooley followed Cantor's lead and struck the show. With strong pro-union feelings, Cantor spent his strike time recruiting for the AEA and giving pep talks to his fellow strikers. On Saturday night, August 16, he spoke to some reporters and said, "I am with the Equity Association and will go back to the cloak-and-suit trade if they lose their fight against the managers." The *Follies*, minus Cantor and the Dooleys, ran for one more week before it went dark.

When Cantor and the *Follies* resumed the run in September after the strike was over, it was strictly a business relationship between Flo and Eddie (compared to one that was described as being close to father/son before the strike). Ziegfeld did not speak to Cantor for the remaining 12 weeks of the *Follies* run on Broadway.[17]

In a PMA statement on August 10 or 11, the managers again displayed how faithfully they tried to follow the advice from Albee and the VMPA, at least in the area of attack. Said the statement, "To further make forever impossible any relationship between the Managers and the Actors' Equity Association, Mr. Wilson took into his councils two notorious agitators and trouble-makers who before their downfall had created great havoc in the vaudeville profession." Blaming the "mark" of those two men (Mountford and Fitzpatrick) for leading to the strike, the "mark" was described as the "complete repudiation of Actors' Equity contracts by which the managers were faithfully abiding, vulgar street displays, five-hundred-dollar-a-week actors accosting thirty-dollar-a-week chorus girls at stage doors and asking them to go out in sympathy, threats of assault on managers, wrecking of theaters, vilest of all anonymous letters and the complete demonstration of all the misery an unscrupulous agitator can create, particularly when he has as his plaything an unusually emotional class." There was no truth in any of those charges. "So far as the managers are concerned, the Actors' Equity Association has proven itself the enemy of the actor and the manager.... The actor is no longer free," continued the statement. And, it believed the affair was no longer a struggle between the actor and the manager because, "The manager must fight now to deliver the actor from the grip of the unscrupulous agitators and restore him to a position of personal liberty. The Producing Managers' Association will continue to keep the theaters open and will give performances. They will not quarrel, nor have they had any quarrel with organized labor...."[18]

Suits for damages totalling $300,000 were filed early in August by the Shuberts against about 500 persons of greater or lesser fame on the stage, according to Equity. Persons named in the litigation included actors presently appearing in New York, many others then in different parts of America, and some who were then in Europe. Names on the list included Grant Mitchell, Norman Trevor, Eddie Foy, Forbes Robertson, Leo Ditrichstein, Chauncey Olcott, and Trixie Friganza.[19]

A report around the same time in another publication said the suits totalled $5 million against Equity as an organization and $6 million in total against nearly 200 named actors. Included in the list of names from this

report were Ernest Truex, Eddie Foy, Francis X. Bushman, Douglas Fair-
banks, Tyrone Power, Charlie Ruggles, William S. Hart, Blanche Ring,
Dustin Farnum, Trixie Friganza, De Wolf Hopper, Conrad Nagel, and Alla
Nazimova.[20]

The August 12 edition of the *New York Times* contained a full-page ad
from the PMA. Besides listing all 37 producing managers, the advertisement
contained the bold heading "WARNING!" and explained that members were
personally liable for all damages caused by the strike: "Do not be misled—
consult your own lawyer."[21]

When a journalist with the *New York Times* observed the striking actors
engaged in picketing, also on August 12, he described the scene as follows:

> Actor pickets thronged the streets again last night, although in lesser numbers
> than on the preceding night. Forty-Fifth Street, in front of strike headquarters,
> was packed from building line to building line all evening by actors and crowds
> of the curious. Sight-seeing automobiles loaded with cheering actors rolled
> through the streets to the accompaniment of applause from the sidewalk.[22]

For the first week of the strike Equity kept 10 houses completely closed
over the seven days, with the count going to 12 houses dark on Wednesday,
August 13. During the strike there were said to have been a few resignations
from AEA, but overall, membership had surged dramatically, from about
4,200 when the strike started to 6,000 by the 13th. The main focus for the
union had settled down to two points—union recognition and pay for extra
shows (defined as any number over eight per week). Managers had made
some publicity efforts to enlist public sympathy with advertisements and
press releases, while Equity tried for educational propaganda through the use
of signs and banners. As well, Equity made extensive use of actors driving
along main streets displaying banners saying the managers did not want the
players to organize. While the AFL had openly expressed its sympathies with
the actors' strike and had promised support, it remained vague and noncom-
mittal on that point. Still struggling to form a company union was the PMA.
It had placed actor E. H. Sothern (also looked upon as a producer) at the
head of it. Managers apparently hoped actors would break away from the
AEA soon after the strike began. They would all be broke, reasoned the
PMA, and getting desperate for money. However, that did not happen to
the slightest degree; Equity was a well-financed organization. On Monday
night, August 11, the Winter Garden venue, unable to mount a production
it had been rehearsing, advertised a vaudeville show for that evening, one
that was supplied "Through the kindness of E. F. Albee." Despite the theater area being mostly dark, the neighborhood was thronged with people,

picketers being outnumbered by curious spectators. "At night, along Broadway and near the picketed theaters, the people made the streets look like a gala night," said one account. "Pickets to the number of 700 or 800 patrolled nightly, each carrying an A.E.A. white printed band on hat or sleeve."[23]

Tuesday night, August 12, saw Equity extend the strike to Chicago (as in New York, just against productions by PMA members). Two shows were closed that night, with the houses going dark —*A Prince There Was* (Cohan's Grand theater, Cohan and Harris producers) and *Cappy Ricks* (Cort theater, Morosco producer). Nine shows were running on the legitimate stage in Chicago when the strike was called. A third show would have closed that night except AEA officials could not reach the cast in time — *Up in Mabel's Room* (Woods Theatre, A. H. Woods producer). An indication of the strength of the union could be seen from the fact that whenever Equity held a mass meeting (to deliver information, and so on) in New York, Chicago, and elsewhere, such gatherings were always filled to overflowing.[24]

At that time there were about 400 Equity members (less than 7 percent) employed as film actors. AEA worried a bit that the supposed affiliation of four industry factions — the National Association of the Motion Picture Industry being one — might lead, as a show of affiliation strength, to barring all AEA members from the film industry. But nothing like that happened, as the industry affiliation was more show than substance. Meanwhile, from Monday, August 11, onward, engagements made in some of the legitimate offices carried the condition that the artist had to agree in writing to support the new actors' society being formed under the leadership of E. H. Sothern. A number of telegrams signed E. H. Sothern were received on August 11 by players. Those wires suggested that the recipients join the newly proposed society of dramatic players. Many of those who received the wires had never met him, and it was presumed his name had been signed, by permission, to a list of AEA members prepared by an unknown person. It was said that a number of "facetious answers" were returned to Sothern.[25]

More of the VMPA's 1917 tactics were visible in a full-page ad that appeared in *Billboard* in the August 16 issue. It was a blow-up of a letter from Howard Kyle (a long-time AEA member who served in various capacities with the union before resigning) to E. H. Sothern (also resigned from the AEA). The letter attacked Equity and was designed to undercut the union and its position. This ad was at least signed at the bottom by the placer of the advertisement, the United Managers' Protective Association — a group, of course, that no longer existed."[26]

A major strike development that favored actors took place on Saturday,

August 16, when the stagehands and musicians at four theaters — Century, Winter Garden, Knickerbocker, and Cohan and Harris — struck in sympathy with AEA after Charles Shay, president of IATSE (International Association of Theatrical Stage Employees) had failed to persuade the managers to confer with any representative of Equity. According to a reporter, "Mr. Shay says he and a representative of the Musicians Union had talked with the managers for two hours, pointing out that the actors did not demand a closed shop, but only asked for a conference. The managers replied that though the actors do not now expressly demand a closed shop, recognition of the association would automatically create this condition." More and more of the superstar players were coming out publicly in support of AEA and the strike. The latest to do so were John Drew, John Barrymore, and Lionel Barrymore.[27]

Strikers paraded on Broadway late on the afternoon of August 16 for the Equity benefit show slated to begin on Monday, August 18, and run for a week before being replaced by a new Equity show. It was a way for the union to raise money to finance the strike. Opening night drew an enthusiastic full house. The scene at the end of the show had hundreds of Equity members on stage, with an actor delivering a variation on a Shakespeare line: "I come not to bury Equity, but to raise him." All on stage pledged themselves anew to Equity. As part of the bill, the second act of *Camille* was played by Ethel Barrymore and her brother Lionel Barrymore. In a dig at scalpers, the report about the benefit remarked, with mock amazement, "Tickets could actually be bought at the box office." Other actors on the bill included striking chorus girls working behind Marie Dressler, Eddie Foy and all the Little Foys, Frank Tinney, Pearl White, Van and Schenk, W. C. Fields, Joseph Santley, Ivy Sawyer, Frank Fay, Eddie Cantor, Charles Winninger, Barney Bernard, and Ed Wynn. Although he had been legally enjoined that day by the managers from appearing on the stage, Wynn got around the problem by entertaining the crowd from a seat down front.[28]

Those benefit shows were held at the Lexington, with performances nightly except Sundays, and with Wednesday and Saturday matinees. Full houses continued to turn out during the first few days at least, and Equity was expected to draw $40,000 for its coffers from just the first week's run of the benefit show. By Wednesday, August 20, the strike had closed 21 theaters in New York and all the houses in Chicago.[29]

One of the young and unknown actors just starting her career in the summer of 1919 was Tallulah Bankhead. In August, after she had played only 12 performances of *39 East* on Broadway, Bankhead received from AEA a union card and a letter stating, "You are hereby instructed to stop playing at once until further notice. By order of the strike committee." All company members walked out. Later, at the opening night of the benefit, show Tallulah was one of many ingénues there who collected money and showed people to their seats. One of the comments to the audience came from Lionel Barrymore, who said, "We're proud to be here. We'll be here forever if necessary." Carried away in that atmosphere, Tallulah pledged $100, which she could ill afford. So she wrote to her grandfather for the money. Bankhead's letter said, in part:

> I joined Actors Equity because it was the right thing to do ... all the very biggest stars in the profession belong and it's a wonderful organization. The Barrymores all belong and if you don't you are called a scab and are blacklisted, and they called *39 East* to strike and of course I did. I couldn't play alone anyway, and, besides, it was the right thing to do.[30]

The Barrymore family was very visible in support of the union and the strike. Siblings John, Lionel, and Ethel all worked actively for the union, as did actor John Drew, their uncle. The father of the siblings, Maurice Barrymore, had been equally active and passionate in support of the White Rats and their 1901 strike. Just prior to the Equity strike, Ethel was said to have graduated from society girl to mature woman, with more weighty and serious roles on the stage. With respect to her support of the strike, journalist Robert Cole wrote:

> Perhaps the most curious fact of the revolution is the presence of the traditional aristocrat, whose interest would seem to lie with the establishment. This woman, who speaks so earnestly for the actor, is an aristocrat of the stage.... If she ever seemed to be pledging herself, speaking out of her heart from the stage, it was in the character of the woman who left every comfort to become a poor stenographer, because she hated the world where material success was everything, whose invisible realities were despised. In the same accent she despises the man who sees nothing but money in the theater."

Ethel performed at benefits, contributed money and raised money, wrote letters to the newspapers, and gave supportive interviews to reporters. As well, she helped Dressler and others organize the chorus people. At one of those meetings Ethel told the choristers, "I don't know how to make a speech really, but I am with you heart and soul, and more than that. Don't be discouraged. Stick! It's all coming out just the way it ought to for us."[31]

When the strike began Equity reportedly had just $13,500 in the bank, which made the benefit shows crucial events to swell the coffers. At the opening night benefit show Ethel Barrymore addressed the crowd, saying:

I know that we are all loyal and that we will win the strike. But our communication is money. I know a lot of persons here feel impoverished by recent events, but I think that some of us who have a little to spare should give this communication. If I can get one hundred and ninety-nine actors and actresses to give five hundred dollars each, I am ready to sign my check for that amount.

Comedian Ed Wynn was the first to contribute, followed by her brother Lionel. It was in that emotional atmosphere that Bankhead pledged the $100 she did not have.[32]

Sime Silverman published an editorial on the strike situation in the August 22 edition of *Variety*, and he, too, was sympathetic to the players. He began his piece by saying, "It should never have started. The managers brought it upon themselves and through that, left the actor, represented by the Actors' Equity Association, with the best basis there can be for a strike, a just cause." He agreed with Equity's major points and liked the fact they had enrolled so many chorus girls, feeling they needed protection the most. Agreeing with the players' demand for extra pay for all extra performances, he commented, "The managers have gotten away with the extra shows for years without paying the professionals for them." Silverman argued that the managers invited the strike by their attitude of arrogance, their imperial nature, attempts to crush AEA, the refusal to recognize the union, and so on. With respect to the union and the closed shop, Sime said, "The A.E.A. says it does not want a closed shop and is willing to agree to that provision in a contract. We are inclined to side with the A.E.A. on the closed shop proposition. The A.E.A. assumes a sensible position when it waives aside the closed shop." He had nothing to say that was negative about the Equity union and the strike.[33]

Sime explained his different position, compared to the WR strike in 1917, by saying the earlier walkout "was the strike of an unbalanced and wild agitator who had gone so far he could not recede, though he had sense enough to do anything." Given Harry's attitude, thought Silverman, "it was impossible" for him to have had anything to do with the success of the AEA's strike. *Variety* stood against the Rats in its strike, he continued,

principally through the Rats having had no just cause in the beginning, and secondly that Mountford, besides the many broken verbal promises made to us when we agreed to support the Rats in the rebuilding process under his guidance, also intended to revive *The Player*. [Apparently Silverman was still smarting from when that old agreement went wrong.] But we opposed the White Rats because we didn't think they were right under their leadership. The Rats never had a solid front. Their agitation divided the vaudeville actor.... The A.E.A. presents a solidified front. It's a wonderful spirit of loyalty among actors.[34]

As far as he was concerned, during the Equity strike the sympathy of the public, if it cared at all, seemed to be with the actor.

In its continued praise of the actors' strike and its progress, *Billboard* hit new heights of hyperbole as it enthused:

> Precedent was smashed and tradition tossed into the ash barrel. With one blow the players freed themselves. And they will never be shackled more. Woe to it who attempts it.... The actor has secured his Magna Carta. He no longer lives at the will of an overlord. He is free.

George M. Cohan continued to be in a huff and grumbled, "Before I will ever do business with the Actors' Equity Association I will lose every dollar I have even if I have to run an elevator to make a living." After he resigned from the Lambs and the Friars clubs a committee from the latter called on Cohan and asked him to reconsider, but he stood firm. "You are too late," he replied." I am in a fight to a finish, and whatever the results I will leave with my manhood. I am not going to associate as a club member with actors who cut me on the street and insult my family."[35]

Reiterating that Equity would not end its strike unless the demands of the Chorus Equity Association were also met, AEA president Frank Gilmore said, "Before we agree to any settlement with the managers we will insist that the chorus girls shall rehearse no longer than four weeks without pay. After that they must be paid half salary, and the management must pay for all costumes, shoes and stockings." At that organization's first meeting about 500 choristers were on hand. Speakers said the average wage of chorus girls was from $25 to $30 a week, and out of that money they had to buy their own shoes, stockings and tights. At that meeting, at which former chorus member Marie Dressler was selected as president, a reference was made to the problem that Albee and Silverman had each declared, on separate occasions, did not even exist: "Several of the speakers proclaimed it their object 'to make the chorus a safe place for womanhood.' Several times Miss Dressler hinted at indignities to which the girls are subjected."[36]

Meanwhile, the PMA continued its efforts to form a company union, through E. H. Sothern, but with little success. From the PMA's publicity office came the following statement about him: "Mr. Sothern declares that any impression that he is the tool of the managers in this step and that he is creating a society for the purpose of disrupting any present organization is without foundation." To that Gilmore retorted:

> It is interesting to note that the announcement of the new actors' organization, fathered by Mr. Sothern, came from the manager's press department. I think

this clearly shows its origin, and I heard that E. F. Albee suggested its organization. It is quite evidently a managerial association of actors, like the National Vaudeville Artists.

Following the lead of the producers' strike committee, and Sothern, who had previously visited all the newspaper offices in a body to publicize their position, the actors did the same, represented by Bruce McRae, Dressler, and Ed Wynn. As of Wednesday, August 13, in New York 13 houses were closed, eight plays were being run, and six productions were on the exempt list (that is, shows not under the control of PMA members and having no strike notice served against them). Two houses remained dark in Chicago where managers obtained a temporary injunction to prevent more venues going dark. Equity decided not to call out any more Chicago casts until a court decision was rendered.[37]

By this time the strike was around two weeks old, and it started to receive coverage in the national magazines, both the weeklies and the monthlies. Writing in the *Nation,* F. T. Vreeland gave an accurate recap of the strike and the demands from both sides. Vreeland went on to express the idea that he and the public were amazed that such a thing could have happened at all, as it shattered the belief that actors "were so self-centered that two of them could get along together only if one were deaf and dumb." He added, "They have suddenly a class consciousness, which leads to the suspicion that some of them secretly indulge in the perusal of Karl Marx. The worlds 'capital' and 'labor' are frequently heard at their mass meetings, quite as though grease paint were entirely compatible with the terms."[38]

A piece in the *New Republic* started with the observation that producing managers without actors could produce nothing, but that without producing managers it was still possible for actors to produce a play. He added the thought that theatrical managers as a class,

> even those who know most about the stage, are under the unfortunate disadvantage of being to a considerable extent parasites.... But the profession, as a rule, has been cruelly subordinated to the exigencies of the business. And that art has simply gone to pot. What the managers have given the American public is, with few exceptions, an immense amount of business promotion to a small accompaniment of art.... And the actors have lost out both as artists and as employees.

One result he hoped to see emerge from the strike was a fundamental readjustment of the theater in line with the actors' best conception of their art: "The measure of the success of the strike may well be the extent to which the managers are reduced from their position as bosses all along the line."

Another outcome he hoped to see arise was the experiment of play-producing by the actors themselves, with the management in the hands of their own agents: "By virtue of such enterprise the American theater may at last come to be the home of American dramatic genius, instead of American commercial genius scowling on the vulgarity of a new labor union."[39]

At the end of the third week of the strike, as of Wednesday, August 27, *Variety* made an estimate of the money losses to that date. Losses to those directly concerned with the strike were put at about $1.5 million. In addition to that were losses to the taxis in the theater districts, to restaurants, hotels, candy shops, dry cleaners, and so on. *Variety* estimated the loss was about $250,000 weekly in gross receipts to the producing managers; $100,000 weekly to the actors; and between $45,000 to $50,000 weekly to the stagehands and musicians on the 21 shows that were closed by the strike, not including the announced productions that had not eventuated. Overhead charges on the houses that were closed in New York City alone were about $4,000 weekly, including salaries that managers were paying to a number of those that remained loyal to them during the strike, a gross overhead of $140,000. Newspapers alone were losing about $2,000 weekly on amusement ads, while the government was out about $75,000 in taxes. Theater ticket agencies were said to have lost about $30,000 in the three weeks.[40]

Up until that Wednesday, August 27, there had been 26 attractions stopped in New York — 20 were prevented from continuing through walkouts of actors or stagehands and musicians; six could not open as announced due to the strike. In Chicago eight attractions were out. The American Federation of Labor, through Gompers, continued to express full support. Perhaps the most significant event of that third week of the strike was the formation of the Actors Fidelity League (or FIDO, as it came to be known). George M. Cohan was elected president of this new organization. Gone and forgotten quite suddenly were E. H. Sothern and his fledgling group. Apparently the managers felt it would never get off the ground, and rolled out company union number two instead. Cohan declared he would accept the presidency of FIDO and come before the League as an actor only, when his resignation as a member of the managers' association had been acted upon (that is, accepted). Observed a reporter, "The A.F.L. [FIDO] is admittedly an affiliation of the managers' association. It refused a tender of $100,000 from Mr. Cohan for financial support in the belief it could be maintained by financial dues."[41]

Formation of the Fidelity League had taken place on Saturday, August 23, with an announced membership of 733. Louis Mann was elected vice president; the Board of Directors numbered 21, and included Fay Bainter and Otis Skinner. Mann declared the league was "an organization never to strike but to secure results through co-operation. That it was an actors' organization first, last and always." After FIDO had rejected Cohan's offer of $100,000 (on the day before), Mann used that rejection as a basis to say the league was in no way connected with the managers, and that it was not formed at the managers' suggestion. After being elected, Cohan addressed the meeting and said:

> I am not here representing anybody at all. I am representing myself. I am a member of the Producing Managers' Association and am very proud of that. Up to a few weeks ago it was said that I was always fair in my dealings and fair to my fellows. Since then they have called me a scab, cutthroat, bandit and the like. But at that I am more a friend of the actor than ever.[42]

By 1919 Cohan's reputation as one of America's greatest showmen was well established; he was a millionaire many times over. Cohan and Harris productions were very successful in New York and on the road. He specialized in producing light entertainment productions, and, as critic George Jean Nathan sarcastically commented, "of writing in at least one mention of a million dollars and one cheer for the United States, and of deleting twenty or thirty lines of dialogue and substituting pantomime" in each of his productions. At the time of the Equity strike, said his biographer, John McCabe, Cohan had not thought of himself as a performer for a long time; he did not like being told what to do, and his resentment of the strikers became implacable. When Cohan made his remark about quitting the theater business to run an elevator if necessary, actor Eddie Cantor quipped, "Somebody'd better tell Mr. Cohan that to run an elevator he'd have to join a union." After the strike was settled, and for the rest of his life, said McCabe, "although every actor in each of his productions was an Equity member, Cohan performed without the standard contract.... Nor did Equity ever insist — as it could have — that Cohan sign their contract."[43]

With respect to Cohan heading the new company union, *Billboard* declared, "Many of his most sincere friends and admirers are greatly saddened over the intelligence. The new society is a lie, a transparent, palpable lie on its very face, which, while claiming hundreds, does not actually number dozens of real players." The publication continued to be a zealous cheerleader for the strike:

> As the strike approaches its fourth week, expert observers find the actors stronger, more determined and solidly cohered and united than ever. Their enthusiasm has suffered not one whit of diminution, while their organization

has been highly perfected and their experience is lending them vast improvement in point of efficiency. It has really been marvellous.... We have been taught to expect so little in the way of practical accomplishment, carefully conceived planning and business acumen from players that the spectacle they are not offering is bewildering. And the producing managers marvel also — marvel, moan and mourn — and are taking on haggard and anxious countenances and dejected miens. The Louis Mann dual association is regarded as a joke — as the last futile and silly offensive of a badly worsted cabal.[44]

When the *Literary Digest* discussed the strike at the end of August it pointed out that offers of mediation, arbitration, and so on to end the dispute were plentiful. Equity had always been agreeable to using such methods, but the managers had always refused, saying it would deal with any problems that arose by itself with the actor alone and never recognize or deal with or through AEA. In its press statements released and printed in all the New York papers over the signature of Arthur Hopkins, it tried to paint Equity as equivalent to a dictatorship:

A member of the Actors' Equity Association can no longer freely enter into any contract with a manager, which he is certain of fulfilling.... The contract between actor and manager ceases to be a contract between two parties. The Actors' Equity Association is the third party and the predominant one. No matter how profitable and pleasant the relations between the individual actor and manager may be, these relations are at all times exposed to immediate destruction by a third party. The Actors' Equity Association has demonstrated that it will not hesitate to destroy those relations.[45]

On the other hand, press material over the name of Hopkins continued to insist the PMA would submit matters of contract fulfillment to a joint board of actors and managers, with an outside umpire, if there was "a dependable actors' organization:"

Bring us an actors' association that is founded on the same principle [contract enforcement]. We will offer it a form of contract that is better than the former Actors' Equity Association contract. But it must be an organization in which the managers have faith. It can not be the Actors' Equity Association. The Actors' Equity Association has proved that for all time.[46]

Ethel Barrymore published an article on the strike in the September 3 issue of *The Outlook*. She traced the troubles to the time of the combinations, and recalled the old days of the individual manager when there was a sense of courtesy and high tradition:

The change began with the great combinations of managers. From that time on, making more money, at any sacrifice of standards, has been the one end.... A good many managers appear to think they are simply merchants and the actors are their stock in trade. They must make all the decisions and everybody else must accept them. They think nothing of the honor of the theater as an institution. Of all the childish things that have been said against us, the funniest is that the actors are forgetting the dignity of their art! What has any of these managers done to keep the stage on a high level?

Speaking of conditions she observed that with respect to the half-salary weeks, some managers had "improved" on the idea

until some contracts called for no less than seven half-salaried weeks during the season. Again, in one-night stands in the West, where Saturday is the worst night in the week theatrically on account of all the stores being open, certain managers made it a practice to cut Saturday-night performances, take a sleeper-jump to a town where Sunday performances could be given (the actor of course paying for his sleeper), and then docking the actor for the Saturday night lost and not paying him for the Sunday performance — or performances — given.[47]

When Barrymore considered the reasons for the PMA's refusal to recognize the union, she said:

They first announced it was because of our unreasonable demands; next because Francis Wilson was our President; later, because we had entered the American Federation of Labor; and then, because our policies were dictated by Harry Mountford; finally, because we had broken existing contracts. As to this last statement, the contracts we were accused of having broken are the same contracts which the managers had announced in the most public manner that they did not intend to live up to. The real reason is obviously none of these. The managers, though strongly organized for their own protection, deny the same right to the actors.... We are striking for recognition. It is for the actors, and not for the managers to decide whether or not the Actors' Equity Association represents the actors. The actors have answered that it does, and are standing fast to the demand for recognition. This is what we are striking for....[48]

As time passed, public sympathy moved increasingly to the side of the actor. Rumors circulated that the managers were close to capitulating, with 36 managers favoring the recognition of Equity and six opposed. Another rumor had it that only two managers were hold-outs, but that those two were the biggest PMA members and controlled most of the houses. H. Irving Stockwell, representing the salesmen of wholesale grocers' firms in the states of New York and New Jersey, sent word to AEA that members of his salesmen's organization had been requested not to buy tickets to any performance given in New York theaters under non–Equity auspices — further evidence of public sentiment.[49]

A full-page ad appeared in the September 5 issue of *Variety* for FIDO, which also contained a membership blank. Dues were $5 a year for anyone who had been employed for 26 weeks or more on the professional stage. According to the ad, "The League is an independent organization of actors who believe that an equitable co-operative spirit should prevail in the theater. It holds the conviction that a standard, uniform, and mutually adopted theatrical employment contract can be established and enforced without compromising the actor's cause by any incongruous affiliations." Also appearing in that issue was a piece that purported to publish a complete list of every member of FIDO. Taking up nearly one full page, about 700 names were listed, although the membership total was said to be 2,500. "The League is looked upon as an arm of the Producing Managers' Association," added *Variety*.[50]

In Washington, D.C., on August 27, the Shubert-Belasco house was closed on the order of the stagehands' union. Equity said no strike had been called there by it, but the players immediately left the house to prevent any attempt to run the show with non-union stagehands. Then on Labor Day, Monday, September 1, in Boston, six shows were closed for the matinee when Equity called its members out. Not one of the shows controlled by the PMA in that city was able to give a matinee on the holiday.[51]

More cheerleading came from *Billboard* in its September 6 issue: "Last week demonstrated anew that the actors, with right on their side, are invincible.... George M. Cohan's attempt to stay the victorious advance of Equity members proved the sorriest kind of a fiasco, and he himself has lost standing and prestige very widely and plainly." Among the many subheads of the article were, "Actors launch blow after blow against their [managers] positions, causing dire devastation and havoc," and, "Press and public solidly with Equity while the new 'Fido League' of Pal-Betrayers is recognized for what it is and quite generally execrated." Also on September 1, four new shows by striking actors were opened on a profit-sharing basis in New York and Brooklyn. At that time Equity membership was said to be 7,912, while FIDO had 1,093.[52]

Then, on Saturday, September 6, 1919, it was announced that the strike had been settled, after 30 days, during which time 44 or more theaters and attractions were stopped. The only complaint about the settlement by AEA members was the fact that FIDO would continue to exist as a body, although it was not mentioned by name in the settlement. Some Equity members worried discrimination would be used against them by the producing managers in favour of the Actors' Fidelity League members. Equity gained everything it went after in the strike.[53]

The main points of the agreement were that the AEA was recognized in a five-year agreement that expired in June 1924 at the end of the theatrical season. Players would not go on strike over those five years unless there was a contract breach. All lawsuits developing from the strike were to be dropped. There would be an open shop with no blacklist. Chorus members also had their organization recognized, with a minimum salary for chorus members to be set at $30 a week in New York and $35 a week on the road. Contract disputes would be settled by a board of arbitration composed of a panel of three. Full salaries were to be paid to actors after four weeks of rehearsals for a drama and five weeks of rehearsals for a musical production. No half-salary weeks were allowed. Eight performances constituted a week's pay, and any and all performances above that number had to be paid for at the rate of one-eighth of a player's salary. Costumes were to be bought by managers and supplied at no cost to the players, everything from shoes to wigs.[54]

Celebrating the end of the strike in print, *Billboard* declared the dispute had been won, and not settled, because AEA secured all of its original demands, and, "It was won in a remarkably clean fight of the actors and their loyal supporters, the stage hands, the musicians, billposters and a handful of guerrilla radical vaudeartists against as unscrupulous tactics and methods as men can well stoop to. It was won decisively." Commenting on the fact that FIDO was to continue caused the publication to mock,

> the Infidelity "Leak," [FIDO] false, beaten, exposed and discredited — its members the butt of ridicule and scorn.... The Fidelity Leak is dead. It is unsung. It is unmourned. It will long remain a foul blot on the stage's history — one that time and charity alone will expunge. No one wants to crow over the carcass of such a contemptible and ignoble adversary. Everyone wants to be permitted to forget it as soon as may be.[55]

In a separate article, *Billboard* praised Equity's leaders in a piece set off in a special bordered box to draw attention to it:

> The members of the Actors' Equity Association are blessed with rarely competent and capable leaders ... many instances of the exercise of rare judgment, of fine foresight, of firm and resolute fortitude, of subtle finesse and great executive ability are passing unnoticed. Ever unselfish, every wholly disinterested, ever entirely unselfish, they have inspired the confidence and held the perfect trust of their adherents.... The fight has been conducted in a most masterly manner, under great difficulties and against great odds.... Equity's leaders have been a very great Equity asset.[56]

The author of an article in *Current Opinion* after the strike was over felt the concrete gains won were not the important things but rather, "the educational value of the gesture itself, in the eloquent assertion of cooperative endeavor and power." Also, the writer hoped the end of the strike would be followed by the elimination of "those Tired Business Men of Broadway, the managers, who have erected their own flaccid tastes and moral prejudices into a criterion of public entertainment." Mocking the current Broadway season, if it ran according to the formulas of the past, *Current Opinion* observed it would include "an obstetrical problem play, in which the young heroine would have died under the most tragic circumstances," three war plays, a bedroom farce called *Mable's Mattress*, a light English farce comedy entitled *And a Little Lemon*, and a special matinee of *Hamlet*.[57]

Marie Dressler, head of the Chorus Equity Association, reported a few weeks after the strike that all the managers were living up to the conditions of settlement with Equity — except the Shuberts, John Cort, and Flo Ziegfeld, all of whom, she said, refused to accept boys under the heading of the chorus and therefore paid them just $25 a week.[58]

A conference held on Friday, October 3, in New York between Equity and the PMA settled the last of 2,400 cases of actors thrown out of work or otherwise affected by the strike. That meeting marked the formal ending of all negotiations between the players and producers as a result of the strike. When the strike ended the managers had to re-employ all players affected within 30 days, as per the strike settlement, or, failing that, had to find employment for them elsewhere on equally favourable terms, or pay a money consideration to be decided upon by committees from each side. One of the last cases settled involved Ed Wynn, whose strike activities generated bitterness between himself and the Shuberts. When the strike started Wynn had been one of the featured members of Shuberts' *Gaieties of 1919*, but he did not return to the cast at the end of the strike. His case was one of the last 10 settled. Agreement was reached that Wynn would not be re-employed by the Shuberts but moved to be under the management of A. L. Erlanger.[59]

Trouble arose in October in the form of a clash at New York's Winter Garden venue between the Shuberts and the Chorus Equity Association. Members of the chorus refused to accept their salaries one Saturday night that month after they learned they were not to be paid for an extra matinee performance they gave. Originally the *Gaieties of 1919* played at the Forty-Fourth Street Theatre on a standard schedule of six evening shows and two matinees. When it moved to the Winter Garden on the previous Monday it arrived at a venue that scheduled three matinees. Equity stepped in, and, after a couple of days of stalling and talks, the Shuberts agreed to pay for the extra matinee. At the same time, Equity took up the matter of the chorus boys, who were all getting $25 a week instead of $30 as per the contract. Shubert agreed to henceforth pay the boys $30 a week and give them back pay for all the weeks they had received only $25.[60]

Two months after the strike ended, Frank Gilmore, AEA executive secretary, said Equity had entered the strike with 2,900 paid-up members and $13,600 in the bank. By November, excluding chorus people and vaudeville members, Equity had over 7,000 legitimate stage performers enrolled, (out of an estimated 11,000 legitimate players in America). They had $100,000 in the bank, despite spending money during the strike "like drunken sailors," said Wilson. At the close of the strike there was just one hostile production running that had not been shut down — William A. Brady's *At 9:45*, which had a couple of managers in the small cast and which played in a single set that was never struck. That is, stagehands had no reason to go near it.[61]

For two years after the strike Equity operated on an open basis, and union and non-union actors played side by side. But that method did not work well because, with Equity gains applied to union and non-union players alike, there was little incentive for outsiders to join the union, and membership started to decline. To remedy the situation the closed-shop method (called the Equity Shop) was applied to all companies in 1921 except those managed by members of the PMA, to whom Equity was bound by the contract. Once that contract expired in 1924 negotiations began with the PMA for a closed shop, but were acrimonious. Some PMA members were adamantly opposed to the idea; some were willing to accept the Equity shop. Some managers broke away to form a new managerial group — the Managers' Protective Association (MPA; the PMA was defunct by 1926) — and negotiated a new agreement in which it was specified that at least 80 percent of all casts would be union members. Non-members of the MPA had to employ 100 percent Equity players if they wished to use any union actors. Membership in FIDO drifted down from an estimated 400 right after the strike to less than 100 by 1926; Equity at that time still had a membership of over 7,000, estimated to include 98 percent of those who earned a living as players on the legitimate stage. Non-members with whom Equity players could appear in casts (through the courtesy of the Equity Council) were the 83 actors who were paid-up members of the Actors' Fidelity League on September 1, 1923, which was part of the deal struck by Equity with the MPA. One estimate put the total cost of the strike to everyone concerned at $3 million.[62]

12 | Conclusion

The period covered by this book saw a dramatic rise in the number of people in the organized labor movement, with membership moving from, according to one account, 200,000 members in 1881 to 2,000,000 in 1916. That increase came mostly in response to the growing power of the capitalist class, as trusts and combinations were formed, strengthened and came to dominate industry after industry. Labor and capital clashed repeatedly, and violently, in this very turbulent era, as conditions for employment remained bleak, or even worsened for many in the working class.

In the theatrical industry things unfolded exactly as they did in the steel industry, or the shoemaking industry, at least from the capitalist side of the fence. Producers and managers in vaudeville and the legitimate stage formed large and dominant combinations, or trusts, that were determined to control every aspect of their industry and crush all opposition that tried to stand in their way. Actors were slow to organize, compared to other occupational groups. Conventional wisdom explained that situation by declaring it was due to the personalities of the actors. They were too egocentric, too wrapped up in themselves to ever be able to display the solidarity and cooperation necessary for successful union behavior. Of course, that was nonsense.

A major reason for the slowness displayed by actors in unionizing had to do with the structure of their workplace. Players moved from theater to theater and from city to city, which created great difficulties in getting a lot of them together for a meeting, something that was relatively simple and straightforward for most unions. Workplaces were small and shifting, and the workers therein were constantly changing. Actors who appeared at union venues or refused to play "unfair" houses became known to managers, and faced going on a blacklist and having their careers ended. When a mill hand got blacklisted out of a mill and/or town for union activities he could move on to another town and start over with a new name. Identification documents did not really exist to any extent in this period, and a person could easily adopt a different name. However, actors could not do so as easily. Also, they became known for their material and style as much as for their name. Thus, it was a major step for an actor to declare for a union. While capitalists in all industries tried to harass and intimidate employees who thought about unionization, it was easier for such harassment to be effective in the small and diverse workplaces found in the theatrical field.

Yet conditions in the theatrical industry were bad enough that a few informal, and unsuccessful, attempts to start a union took place before 1900. None of those fledgling groups described themselves as a union, but insisted they were fraternal or social organizations only, with some business concerns. Mostly they tried to hide any union-style activities under the cloak of social service behavior, perhaps worried over possible reprisals from the managers. One group, the Actors Society, started out as such a hybrid, but in 1898 it collapsed when it split into two factions, with one wanting the group to be a union, the other wanting it to stay a fraternal lodge. In the end it went nowhere. As 1900 approached, capitalist trust formations speeded up in industries all over America. In 1898, in an effort to fight the Theatrical Trust, a number of actors took a stand against them by refusing to play in trust houses. But they took that stand individually and not collectively, and, as a result, were picked off one by one by the Trust with its big contract offers. Illustrated by that example was the hatred of conditions in the theatrical industry and the vulnerability and inadvisability of acting alone.

Thus, the White Rats organization emerged in June 1900, in direct response to the latest and biggest combination in vaudeville, the VMA. Despite the fact George Fuller Golden and others formed the WR to combat the trust, it took pains to point out it was not a union, that it was not radical, and that it was very non-aggressive. Like many unions of the time, the Rats were racist and sexist, open only to white males as members. While it apparently never had a black member, it was more ambivalent over the woman question, struggling for years over whether or not to admit them as members. In the end it created a sort of ladies auxiliary for them, and still later let them participate in voting in the order.

The biggest issue for the WR in the 1900–1901 period was the much hated 5 percent commission levied on acts by the newly established trust, the VMA. Players saw it for what it was — an indirect way of imposing a 5 percent pay cut on the players. A brief strike of a few hours' duration on February 14, 1901, abolished that commission, or so the Rats thought. But it remained, and a larger strike took place on February 21. After two weeks it was settled, with the commission again supposedly abolished. While many acts walked out in response to the strike call, none of the venues were shut down, as all were able to run with substitute acts. Managers again failed to live up to anything they granted in the settlement. Further, they subjected many of the WR members most active in the strike to a blacklist. Within a few months all gains won by the WR had been lost, and many acts were blackballed for years; some never worked again in vaudeville. The Rats also failed to win recognition from the managers as to their status of being the actors' representative. Chief architect of the managers' strike strategy was E. F. Albee. By the end of 1901 the White Rats were weakened, directionless, and dispirited. Membership was down dramatically.

For the next five years actors' attempts to unionize stagnated, with little progress made. The Vaudeville Comedy Club was established as a partly fraternal, partly business (or union-like) organization. So co-opted had it become within a few years that it admitted lay people and even managers as members. So moribund had the movement to unionize actors become that the trade publication *Variety* published a series of editorials in every issue for months pointing out the bad conditions suffered by actors and the urgent need for them to organize. Some thought was given to the idea the Rats could be the organization to fill that need, but mostly it was ignored. When R. C. Mudge became WR president in 1906 the union revived a bit, and it became a little militant. Then Mudge was accused of corruption by some WR members and resigned suddenly early in 1908. Once again the Rats were weakened, and also leaderless. English entertainer Harry Mountford arrived in America very late in 1907. As of February 1908 he was a WR executive and soon came to dominate the organization. Later that year he started a series of meetings with Albee in an effort to win an equitable contract for the players. In a move that further enraged the managers, Harry set in motion plans to buy into theaters and run vaudeville programs in direct competition against the trust, and to use an in-house booking agency. A few years earlier Golden had explored the same options, but Mountford took them much farther. In the eyes of the managers it was bad enough for an actor to dare to join a union, but to try to muscle in on the capitalist side of the fence as Harry intended, was especially unforgivable. Both endeavors failed within a couple of years, mainly because anyone connected with them could be easily blacklisted by the managers. The animosity Harry earned from that episode stuck to him permanently.

One thing the Rats did achieve, after two years of long and expensive lobbying of the New York State Legislature, was the enacting of a law that limited commissions to a maximum of 5 percent of a player's salary, no matter how many agents were involved. However, once again the trust ignored the measure, treating it as a joke. It led to more frustration for the Rats. The WR merging with the small rival group in 1910, combined with its increasing militancy, caused the Trust to reorganize itself and take a harder line. The Trust refused to meet with the Rats in order to emphasize that it did not recognize the union, and launched a vicious media campaign in which it issued threat after threat against the actor about all types of reprisals that would befall actors treating with the Rats. Also, the managers launched an endless stream of personal attacks against Harry, all lies. Then, suddenly, in September 1911 Harry Mountford resigned under obscure circumstances never explained (perhaps an internal power struggle, or was he ousted surreptitiously by the managers?).

Several more years of stagnation followed for the White Rats and actors' unions in general, although players in the legitimate theater formed Actors' Equity Association in 1913. Once again *Variety* delivered a series of editorials about the abuses actors were subjected to, and about the need for actors to organize, as if the WR did not exist. Film players made a couple of efforts to organize their own field but gave up when the power of the blacklist was brought into play. When actors did organize they were never able to reach out to players in other areas of the industry. Vaudeville actors never joined any other union, to any extent, except the Rats; legitimate players only joined Equity; film actors were never unionized until 1934, when they formed their own organization, SAG (Screen Actors' Guild). After swearing it would never cut salaries, the Trust turned around and did just that, suddenly, in October 1914. An impotent White Rats union produced little in the way of response, and an intensified sense of frustration and desperation set in. Just as suddenly as he had left, Harry Mountford returned to lead the Rats, in October 1915, at the request of the union. It signalled a return to militancy in the form of threats, but first they launched a major, and successful, drive to increase membership.

A strident and bellicose war of words took place between the WR and the VMPA in 1916, conducted in the pages of *Variety*. Worried managers issued more threats against actors and waved the blacklist over their heads. Lies and personal attacks on Harry increased, all displaying bile and venom. The three major trade publications that covered the theatrical industry stood together against Mountford and the Rats. All of the media boycotted the union, never allowing it access to its pages to give its side of the story. Stool pigeons were everywhere, with the result being the Rats could make no move the managers did not quickly know about. In the middle of 1916 the VMPA set up a company union, the National Vaudeville Artists, pretending it was an independent group that had been spontaneously formed by actors opposed to Harry and the Rats.

Unable to arrange any meetings with managers — since the Trust felt even to meet with the Rats implied they recognized the group — the union called a series of strikes in Oklahoma City and Tulsa in the second half of 1916. None were successful to any degree, and all petered out months later. Managers were ready with complete duplicate bills on stand-by. It was an expensive strategy, but one the trust was willing to implement. For their part the Rats seemed to have no well-constructed strategy to implement, no clear strike plan. By December 1916, rumors of a larger strike by the Rats abounded, but it failed to materialize. As 1916 ended, the WR seemed to be on the decline.

Suddenly, on January 1, 1917, the Rats launched the first in what would be a series of strikes against the VMPA. As before, no clear plan seemed to be present. Quite a few acts did heed the strike call and walk out, but vaudeville was not disrupted, as the managers still had full compliments of duplicate bills on stand-by. That, combined with continued use of the blacklist and relentless personal attacks on the Rats and its executives saw those strikes all come to an end in April 1917, with the Rats having gained nothing, not even recognition. To save face the Rats announced the strikes were suspended, not ended, as a patriotic gesture, since America was then at war. Although the WR continued to exist for some time to come, in various forms and under different names, as of April 1917 it was effectively dead.

After Equity formed in 1913 it found itself faced with the same situation as that of the Rats; that is, it spent years meeting with, or trying to meet with, the legitimate stage's trust and getting mostly nowhere. After four years the two sides announced an agreement had been reached and an equitable contract issued. However, some managers ignored it from the start, and all repudiated it within two years. In order to do so without seeming to be guilty of violating the agreement, the managers accomplished full repudiation of the contract in 1919 by a minor reorganization of the trust, including a new name, and the statement that the managers' group that had signed the 1917 pact no longer existed (so the deal was no longer valid).

Soon, Equity found itself, like the Rats before, with its back to the wall and forced to call a strike, in August 1919. This "new" trust, the PMA, called in vaudeville's E. F. Albee for advice and tried to use exactly the same tactics as Albee had used so successfully against the Rats. However, things were different. Vaudeville acts were all independent parts of the whole, and were easily replaced one with another — although, of course, quality was highly variable. On the legitimate stage there were never enough understudies to replace several actors leaving a production at the same time. Although the PMA launched personal attacks against Equity executives and set up a company union, it did not work. For one thing, those tactics were crudely implemented and seen for what they were. For another, they were no longer new tactics and thus held no element of surprise. Striking legitimate actors were not shut out of the media; it was quite the opposite, with many national publications giving the actors space and sympathy. Nor was the public apathetic and indifferent to the Equity strike, as it had always been to any Rat walkouts. For the most part, they seemed to favor the players, which may have had something to do with the positive media coverage Equity received. When the strike ended Equity emerged the clear winner; it had achieved all of its demands.

Another difference between the Equity and Rat strikes, besides those already mentioned, was the ability of the legitimate players to shut down productions. By the end of the strike all productions targeted in New York and Chicago had been shut, except one. The PMA made a major mistake in trying to blindly follow the strategy used by Albee in the vaudeville strike without taking into account the differences between the two arenas. For example, while *Variety* and *Billboard* had been remorseless and venomous in their attacks on the Rats, both were supportive and enthusiastic supporters of Equity. After the Equity strike things became easier for actors when it came to unionization, although never easy in an absolute sense.

Chapter Notes

Chapter 1

1. "An Actors Strike and a Stabbing Affair in a Richmond Theatre." *New York Times*, November 5, 1872, p. 2.
2. "Unpaid Salaries." *New York Dramatic Mirror*, July 15, 1882, p. 6.
3. "A Cold Day for *Russia*." *Washington Post*, August 27, 1887, p. 2.
4. Ibid.
5. "Trouble in a Company." *New York Dramatic Mirror*, October 14, 1893, p. 3.
6. "Arab Acrobats Sue for Services." *New York Dramatic Mirror*, December 2, 1893, p. 2.
7. "An Actor's Troubles." *New York Dramatic Mirror*, January 27, 1894, p. 8.
8. "Companies Stranded." *New York Dramatic Mirror*, October 12, 1895, p. 13.
9. "Jewish Actors on Strike." *New York Dramatic Mirror*, January 4, 1896, p. 3.
10. "A Strike at Seattle." *New York Dramatic Mirror*, July 25, 1896, p. 14.
11. "Actors Who Object." *New York Dramatic Mirror*, April 29, 1882, p. 6.
12. "Decent Dressing Rooms Wanted." *New York Dramatic Mirror*, January 27, 1883, p. 6.
13. "Be More Cautious." *New York Dramatic Mirror*, September 22, 1888, p. 6.
14. "A Young Actress Complains." *New York Dramatic Mirror*, September 29, 1894, p. 3.
15. "Left Destitute in Port Jervis." *New York Dramatic Mirror*, October 12, 1895, p. 13.
16. "Performers in Distress." *New York Dramatic Mirror*, October 27, 1906, p. 20.
17. "Miss Craigen's Broken Contract." *New York Dramatic Mirror*, September 20, 1890, p. 8.
18. "The Two Weeks Clause Again." *New York Dramatic Mirror*, December 6, 1890, p. 2.
19. "The Rascals Must Go." *New York Dramatic Mirror*, June 25, 1892, p. 4.
20. "Drive Out the Swindlers." *New York Dramatic Mirror*, July 2, 1892, p. 4.
21. "To Punish Frauds." *New York Dramatic Mirror*, July 9, 1892, p. 8.
22. "The Swindlers Must Go." *New York Dramatic Mirror*, July 16, 1892, p. 2.
23. "But Two Salary Days." *New York Dramatic Mirror*, July 16, 1892, p. 6.
24. "An Old Question." *New York Dramatic Mirror*, September 20, 1896, p. 12.
25. "Sunday Performances." *New York Dramatic Mirror*, July 3, 1886, p. 1.
26. "Outrageous." *New York Dramatic Mirror*, April 8, 1897, p. 12.
27. "Sunday Performances." *New York Dramatic Mirror*, December 8, 1900, p. 14.
28. "Police Inspect Sunday Concerts." *New York Dramatic Mirror*, March 14, 1903, p. 22.
29. "More Arrests on Sunday." *New York Dramatic Mirror*, January 9, 1909, p. 17.
30. "Actress Accuses U.B.O. Man of Attempted Assault." *Variety*, June 27, 1913, p. 3.
31. "Vaudeville's Seamy Side." *Variety*, June 6, 1913, p. 6.
32. Ibid.
33. Ibid.
34. Ibid.
35. "W.R.A.U. Offers Protection to the Legitimate Player." *Variety*, December 12, 1913, p. 14.

36. Don B. Wilmeth and Christopher Bigsby, eds. *The Cambridge History of American Theatre volume 2: 1870–1945*. Cambridge: Cambridge University Press, 1999, p. 219.

37. Joe Laurie Jr. *Vaudeville: From the Honky-Tonks to the Palace*. New York: Henry Holt, 1953, pp. 310–311.

Chapter 2

1. Don B Wilmeth and Christopher Bigsby, eds. *The Cambridge History of American Theatre volume 2: 1870–1945*. Cambridge: Cambridge University Press, 1999, pp. 219–220.

2. "The Theatrical Protective Association." *New York Times*, July 22, 1864, p. 8.

3. "A Timely Hint." *New York Dramatic Mirror*, June 12, 1886, p. 1.

4. "The Strike for Higher Salaries." *New York Dramatic Mirror*, June 17, 1882, p. 6.

5. "Why Not Arbitrate?" *New York Dramatic Mirror*, October 28, 1882, p. 6.

6. "Theatrical Litigation." *New York Dramatic Mirror*, April 11, 1885, p. 11.

7. "The Proposed League." *New York Dramatic Mirror*, June 27, 1891, p. 5.

8. "The Arbitration Scheme." *New York Dramatic Mirror*, July 25, 1891, p. 7; "The Managers' League." *New York Dramatic Mirror*, August 8, 1891, p. 4.

9. "Protection for Our Actors." *New York Dramatic Mirror*, December 22, 1888, p. 6.

10. "NYM Crinkle's Feuilleton." *New York Dramatic Mirror*, December 29, 1888, p. 1.

11. "A Ballet Girls' Union." *New York Dramatic Mirror*, August 11, 1894, p. 4.

12. "The Agency Abuses." *New York Dramatic Mirror*, August 1, 1885, p. 10.

13. "The Actors' Association." *New York Dramatic Mirror*, September 1, 1894, p. 12.

14. "The Actors' Association Is Growing." *New York Dramatic Mirror*, February 22, 1896, p. 3.

15. "The Actors' Society." *New York Dramatic Mirror*, May 16, 1896, p. 11.

16. "The Actors' Society." *New York Dramatic Mirror*, May 23, 1896, p. 14.

17. "The Actors' Society." *New York Dramatic Mirror*, August 29, 1896, p. 2.

18. "An Important Event." *New York Dramatic Mirror*, November 21, 1896, p. 14.

19. "Actors' Society of America." *New York Dramatic Mirror*, November 28, 1896, p. 4.

20. "Scope of the Actors' Society." *New York Dramatic Mirror*, November 28, 1896, p. 14.

21. "A Proper Protest." *New York Dramatic Mirror*, January 23, 1897, p. 12.

22. "A Professional Question." *New York Dramatic Mirror*, October 2, 1897, p. 14.

23. Ibid.

24. "The Actors' Society." *New York Dramatic Mirror*, August 27, 1898, p. 13.

25. Benjamin McArthur. *Actors and American Culture, 1880–1920*. Philadelphia: Temple University Press, 1984, pp. 217–218.

26. "Actors to Amuse Strikers." *New York Dramatic Mirror*, March 31, 1900, p. 18.

27. "The Story of the Trust." *New York Dramatic Mirror*, November 13, 1897, p. 29.

28. Benjamin McArthur, op. cit., pp. 213–215.

29. Ibid., p. 216.

30. Ibid., pp. 221–222.

31. "Vaudeville Managers Confer." *New York Dramatic Mirror*, May 26, 1900, p. 17.

Chapter 3

1. "White Rats News." *Variety*, September 22, 1916, p. 15.

2. George Fuller Golden. "The Original Eight." In Charles W. Stein, ed. *American Vaudeville as Seen by Its Contemporaries*. New York: Alfred A. Knopf, 1984, pp. 131–132.

3. "The White Rats of America." *New York Dramatic Mirror*, June 30, 1900, p. 16.

4. "The Vaudeville Actors' Movement." *New York Dramatic Mirror*, July 14, 1900, p. 12.

5. Ad. *New York Dramatic Mirror*, July 28, 1900, p. 24.

6. "The White Rats' Testimonial." *New York Dramatic Mirror*, September 15, 1900, p. 18.

7. "The Little Mice." *New York Dramatic Mirror*, October 6, 1900, p. 18.

8. "Big White Rats." *New York Dramatic Mirror*, January 19, 1901, p. 18; "White Rats to Admit Women." *New York Dramatic Mirror*, January 26, 1901, p. 18; "White Rats Make Important Move." *New York Dramatic Mirror*, February 2, 1901, p. 20.

9. "White Rats Make Important Move." *New York Dramatic Mirror*, February 2, 1901, p. 20.

10. Epes W. Sargent. "Why the Vaudeville Artists of America Should Organize." *Variety*, February 24, 1906, p. 4.

11. "The White Rats." *Washington Post*, February 17, 1901, p. 26.

12. Ibid.

13. Ibid.

14. Ibid.

15. "White Rats Win Their Point." *New York Dramatic Mirror*, February 16, 1901, p. 20.

16. Ibid.

17. "White Rats Rejoice." *New York Dramatic Mirror*, February 23, 1901, pp. 18, 20.

18. "A Lesson for Legitimate Actors." *New York Dramatic Mirror*, February 23, 1901, p. 18.

19. Ibid.

20. "Strike of the White Rats." *Washington Post*, February 23, 1901, p. 11.

21. "White Rats News." *Variety*, September 22, 1916, p. 15.

22. Ibid.

23. "The Strike of the Vaudeville Actors." *New York Times*, February 23, 1901, p. 9.

24. "The White Rats Are Standing Firm." *New York Times*, February 24, 1901, p. 7.

25. "The Troubles in Vaudeville." *New York Dramatic Mirror*, March 2, 1901, p. 18.

26. Ibid.

27. Ibid.

28. Ibid., p. 20; Hollis Alpert. *The Barrymores*. New York: The Dial Press, 1964, p. 87.

29. "Aimed at Vaudeville Managers." *Washington Post*, February 25, 1901, p. 8.

30. "The Troubles in Vaudeville." *New York Dramatic Mirror*, March 2, 1901, p. 20.

31. "The Vaudeville Troubles." *New York Dramatic Mirror*, March 2, 1901, p. 14.

32. "The White Rats Strike." *Billboard*, March 2, 1901, p. 9; "Saturday, March 9th 1901." *Billboard*, March 9, 1901, p. 4.

33. "White Rats' Strike Ended." *New York Times*, March 7, 1901, p. 2.

34. "Vaudeville Strike Declared Off." *Washington Post*, March 8, 1901, p. 3.

35. Willard Holcomb. "Trials in Vaudeville." *Washington Post*, March 10, 1901, p. 27.

36. "White Rat Bookings." *Billboard*, March 23, 1901, p. 24.

37. "What the Rats Are Doing." *New York Dramatic Mirror*, March 30, 1901, p. 18.

38. Epes W. Sargent, op. cit.

39. Armond Fields and L. Marc Fields. *From the Bowery to Broadway: Lew Fields and the Roots of American Popular Theatre*. New York: Oxford University Press, 1993, p. 170.

40. Abel Green and Joe Laurie Jr. *Show Biz from Vaude to Video*. New York: Henry Holt, 1951, p. 95.

41. Joe Laurie Jr. *Vaudeville: From the Honky-Tonks to the Palace*. New York: Henry Holt, 1953, p. 312.

42. "George Fuller Golden." *New York Dramatic Mirror*, July 20, 1901, p. 13.

43. "George Fuller Golden." *Variety*, February 24, 1912, p. 6.

Chapter 4

1. "The Actors' Society." *New York Dramatic Mirror*, June 14, 1902, p. 12.

2. "A Chorus Girls' Union." *New York Dramatic Mirror*, April 5, 1902, p. 15.

3. "A Union of Chorus Girls?" *New York Dramatic Mirror*, June 28, 1902, p. 15.

4. "Performers Go on Strike." *New York Dramatic Mirror*, July 4, 1903, p. 16.

5. "Western Actors Join Union." *New York Dramatic Mirror*, August 6, 1904, p. 17.

6. "Actors' Union Mass Meeting." *New York Dramatic Mirror*, January 21, 1905, p. 20.

7. "Speakers Urge Actors to Unionize the Stage." *New York Times*, January 14, 1905, p. 9.

8. "Unions Tackle Conreid with Chorus' Demands." *New York Times*, December 25, 1905, p. 4.

9. "The Union and Mr. Conreid." *New York Times*, September 13, 1906, p. 6.

10. "Actors' Union in Philadelphia." *New York Dramatic Mirror*, December 29, 1906, p. 20.

11. "Actors' Union Going West." *Variety*, March 9, 1907, p. 5.

12. "Actors' Union Active." *Variety*, October 26, 1907, p. 7.

13. "Actors' Union Strengthened." *Variety*, November 30, 1907, p. 6.

14. "An Important Step Toward Organization." *Variety*, June 2, 1906, p. 2.

15. "Comedy Club's Birthday." *Variety*, May 18, 1907, p. 7.

16. "The Vaudeville Comedy Club." *New York Dramatic Mirror*, June 8, 1907, pp. 8–9.

17. Ibid.

18. "Vaudeville Protective Ass'n Is Artists' Secret Society." *Variety*, May 16, 1913, p. 4.

19. "White Rats News." *Variety*, September 22, 1916, p. 16; "R. C. Mudge on White Rats." *New York Dramatic Mirror*, October 10, 1908, p. 19.

20. Ad. *Variety*, January 20, 1906, p. 3.

21. Epes W. Sargent. "Why the Vaudeville Artist of America Should Organize." *Variety*, February 24, 1906, p. 4.

22. Sime Silverman. "Why the Vaudeville Artist of America Should Organize." *Variety*, March 3, 1906, p. 4.

23. Epes W. Sargent. "Why the Vaudeville Artist of America Should Organize." *Variety*, March 10, 1906, p. 4.

24. Sime Silverman. "Why the Vaudeville Artist of America Should Organize." *Variety*, March 17, 1906, p. 4.

25. Epes W. Sargent. "Why the Vaudeville Artist of America Should Organize." *Variety*, March 24, 1906, p. 4.

26. Epes W. Sargent. "Why the Vaudeville Artist of America Should Organize." *Variety*, April 7, 1906, p. 4.

27. Epes W. Sargent. "Percy Williams' Views on the Organization of Vaudeville." *Variety*, April 28, 1906, p. 4.

28. Sime Silverman. "Why the Vaudeville Artist of America Should Organize." *Variety*, May 12, 1906, p. 4.

29. Sime Silverman. "Why the Vaudeville Artist of America Should Organize." *Variety*, June 2, 1906, p. 4.

30. Sime Silverman. "Why the Vaudeville Artist of America Should Organize." *Variety*, June 23, 1906, p. 4.

31. "R. C. Mudge on White Rats." *New York Dramatic Mirror*, October 10, 1908, p. 19.

32. "Plans for Affiliation." *Variety*, September 15, 1906, p. 2.

33. R. C. Mudge. "Benefits of Organization." *Variety*, December 15, 1906, p. 24.

34. "Williams and Albee Talk." *Variety*, February 16, 1907, p. 6.

35. "After Equitable Contract." *Variety*, February 23, 1907, p. 6.

36. "United Agrees to Be Fair." *Variety*, March 9, 1907, p. 5.

37. "Percy G. Williams' New Contract Form." *Variety*, March 23, 1907, p. 4.

38. "Want Rats in Labor Union." *Variety*, April 20, 1907, p. 6.

39. "White Rats After Irresponsible Agents." *Variety*, July 13, 1907, p. 2.

40. "Planning to Forbid Sunday Shows." *Variety*, September 14, 1907, p. 6.

41. "Protection of White Rats Offered Women of the Profession." *Variety*, December 28, 1907, p. 2.

42. "President Mudge Marries May Belfort." *Variety*, November 2, 1907, p. 6.

43. "White Rats News." *Variety*, September 22, 1916, p. 16.

44. Harry Mountford on His Way." *Variety*, December 28, 1907, p. 6.

Chapter 5

1. "Emergency Committee in Charge of White Rats." *Variety*, February 22, 1908, p. 8.

2. "White Rats Draw Up Special Form of Contract." *Variety*, March 28, 1908, p. 3.

3. "Notes of the White Rats." *New York Dramatic Mirror*, June 13, 1908, p. 17.

4. "White Rats Annual Meeting." *Variety*, June 20, 1908, p. 8.

5. "Special Representatives for Rats." *Variety*, June 27, 1908, p. 3.

6. "Fred Niblo Elected Rats' Big Chief." *Variety*, July 4, 1908, p. 4.

7. "White Rats' Meeting Draws Crowd at Chicago." *Variety*, July 11, 1908, p. 8.

8. "Investment Fund Moves in Managerial Direction." *Variety*, July 11, 1908, p. 4.

9. "Managers Much Worried by Artists' Aggressiveness." *Variety*, July 25, 1908, p. 8.

10. "$100,000 in Reserve for Rats' Investment Fund." *Variety*, August 1, 1908, p. 4.

11. "White Rat Notes." *New York Dramatic Mirror*, August 1, 1908, p. 16.

12. "The Question of Opposition." *New York Dramatic Mirror*, August 15, 1908, p. 14.

13. "The Vaudeville Situation." *New York Dramatic Mirror*, September 5, 1908, p. 17.

14. "From George Fuller Golden." *New York Dramatic Mirror*, October 3, 1908, p. 19.

15. "Small Time Forming Union with White Rats Agency." *Variety*, June 5, 1909, pp. 3, 11.

16. "White Rats Theatres Pass to Feiber & Shea." *Variety*, March 2, 1912, p. 5.

17. "An Equitable Contract as Drawn by the Artists." *Variety*, August 8, 1908, p. 9.

18. "Rats in Politics." *Variety*, August 15, 1908, p. 4.

19. "Actors Political Meeting First to be Held by Artists." *Variety*, September 12, 1908, p. 8.

20. "Bars a Salomer." *Variety*, August 15, 1908, p. 4.

21. "Actors' Union Bars Salome." *Variety*, August 22, 1908, p. 9.

22. "150 Houses Bar Salome." *Variety*, September 26, 1908, p. 3.

23. "Rats Expel Two Members." *Variety*, October 17, 1908, p. 4.

24. Harry Mountford. "The White Rats' Year." *Variety*, December 12, 1908, p. 52.

25. "The Actors' Society." *New York Dramatic Mirror*, May 1, 1909, p. 5.

26. "Actors Against Big Fee." *New York Dramatic Mirror*, March 13, 1909, p. 14.

27. "Passage of Voss Agency Bill Promises Artists Protection." *Variety*, May 1, 1909, p. 6.

28. "Mayor McClellan Signs Voss New Agency Bill." *Variety*, May 15, 1909, p. 4.

29. "Actors Demand More Pay." *Variety*, May 15, 1909, p. 6.

30. "Actors Threaten Strike." *Washington Post*, June 27, 1909, p. 5.

31. "E. F. Albee's Views." *New York Dramatic Mirror*, August 15, 1908, p. 14.

32. "Second Annual Convention of White Rats at Chicago." *Variety*, July 30, 1909, pp. 9, 12.

33. "Blacklist Might Be Broken Upon Demand of White Rats." *Variety*, October 16, 1909, p. 3.

34. "Acts Still Holding Out." *Variety*, September 18, 1909, p. 4.

35. "Boycott of Chicago Agent." *Variety*, October 16, 1909, p. 4.

36. "Artists Win Strike." *Variety*, October 23, 1909, p. 4.

37. "Agent Unfair Again." *Variety*, October 30, 1909, p. 8.

38. "Agency Bill Introduced in New York Legislature." *Variety*, January 22, 1910, p. 5.

39. "White Rats Introduce New Agency Measure in Albany." *Variety*, March 5, 1910, p. 9.

40. "The Artists' Associations Agree on De Veaux's Bill." *Variety*, March 26, 1910, p. 5.

41. "New Agency Law Makes Personal Representatives." *Variety*, July 2, 1910, p. 5.

42. "Chicago Artist-Agent Row Threatens Serious Trouble." *Variety*, March 19, 1910, p. 5.

43. "Wants All Agencies to Become Unionized Ones." *Variety*, June 11, 1910, p. 4.

44. "Chicago's Labor Union and White Rats Fail to Agree." *Variety*, July 2, 1910, p. 6.

45. "Agency Strike in Boston." *Variety*, August 13, 1910, p. 9.

46. "Striking Boston Artists Formed into Actors' Union." *Variety*, August 20, 1910, p. 8.

47. "Application of White Rats Made to Federation of Labor." *Variety*, September 24, 1910, p. 5.

48. "Unionizing Again." *Variety*, October 22, 1910, p. 6.

49. "The White Rats Society Joins Labor Organization." *Variety*, November 12, 1910, p. 5.

50. "Old Union to Be Revived." *Variety*, January 28, 1911, p. 5.

51. "Leading Vaudeville Artists Forming Association of 100." *Variety*, January 7, 1911, p. 4.

52. "New Actors' Society Making Some Headway." *Variety*, January 14, 1911, p. 8.

53. "Vaudeville Actors' Fund Suggested by Managers." *Variety*, March 4, 1911, p. 12.

54. "Chicago Managers Accede to Demands of Actors." *Variety*, February 11, 1911, p. 9.

55. "V.M.P.A. Issues a Statement on Strikes and Unionism." *Variety*, April 22, 1911, p. 9.

56. Ibid.

57. Ibid.

58. "Vaudeville Managers Talk on Proposed Unionizing." *Variety*, April 29, 1911, p. 3.

59. Ibid.

60. "Salaries Will Not Be Cut, Officially Says V.M.P.A." *Variety*, June 3, 1911, p. 17.

61. "Common Sense Versus Hot Air." *Variety*, July 8, 1911, p. 19.

62. "Vaudeville Managers Won't Recognize Rats as a Union." *Variety*, September 2, 1911, p. 3.

63. "Clause for Picture-Actors in Frohman's New Contracts." *Variety*, August 5, 1911, p. 9.

64. "Warning Legitimate Players Against Picture Connection." *Variety*, January 6, 1912, p. 10.

65. "White Rats Reshaping Itself After Change of Direction." *Variety*, October 7, 1911, p. 9.

66. Sime Silverman. "Mountford's Rise and Fall." *Variety*, December 23, 1911, p. 47.

67. Ibid., p. 122.

Chapter 6

1. "Conference with Managers Asked for by White Rats." *Variety*, October 28, 1911, p. 5.

2. "White Rats and Managers Taking Positive Stands." *Variety*, November 4, 1911, p. 5.

3. "Rats Ask Minimum Scale for Chicago and Boston." *Variety*, November 4, 1911, p. 13.

4. "Western Vaudeville Man Agrees to Closed Shop." *Variety*, November 11, 1911, p. 5.

5. "Agreement at Atlanta by Theatrical Unions." *Variety*, November 25, 1911, p. 6.

6. "White Rats Investigation by Union Labor People." *Variety*, May 18, 1912, p. 3.

7. "White Rats New Club House Astonishes, and Is Admired." *Variety*, December 13, 1912, p. 8.

8. "How the United Bleeds the Agents and Actors." *Variety*, October 18, 1912, p. 7.

9. Sime Silverman. "What the Actor Must Do." *Variety*, February 7, 1913, p. 6.

10. Sime Silverman. "What the Actor Must Do." *Variety*, February 14, 1913, p. 8.

11. Sime Silverman. "What the Actor Must Do." *Variety*, February 21, 1913, p. 8.

12. "Vaudeville Protective Ass'n Is Artists' Secret Society." *Variety*, May 16, 1913, p. 4.

13. "Photoplay Actors Fail to Form New Organization." *Variety*, July 25, 1913, p. 8.

14. "Protection for Chorus Girls in Federation of Labor." *Variety*, November 21, 1913, p. 4.

15. "Chorus Girls Form Union to Enforce Many Reforms." *Variety*, November 28, 1913, p. 11.

16. "White Rats Give up *Player*; Using *Variety* for Its News." *Variety*, November 21, 1913, p. 3.

17. "Procrastinating Players Losing White Rats Benefits." *Variety*, December 19, 1913,
p. 18.

18. "Gompers Draws the Color Line." *New York Times*, November 19, 1910, p. 4.

19. Ernest Hogan. "The Negro in Vaudeville." *Variety*, December 15, 1906, p. 22.

20. Ad. *Variety*, December 26, 1913, p. 40.

21. Sime Silverman. "Mr. Fogarty and the Rats." *Variety*, September 26, 1914, p. 7.

22. "Salary Cutting Sole Topic This Week in Vaudeville." *Variety*, October 17, 1914, p. 3.

23. "White Rat News." *Variety*, June 25, 1915, p. 6.

24. "Mountford Back in Harness for Aggressive Campaign." *Variety*, October 22, 1915, p. 4.

25. "To the Actor and Actress of the U.S." *Variety*, October 22, 1915, pp. 12–13.

26. "White Rats Begin Crusade." *New York Times*, October 16, 1915, p. 11.

Chapter 7

1. "To Non-Members of the W.R.A.U. and A.A.A." *Variety*, October 29, 1915, pp. 14–15.

2. "Rats Give Local Autonomy; Admit Women to Meetings." *Variety*, January 14, 1916, p. 5.

3. "A White Rat Loses Route Through Impassioned Speech." *Variety*, November 26, 1915, p. 6.

4. Joe Laurie Jr. *Vaudeville: From the Honky-Tonks to the Palace*. New York: Henry Holt, 1953, p. 313.

5. "White Rats and Labor Leaders' Get-Together Meet in Boston." *Billboard*, February 26, 1916, pp. 3, 63.

6. "Vaudeville Managers' Ass'n Decide on Publicity Campaign." *Variety*, March 3, 1916, p. 5.

7. Charles Leonard Fletcher. "Why I Resigned." *Variety*, March 3, 1916, p. 8.

8. "Reorganization of Protective Association by Managers." *Billboard*, March 4, 1916, pp. 3, 71.

9. "White Rats Recognize Claims of Insurgents." *Billboard*, March 4, 1916, p. 6.

10. "Stop! Read!—And Reflect!" *Variety*, March 10, 1916, pp. 18–19.

11. Ibid.

12. "Managers Take Decided Stand Against Policy of Mountford." *Billboard*, March 11, 1916, pp. 3, 63.

13. "Major Doyle Tells Facts to Enlighten the White Rats." *Billboard*, March 11, 1916, p. 62.

14. "Actors Equity Assn. Meets to Discuss W.R.A.U. Affiliation." *Variety*, March 17, 1916, p. 5.

15. "Colored Artists of America." *Variety*, March 7, 1916, p. 15.

16. "Managers Tabbing Rats." *Variety*, March 24, 1916, p. 5.

17. "To the Vaudeville Artist." *Variety*, March 24, 1916, p. 19.

18. "Screen Club Gives Reel." *New York Times*, July 30, 1917, p. 9; "Screen Club's Members Wary of Mountford and His Order." *Billboard*, March 25, 1916, p. 3.

19. "W.R.A.U. Will Resort to Conscription After May 26." *Variety*, March 31, 1916, p. 5.

20. Ibid.

21. "White Rats Being Barred from Vaudeville." *Billboard*, April 1, 1916, p. 3.

22. Ibid., pp. 3, 70.

23. "White Rats Desert Ranks in Fear of Cancellation." *Billboard*, April 8, 1916, p. 6.

24. "Managers' Axe Still Falling on Members of the White Rats." *Billboard*, April 15, 1916, pp. 3, 62.

25. "Fitzpatrick Elected President of the White Rats." *Billboard*, April 15, 1916, pp. 6, 62.

26. "Managers Securing Reports of White Rats Meetings." *Variety*, April 21, 1916, p. 5.

27. "White Rats News." *Variety*, April 21, 1916, p. 16.

28. "Have Won Big Victory Over Rat Agitators, Say Managers." *Billboard*, April 22, 1916, pp. 3, 67.

29. "Startling Disclosures on Dwindling Rat Membership." *Billboard*, April 29, 1916, pp. 3, 67.

30. "The *Billboard*'s Defi to Mountford." *Billboard*, April 29, 1916, p. 6.

31. "National Vaudeville Artists, Title of New Organization." *Billboard*, May 6, 1916, p. 6.

32. Ibid., pp. 6, 78.

33. "The Vaudeville Artists' New Association Now a Reality." *Billboard*, May 13, 1916, p. 14.

34. Ibid.

35. "Mountford Back in New York Addressed Big Open Meeting." *Variety*, May 12, 1916, p. 5.

36. "Mr. Gompers." *Billboard*, May 13, 1916, p. 6.

37. "Organization Details." *Billboard*, May 20, 1916, pp. 6, 67.

38. "Mountford Stages Another Mutual Admiration Meeting." *Billboard*, May 20, 1916, p. 6.

39. Ad. *Variety*, May 26, 1916, p. 13.

40. Ad. *Variety*, June 9, 1916, pp. 20–21.

41. "Artists' New Contract Discussed by Managers." *Billboard*, June 10, 1916, pp. 6, 71.

42. "Gompers Adopts *Billboard* Suggestion." *Billboard*, June 10, 1916, p. 3.

43. "Will Proceed in Accordance with the Policies of A.F. of L." *Billboard*, June 17, 1916, pp. 3, 59.

44. "Mutually Accepted Contract by Managers and Artists." *Variety*, June 16, 196, p. 3.

45. "Managers Give Artists Better Contract Than Asked by Them." *Billboard*, June 24, 1916, pp. 3, 59.

46. "Pacific Coast Managers Sign White Rats Contract." *Variety*, July 14, 1916, p. 3.

47. "Much Ado About Nothing Furnishes Glee for Rats." *Billboard*, July 29, 1916, pp. 6, 83.

48. "Preference to N.V.A. Acts." *Variety*, August 4, 1916, p. 6.

49. "Willard Mack Elected Head of New Vaude Organization." *Billboard*, August 5, 1916, p. 3; Ad. *Variety*, August 11, 1916, p. 13.

50. "Oh! Rats." *Billboard*, July 1, 1916, p. 6.

Chapter 8

1. "White Rats' Representative Declares Okla. City Unfair." *Variety*, July 28, 1916, p. 6.

2. "Oklahoma Strike Continues with Managers Watching." *Variety*, August 4, 1916, pp. 3, 6.

3. Carl L. Shannon. "Oklahoma Strike Settlement in Two Weeks Predicted." *Variety*, August 11, 1916, p. 5.

4. Ibid.

5. W. M. Smith. "Oklahoma City Strike Going Along Without Much Change." *Variety*, August 18, 1916, p. 6.

6. Carl L. Shannon. "Oklahoma City Strike Going Along Without Much Change." *Variety*, August 18, 1916, p. 6.

7. Ibid., pp. 6, 13.

8. Carl L. Shannon. "Strikers Pulling Acts Out in Oklahoma City Fight." *Variety*, August 25, 1916, p. 5.

9. "Situation Unchanged." *Billboard*, August 26, 1916, p. 6.

10. "Managers Make Two Requests for Conferences to End Fight." *Variety*, September 1, 1916, p. 5.

11. "White Rats to Be Boycotted in Managers' Ass'n Threat." *Variety*, September 15, 1916, p. 3.

12. "Oklahoma Managers Send Defi to State Arbitration Board." *Variety*, September 15, 1916, p. 7.

13. "Managers' Defiance Holds Up Strike Decision Till Sept. 23." *Variety*, September 22, 1916, p. 6.

14. "State Board of Arbitration Is Considering Okla. Strike." *Billboard*, September 30, 1916, p. 6.

15. "Arbitration Board Counsels Reinstatement of Strikers." *Variety*, September 29, 1916, p. 6.

16. Ibid.

17. Ibid.

18. "Arbitration Board Throws Out Testimony of Mountford." *Billboard*, October 7, 1916, pp. 3, 70.

19. "Protecting Oklahoma City Aim of Chicago's Association." *Variety*, October 6, 1916, p. 6.

20. "Pickets Barred." *Variety*, October 13, 1916, p. 3.

21. "Oklahoma Strikers Abandon Metropolitan; Deny Defeat." *Variety*, October 13, 1916, p. 6.

22. "Again Picketing." *Variety*, October 20, 1916, p. 6.

23. "Oklahoma City Strike Quiet." *Variety*, November 17, 1916, p. 6.

24. "Oklahoma's Unfair Lyric Turns Union, Without Rats." *Variety*, November 24, 1916, p. 6.

25. "Oklahoma Strike Lost." *Variety*, January 5, 1917, p. 7.

26. "Extras Forming Union for Mutual Protection." *Variety*, August 25, 1916, p. 20.

27. Ibid.

28. Ibid.

29. "Supers Call Mass Meetings and Arrange for a Charter." *Variety*, September 1, 1916, p. 13.

30. "Sluts and Other Things." *Billboard*, August 26, 1916, p. 6.

31. "White Rat News." *Variety*, September 22, 1916, pp. 15, 19.

32. "Managers Refuse Invitation for White Rat Conference." *Variety*, September 29, 1916, p. 3.

33. "Rats Refuse Resignations." *Variety*, October 13, 1916, p. 3.

34. "White Rats' Union Tries to Stop Poli's Sundays." *Variety*, October 13, 1916, p. 3.

35. "Waterbury's Sunday Stops." *Variety*, October 20, 1916, p. 6.

36. "The Agi Says." *Billboard*, October 21, 196, p. 6.

37. "On Which Side Is Your Bread Buttered." *Variety*, October 13, 1916, p. 8.

38. "Stuck to Rats; Forced Out." *Variety*, October 20, 1916, p. 6.

39. "Vaudeville Managers Are Not Against Organized Labor." *Variety*, October 20, 1916, p. 8.

40. "Managers Plan Salary Cut to Meet No Sunday Threat." *Variety*, November 10, 1916, p. 6.

41. "White Rats Resign from Organization When Cancelled." *Billboard*, November 11, 1916, pp. 6, 63.

42. "Canceled Rats Passed Upon by Managers' Committee." *Variety*, November 17, 1916, p. 5.

43. "V.M.P.A. Will Give No Quarter to Rats." *Billboard*, December 2, 1916, p. 6.

44. "Theatrical Charter Confined to Rats by A.F. of L. Meeting." *Variety*, November 24, 1916, p. 3.

45. "V.M.P.A. Will Give No Quarter to Rats." *Billboard*, December 2, 1916, pp. 6, 55.

46. "White Rats Ask for Meeting for Submission of Its Demands." *Variety*, December 8, 1916, p. 3.

47. "Managers Say Blacklist for Any Striking Actor." *Variety*, December 8, 1916, p. 6.

48. "Failure to Strike Monday Eases Vaudeville Situation." *Variety*, December 15, 1916, pp. 3, 6.

49. Sime Silverman. "Strike." *Variety*, December 15, 1916, p. 9.

50. Ibid.

51. Ibid., pp. 9, 19.

52. "Actors Should Make Their Peace with Managers and Settle Down to Regular Work." *Variety*, December 15, 1916, p. 17.

53. "Mountford Has Fallen Down in Pre-

vailing Chicago Opinion." *Variety*, December 22, 1916, p. 3.

54. E. F. Albee. "E. F. Albee and Vaudeville." *Variety*, December 22, 1916, p. 5.

55. Sime Silverman. "Merry Christmas." *Variety*, December 22, 1916, p. 9.

56. "Year in Vaudeville." *Variety*, December 22, 1916, pp. 6, 118.

57. "All Is Well." *Billboard*, December 23, 1916, pp. 6, 59.

58. "White Rats Mortgage Clubhouse Furnishings for $5,000." *Variety*, December 29, 1916, p. 3.

59. "Chicago Rats Hear Hot Air." *Variety*, December 29, 1916, p. 6.

Chapter 9

1. "Acts Flatly Refuse to Obey Order to Strike in Boston." *Variety*, January 5, 1917, p. 7.

2. "Strike's Aftermath Finds Chicago Conditions Normal." *Variety*, January 12, 1917, p. 6.

3. "Failure Again Marks Rats' Strike Attempt in Boston." *Variety*, February 9, 1917, p. 3.

4. Ibid.

5. Ibid., pp. 3, 7.

6. Ibid.

7. "W.R.A.U. Levies Assessment of 5 Percent on Workers' Pay." *Variety*, February 9, 1917, p. 5.

8. "Boston Strike Becomes Peaceful Picketing Affair." *Variety*, February 16, 1917, p. 6.

9. Ibid.

10. "Intended Strike in East Flickered and Went Out." *Billboard*, February 17, 1917, pp. 6, 67.

11. "Mountford Causes Ruction in Boston Labor Meeting." *Variety*, February 23, 1917, p. 7.

12. "Rats' Awful Flop in St. Louis." *Variety*, February 23, 1917, p. 7.

13. "Loyal Acts Rewarded." *Variety*, February 23, 1917, p. 7.

14. "Down to Endurance Test in Rats Boston Strike." *Variety*, March 2, 1917, p. 6.

15. "Checking Up Levy Payers." *Variety*, March 2, 1917, p. 6.

16. "More Money from Actors Is Plea of Executives." *Billboard*, March 3, 1917, pp. 6, 79.

17. "More White Rats Strikes with Customary Results." *Variety*, March 16, 1917, p. 6.

18. Ibid., pp. 6, 24; "Strike Fails, Says Loew." *New York Times*, March 10, 1912, p. 9.

19. "Judge Instructs Pickets." *Variety*, March 16, 1917, p. 24.

20. "Acts Added to Blacklist." *Variety*, March 16, 1917, p. 7.

21. Sime Silverman. Editorial page. *Variety*, March 16, 1917, p. 9.

22. Ibid.

23. Ad. *Variety*, March 16, 1917, pp. 12–13.

24. "More Attempted Strikes by W.R.A.U. Are Fiascos." *Billboard*, March 17, 1917, p. 8.

25. "Agents Will Lose Franchises if Booking Blacklisted Acts." *Variety*, March 23, 1917, p. 3.

26. "Disappointed in Boston." *Variety*, March 23, 1917, p. 7.

27. "White Rats Resort to Tactics of Ruffians." *Billboard*, March 24, 1917, pp. 38, 90.

28. "White Rats in Death Throes and Beaten in All Walkouts." *Billboard*, March 24, 1917, pp. 3, 191.

29. Sime Silverman. Editorial page. *Variety*, March 30, 1917, p. 9.

30. "White Rats Admit Defeat; Order Faces Bankruptcy." *Variety*, April 13, 1917, p. 3.

31. "Play Loyal Acts Is Order of Vaudeville Managers' Society." *Variety*, April 20, 1917, p. 7.

32. "Managers Will Continue Fight Against Rats and Supporters." *Billboard*, May 5, 1917, p. 2.

33. "National Vaudeville Artists." *Variety*, May 11, 1917, p. 5.

34. Pat Casey. "Running the V.M.P.A." *Variety*, May 11, 1917, p. 6.

35. Ibid.

36. J. E. Edwards. "National Vaudeville Artists Inaugurated a New Era." *Billboard*, May 12, 1917, p. 4.

37. A. P. Knutt. "N.V.A. Club." *Billboard*, May 12, 1917, p. 18.

38. "Managers Checking Up on Who Aids N.V.A. Benefit." *Billboard*, May 26, 1917, pp. 6, 95.

39. Ibid.

40. "Blacklisted Acts Taken Up After Others Are Placed." *Variety*, June 8, 1917, p. 3.

41. "Fitzpatrick Flays Unions at White Rats' Meeting." *Billboard*, July 7, 1917, p. 6.

42. "The Blacklist Called Off by Managers' Association." *Variety*, August 31, 1917, pp. 3, 20.

43. "Blacklisted Act Barred from V.M.P.A. Theatres." *Variety*, October 19, 1917, p. 6.

44. Ad. *Billboard*, July 19, 1919, pp. 12–13.

45. Ad. *Billboard*, August 16, 1919, pp. 14–15.

46. "The Real Mountford." *Billboard*, December 20, 1919, p. 48.

47. Joe Laurie Jr. *Vaudeville: From the Honky-Tonks to the Palace.* New York: Henry Holt, 1953, p. 312.

48. Douglas Gilbert. *American Vaudeville: Its Life and Times.* New York: Dover, 1940 (1963), p. 391.

49. Harry Mountford. *New York Times*, June 5, 1950, p. 21.

Chapter 10

1. "Actors Equity Association." *Christian Science Monitor*, March 6, 1913, p. 18.

2. Don B. Wilmeth and Christopher Bigsby, eds. *The Cambridge History of American Theatre volume 2: 1870–1945.* Cambridge: Cambridge University Press, 1999, p. 220.

3. "An Actors' Trade Union." *The Outlook* 106 (January 3, 1914): 12.

4. Ibid., pp. 12–13.

5. "Actors Equity Association Has Successful Year." *Christian Science Monitor*, June 6, 1914, p. 20.

6. Benjamin McArthur. *Actors and American Culture, 1880–1920.* Philadelphia: Temple University Press, 1984, p. 219.

7. "No Bar to Negro Actors in Equity." *New York Dramatic Mirror*, September 4, 1919, p. 1391.

8. "Equitable Contract Nearer." *Variety*, November 14, 1914, p. 2.

9. "Actors Equity Assn. Meets to Discuss W.R.A.U. Affiliation." *Variety*, March 17, 1916, p. 5.

10. "Actors' Equity Association Favors Union with A.F. of L." *Billboard*, March 18, 1916, p. 29.

11. "Actors to Be Unionized." *New York Dramatic Mirror*, March 18, 1916, p. 7.

12. Hiram Kelly Moderwell. "Acting as a Trade." *New Republic* 6 (April 22, 1916): 311.

13. Ibid.

14. Ibid.

15. "Actors Join Federated Labor." *New York Dramatic Mirror*, June 3, 1916, p. 9.

16. "Legit Actors' Society Vote for Union Affiliation." *Variety*, June 2, 1916, p. 5.

17. "Actors' Equity Members Favor Alliance with Fed. of Labor." *Billboard*, June 3, 1916, p. 82.

18. "Managers Not Hostile to Actors." *New York Dramatic Mirror*, June 10, 1916, p. 8.

19. "Why the Actors Joined Labor Federation." *New York Times*, June 4, 1916, p. SM8.

20. "A.E.A. and White Rats Join to Form Union Under New Name." *Variety*, July 29, 1919, p. 6.

21. "A.E.A. Film Membership." *Variety*, December 21, 1917, p. 50.

22. "Managers Adopt Contract of Actors' Equity Assn." *Billboard*, June 16, 1917, pp. 4, 78.

23. "Legit Equitable Contract Adopted by Both Factions." *Variety*, October 5, 1917, p. 12.

24. "Smaller Managers Protest the A.E.A.'s Contract Form." *Variety*, March 1, 1918, p. 13.

25. "Legit Try-Out Contract Form Adopted by A.E.A." *Variety*, May 17, 1918, p. 12.

26. "Actors in Binding Pledges Slash Non-Paying Managers." *Variety*, May 31, 1918, p. 13.

27. "Equity Votes to Arbitrate After Contract Is Rejected." *Variety*, May 30, 1919, p.10.

28. "Battle Over Contract Forms Between A.E.A. and Managers." *Variety*, July 18, 1919, p. 13.

29. "A.E.A. and White Rats Join to Form Union Under New Name." *Variety*, July 25, 1919, p. 16.

30. "Managers Cease to Treat with Actors." *Christian Science Monitor*, July 25, 1919, p. 5.

31. "Broadway Still Talking of New A.E.A. Affiliation." *Billboard*, August 2, 1919, p. 3.

Chapter 11

1. Paul F. Gemmill. "Equity: The Actors' Trade Union." *Quarterly Journal of Economics* 41 (November, 1926): 130.

2. John McCabe. *George M. Cohan: The Man Who Owned Broadway*. Garden City, New York: Doubleday, 1973, pp. 147–148.

3. "Strike Flivs Despite Pledge Equity Members Gave to Quit." *Variety*, August 1, 1919, p. 12.

4. "Mobilizing Actors' Equity Association." *Billboard*, August 9, 1919, p. 5.

5. Ibid., pp. 15, 90.

6. "Theatrical Interests Combine to Cope with Expected Strike." *Variety*, August 8, 1919, p. 6.

7. Ibid.

8. "Actors Strike, Theaters Close." *Christian Science Monitor*, August 8, 1919, p. 2.

9. Ibid.

10. "Leading Players Go Out, Closing Big Attractions." *New York Times*, August 8, 1919, p. 1.

11. Ibid., pp. 1, 12.

12. "Theaters Stay Dark." *Washington Post*, August 9, 1919, p. 7.

13. "Striking Actors Keep 9 Shows Dark." *New York Times*, August 9, 1919, pp. 1, 9.

14. "Latest News of the Actors' Strike." *New York Dramatic Mirror*, August 21, 1919, pp. 1313, 1316.

15. "They Did Strike." *Billboard*, August 16, 1919, p. 5.

16. Ibid., pp. 12–13.

17. Herbert G. Goldman. *Banjo Eyes: Eddie Cantor and the Birth of Modern Stardom*. New York: Oxford University Press, 1997, p. 77.

18. "They Did Strike." *Billboard*, August 16, 1919, p. 18.

19. "Actors' Strike Leads to Suits." *Christian Science Monitor*, August 12, 1919, p. 2.

20. "Equity Body and Members Sued by Shuberts for $500,000." *New York Dramatic Mirror*, August 21, 1919, p. 1314.

21. Ad. *New York Times*, August 12, 1919, p. 14.

22. "Chicago Theatres Closed by Strike; Fight Bitter Here." *New York Times*, August 13, 1919, p. 1.

23. "Outcome of Actors Strike Still in Doubt This Week." *Variety*, August 15, 1919, pp. 3, 21.

24. "Strike in Chicago." *Variety*, August 15, 1919, pp. 17, 21.

25. "Events Leading to Strike." *Variety*, August 15, 1919, p. 28.

26. Ad. *Billboard*, August 16, 1919, p. 11.

27. "Realty Interests in Actors' Strike." *Christian Science Monitor*, August 18, 1919, p. 5.

28. "Theaters." *Christian Science Monitor*, August 21, 1919, p. 8.

29. "Theatricals Fiercest Fight Still Holding on Wednesday." *Variety*, August 22, 1919, pp. 3, 9.

30. Lee Israel. *Miss Tallulah Bankhead*. New York: Putnam's Sons, 1972, pp. 63–64.

31. Albert Auster. *Actresses and Suffragists: Women in the American Theater, 1890–1920*. New York: Praeger, 1984, pp. 136–137.

32. Betty Lee. *Marie Dressler: The Unlikeliest Star*. Lexington, Kentucky: The University Press of Kentucky, 1997, p. 140.

33. Sime Silverman. Editorial page. *Variety*, August 22, 1919, p. 12.

34. Ibid.

35. "All Over — Equity Wins." *Billboard*, August 23, 1919, pp. 5, 9.

36. Ibid., p. 9.

37. Ibid.

38. F. T. Vreeland. "The Actors' Strike." *Nation* 109 (August 23, 1919): 243–244.

39. "Plays Without Actors?" *New Republic* 20 (August 27, 1919): 105–106.

40. "Strike Costs Both Parties $1,500,000 in Three Weeks." *Variety*, August 29, 1919, p. 12.

41. "Strike Factions Deadlocked at End of Strife's Third Week." *Variety*, August 29, 1919, p. 3.

42. "Fidelity League Organizes with Geo. M. Cohan President." *Variety*, August 29, 1919, p. 29.

43. John McCabe, op. cit., pp. 142, 151, 152, 156.

44. "Smoke of Burning Money Still Rises in Clouds." *Billboard*, August 30, 1919, pp. 5, 8.

45. "The Actors' Strike." *Literary Digest* 62 (August 30, 1919): 30.

46. Ibid.

47. Ethel Barrymore. "The Actors' Strike." *The Outlook* 123 (September 3, 1919): 11.

48. Ibid., p. 12.

49. "Managers Said to Favour Settle-

ment." *Christian Science Monitor*, September 4, 1919, p. 6.

50. Ad. *Variety*, September 5, 1919, p. 57; "A.F.L. Membership." *Variety*, September 5, 1919, p. 9.

51. "Boston Added to Strike's List." *Variety*, September 5, 1919, p. 27.

52. "Producers Getting Terrible Pounding." *Billboard*, September 6, 1919, pp. 5, 8.

53. "Show Business Resuming Old Trend After Settlement." *Variety*, September 12, 1919, p. 12.

54. "Equity's Victory." *Billboard*, September 13, 1919, p. 5.

55. Ibid., pp. 5, 121.

56. "Equity's Wise and Able Leaders." *Billboard*, September 13, 1919, p. 122.

57. "The Great Spiritual Victory Won by the Striking Actors." *Current Opinion* 67 (October, 1919): 234–235.

58. "Marie Dressler." *Billboard*, October 4, 1919, p. 10.

59. "Last of Strike Cases Settled at Conference." *Billboard*, October 11, 1919, p. 5.

60. "Chorus Equity Scores Victory for Members of Gaieties Co." *Variety*, October 17, 1919, p. 12.

61. M. F. Lennards. "Francis Wilson Speaks." *Billboard*, November 15, 1919, pp. 10, 98.

62. Paul F. Gemmill. "Equity: The Actors' Trade Union." *Quarterly Journal of Economics* 41 (November, 1926): 132–134; Alfred Harding. "Ten Years After." *New York Times*, August 18, 1929, p. X4.

Bibliography

"Actors Against Big Fees." *New York Dramatic Mirror*, March 13, 1909, p. 14.

"The Actors' Association." *New York Dramatic Mirror*, September 1, 1894, p. 12.

"The Actors' Association Is Growing." *New York Dramatic Mirror*, February 22, 1896, p. 3.

"Actors Demand More Pay." *Variety*, May 15, 1909, p. 6.

"Actors Equity Association." *Christian Science Monitor*, March 6, 1913, p. 18.

"Actors' Equity Association Favors Union with A.F. of L." *Billboard*, March 18, 1916, pp. 29, 185.

"Actors Equity Association Has Successful Year." *Christian Science Monitor*, June 6, 1914, p. 20.

"Actors Equity Assn. Meets to Discuss W.R.A.U. Affiliation." *Variety*, March 17, 1916, p. 5.

"Actors' Equity Members Favor Alliance with Fed. of Labor." *Billboard*, June 3, 1916, pp. 3, 82.

"Actors in Binding Pledges Slash Non-Paying Managers." *Variety*, May 31, 1918, p. 13.

"Actors Join Federated Labor." *New York Dramatic Mirror*, June 3, 1916, p. 9.

"Actors' Political Meeting First to Be Held by Artists." *Variety*, September 12, 1908, p. 8.

"Actors Should Make Their Peace with Managers and Settle Down to Regular Work." *Variety*, December 15, 1916, p. 17.

"The Actors' Society." *New York Dramatic Mirror*, May 16, 1896, p. 11.

"The Actors' Society." *New York Dramatic Mirror*, May 23, 1896, p. 14.

"The Actors' Society." *New York Dramatic Mirror*, August 29, 1896, p. 2.

"The Actors' Society." *New York Dramatic Mirror*, August 27, 1898, p. 13.

"The Actors' Society." *New York Dramatic Mirror*, June 14, 1902, p. 12.

"The Actors' Society." *New York Dramatic Mirror*, May 1, 1909, pp. 5–6.

"Actors' Society of America." *New York Dramatic Mirror*, November 28, 1896, pp. 3–4, 23.

"The Actors' Strike." *Literary Digest* 62 (August 30, 1919): 30–31.

"An Actors Strike and a Stabbing Affair in a Richmond Theatre." *New York Times*, November 5, 1872, p. 2.

"Actors' Strike Ends Play." *New York Times*, May 14, 1918, p. 3.

"Actors' Strike Leads to Suits." *Christian Science Monitor*, August 12, 1919, p. 2.

"Actors Strike, Theaters Close." *Christian Science Monitor*, August 8, 1919, p. 2.

"Actors Threaten Strike." *Washington Post*, June 27, 1909, p. 5.

"Actors to Amuse Strikers." *New York Dramatic Mirror*, March 31, 1900, p. 18.

"Actors to Be Unionized." *New York Dramatic Mirror*, March 18, 1916, p. 7.

"An Actors' Trade Union." *The Outlook* 106 (January 3, 1914): 12–13.

"An Actor's Troubles." *New York Dramatic Mirror*, January 27, 1894, p. 8.

"Actors' Union Active." *Variety*, October 26, 1907, p. 7.

"Actors' Union Bars Salome." *Variety*, August 22, 1908, p. 9.

"Actors' Union Going West." *Variety*, March 9, 1907, p. 5.

"Actors' Union in Philadelphia." *New York Dramatic Mirror*, December 29, 1906, p. 20.

"Actors' Union Mass Meeting." *New York Dramatic Mirror*, January 21, 1905, p. 20.

"Actors' Union Strengthened." *Variety*, November 30, 1907, p. 6.

"Actors Who Object." *New York Times*, April 29, 1882, p. 6.

"Actress Accuses U.B.O. Man of Attempted Assault." *Variety*, June 27, 1913, p. 3.

"Acts Added to Blacklist." *Variety*, March 16, 1917, p. 7.

"Acts Flatly Refuse to Obey Order to Strike in Boston." *Variety*, January 5, 1917, p. 7.

"Acts Still Holding Out." *Variety*, September 18, 1909, p. 4.

Advertisement. *Billboard*, July 19, 1919, pp. 12–13.

Advertisement. *Billboard*, August 16, 1919, p. 11.

Advertisement. *Billboard*, August 16, 1919, pp. 14–15.

Advertisement. *New York Dramatic Mirror*, July 28, 1900, p. 24.

Advertisement. *New York Times*, August 12, 1919, p. 4.

Advertisement. *Variety*, January 20, 1906, p. 3.

Advertisement. *Variety*, December 26, 1913, p. 40.

Advertisement. *Variety*, May 26, 1916, p. 13.

Advertisement. *Variety*, June 9, 1916, pp. 20–21.

Advertisement. *Variety*, August 11, 1916, p. 13.

Advertisement. *Variety*, March 16, 1917, pp. 12–13.

Advertisement. *Variety*, September 5, 1919, p. 57.

"A.E.A. and White Rats Join to Form Union Under New Name." *Variety*, July 25, 1919, pp. 6, 16.

"A.E.A. Film Membership." *Variety*, December 21, 1917, p. 50.

"A.F.L. Membership." *Variety*, September 5, 1919, p. 9.

"After Equitable Contract." *Variety*, February 23, 1907, p. 6.

"Again Picketing." *Variety*, October 20, 1916, p. 6.

"The Agency Abuses." *New York Dramatic Mirror*, August 1, 1885, p. 10.

"Agency Bill Introduced in New York Legislature." *Variety*, January 22, 1910, p. 5.

"Agency Strike in Boston." *Variety*, August 13, 1910, p. 9.

"Agent Unfair Again." *Variety*, October 30, 1909, p. 8.

"Agents Will Lose Franchises if Booking Blacklisted Acts." *Variety*, March 23, 1917, p. 3.

"The Agi Says." *Billboard*, October 21, 1916, p. 6.

"Agreement at Atlanta by Theatrical Unions." *Variety*, November 25, 1911, p. 6.

"Aimed at Vaudeville Managers." *Washington Post*, February 25, 1901, p. 8.

Albee, E. F. "E. F. Albee and Vaudeville." *Variety*, December 22, 1916, p. 5.

"All Is Well." *Billboard*, December 23, 1916, pp. 6, 59.

"All Over — Equity Wins." *Billboard*, August 23, 1919, pp. 5, 8–9, 12.

Alpert, Hollis. *The Barrymores*. New York: The Dial Press, 1964.

"Application by White Rats Made to Federation of Labor." *Variety*, September 24, 1910, p. 5.

"Arab Acrobats Sue for Services." *New York Dramatic Mirror*, December 2, 1893, p. 2.

"Arbitration Board Counsels Reinstatement of Strikers." *Variety*, September 29, 1916, p. 6.

"Arbitration Board Throws Out Testimony of Mountford." *Billboard*, October 7, 1916, pp. 3, 70.

"The Artists' Associations Agree on De Veaux's Bill." *Variety*, March 26, 1910, p. 5.

"Artists' New Contract Discussed by Managers." *Billboard*, June 10, 1916, pp. 6, 71.

"Artists Win Strike." *Variety*, October 23, 1909, p. 4.

Auster, Albert. *Actresses and Suffragists: Women in the American Theater, 1890–1920*. New York: Praeger, 1984.

"A Ballet Girls' Union." *New York Dramatic Mirror*, August 11, 1894, p. 4.

Barrymore, Ethel. "The Actors' Strike." *The Outlook* 123 (September 3, 1919): 11–12.

"Bars a Salomer." *Variety*, August 15, 1908, p. 4.

"Battle Over Contract Forms Between A.E.A. and Managers." *Variety*, July 18, 1919, p. 13.

"Be More Cautious." *New York Dramatic Mirror*, September 22, 1888, p. 6.

"Big White Rats." *New York Dramatic Mirror*, January 19, 1901, p. 18.

"The *Billboard*'s Defi to Mountford." *Billboard*, April 29, 1916, p. 6.

"The Blacklist Called Off by Managers' Association." *Variety*, August 31, 1917, pp. 3, 20.

"Blacklist Might Be Broken Upon Demand of White Rats." *Variety*, October 16, 1909, p. 3.

"Blacklisted Act Barred from V.M.P.A. theatres." *Variety*, October 19, 1917, p. 6.

"Blacklisted Acts Taken Up After Others Are Placed." *Variety*, June 8, 1917, p. 3.

"Boston Added to Strike's List." *Variety*, September 5, 1919, p. 27.

"Boston Strike Becomes Peaceful Picketing Affair." *Variety*, February 16, 1917, p. 6.

"Boycott of Chicago Agent." *Variety*, October 16, 1909, p. 4.

"Broadway Still Talking of New A.E.A. Affiliation." *Billboard*, August 2, 1919, p. 3.

"But Two Salary Days." *New York Dramatic Mirror*, July 16, 1892, p. 6.

"Call Off Strike in War." *New York Times*, April 2, 1917, p. 9.

"Canceled Rats Passed Upon by Managers' Committee." *Variety*, November 17, 1916, p. 5.

Casey, Pat. "Running the V.M.P.A." *Variety*, May 11, 1917, p. 6.

"Checking Up Levy Payers." *Variety*, March 2, 1917, p. 6.

"Chicago Artist-Agent Row Threatens Serious Trouble." *Variety*, March 19, 1910, p. 5.

"Chicago Managers Accede to Demands of Actors." *Variety*, February 11, 1911, p. 9.

"Chicago Rats Hear Hot Air." *Variety*, December 29, 1916, p. 6.

"Chicago Theatres Closed by Strike; Fight Bitter Here." *New York Times*, August 13, 1919, pp. 1, 12.

"Chicago's Labor Union and White Rats Fail to Agree." *Variety*, July 2, 1910, p. 6.

"Chorus Equity Scores Victory for Members of Gaieties Co." *Variety*, October 17, 1919, p. 12.

"Chorus Girls Form Union to Enforce Many Reforms." *Variety*, November 28, 1913, p. 11.

"A Chorus Girls' Union." *New York Dramatic Mirror*, April 5, 1902, p. 15.

"Clause for Picture-Actors in Frohman's New Contracts." *Variety*, August 5, 1911, p. 9.

"A Cold Day for *Russia*." *Washington Post*, August 27, 1887, p. 2.

"Colored Artists of America." *Variety*, March 17, 1916, p. 15.

"Comedy Club's Birthday." *Variety*, May 18, 1907, p. 7.

"Common Sense Versus Hot Air." *Variety*, July 8, 1911, pp. 18–19.

"Companies Stranded." *New York Dramatic Mirror*, October 12, 1895, p. 13.

"Conference with Managers Asked for by White Rats." *Variety*, October 28, 1911, p. 5.

"Decent Dressing Rooms Wanted." *New York Dramatic Mirror*, January 27, 1883, p. 6.

"Disappointed in Boston." *Variety*, March 23, 1917, p. 7.

"Down to Endurance Test in Rats Boston Strike." *Variety*, March 2, 1917, p. 6.

"Drive Out the Swindlers." *New York Dramatic Mirror*, July 2, 1892, p. 4.

"E. F. Albee's views." *New York Dramatic Mirror*, August 15, 1908, p. 14.

Edwards, J. E. "National Vaudeville Artists Inaugurating a New Era." *Billboard*, May 12, 1917, pp. 4, 10–11.

"Emergency Committee in Charge of White Rats." *Variety*, February 22, 1908, p. 8.

"An Equitable Contract as Drawn by the Artists." *Variety*, August 8, 1908, p. 9.

"Equitable Contract Nearer." *Variety*, November 14, 1914, p. 12.

"Equity Body and Members Sued by Shuberts for $500,000." *New York Dramatic Mirror*, August 21, 1919, pp. 13, 14.

"Equity Votes to Arbitrate After Contract Is Rejected." *Variety*, May 30, 1919, p. 10.

"Equity's Victory." *Billboard*, September 13, 1919, pp. 5, 121.

"Equity's Wise and Able Leaders." *Billboard*, September 13, 1919, p. 122.

"Events Leading to Strike." *Variety*, August 15, 1919, p. 28.

"Extras Forming Union for Mutual Protection." *Variety*, August 25, 1916, p. 20.

"Failure Again Marks Rats' Strike Attempt in Boston." *Variety*, February 9, 1917, pp. 3, 7.

"Failure to Strike Monday Eases Vaudeville Situation." *Variety*, December 15, 1916, pp. 3, 6.

"Fidelity League Organizes with Geo. M. Cohan President." *Variety*, August 29, 1919, p. 29.

Fields, Armand, and L. Marc Fields. *From the Bowery to Broadway: Lew Fields and the Roots of American Popular Theatre.* New York: Oxford University Press, 1993.

"Fitzpatrick Elected President of White Rats." *Billboard,* April 15, 1916, pp. 6, 62.

"Fitzpatrick Flays Unions at White Rats' Meeting." *Billboard,* July 7, 1917, pp. 6, 75.

Fletcher, Charles Leonard. "Why I Resigned." *Variety,* March 3, 1916, p. 8.

"Fred Niblo Elected Rats' Big Chief." *Variety,* July 4, 1908, p. 4.

"From George Fuller Golden." *New York Dramatic Mirror,* October 3, 1908, p. 19.

Gemmill, Paul F. "Equity: The Actors' Trade Union." *Quarterly Journal of Economics* 41 (November, 1926): 129–145.

"George Fuller Golden." *New York Dramatic Mirror,* July 20, 1901, p. 13.

"George Fuller Golden." *Variety,* February 24, 1912, p. 6.

Gilbert, Douglas. *American Vaudeville: Its Life and Times.* New York: Dover 1940 (1963).

Golden, George Fuller. "The Original Eight." In Charles W. Stein, ed. *American Vaudeville as Seen by Its Contemporaries.* New York: Alfred A. Knopf, 1984, pp. 131–134.

Goldman, Herbert G. *Banjo Eyes: Eddie Cantor and the Birth of Modern Stardom.* New York: Oxford University Press, 1997.

"Gompers Adopts *Billboard* Suggestion." *Billboard,* June 10, 1916, pp. 3, 71.

"Gompers Draws Color Line." *New York Times,* November 19, 1910, p. 4.

"The Great Spiritual Victory Won by the Striking Actors." *Current Opinion* 67 (October, 1919): 234–236.

Green, Abel, and Joe Laurie Jr. *Show Biz from Vaude to Video.* New York: Henry Holt, 1951.

Harding, Alfred. "Ten Years After." *New York Times,* August 18, 1929, pp. X1, X4.

"Harry Mountford." *New York Times,* June 5, 1950, p. 21.

"Harry Mountford on His Way." *Variety,* December 28, 1907, p. 6.

"Have Won Big Victory over Rat Agitators, Say Managers." *Billboard,* April 22, 1916, pp. 3, 67.

Hogan, Ernest. "The Negro in Vaudeville." *Variety,* December 15, 1906, p. 22.

Holcomb, Willard. "Trials in Vaudeville." *Washington Post,* March 10, 1901, p. 27.

"How the United Bleeds the Agents and Actors." *Variety,* October 18, 1912, p. 7.

"An Important Event." *New York Dramatic Mirror,* November 21, 1896, p. 14.

"An Important Step Toward Organization." *Variety,* June 2, 1906, p. 2.

"Intended Strike in East Flickered and Went Out." *Billboard,* February 17, 1917, pp. 6, 67.

"Investment Fund Moves in Managerial Direction." *Variety,* July 11, 1908, p. 4.

Israel, Lee. *Miss Tallulah Bankhead.* New York: Putnam's Sons, 1972.

"Jewish Actors on Strike." *New York Dramatic Mirror,* January 4, 1896, p. 3.

"Judge Instructs Pickets." *Variety,* March 16, 1917, p. 24.

Knutt, A. P. "N.V.A. Club." *Billboard,* May 12, 1917, p. 18.

"The Last Arbitration Scheme." *New York Dramatic Mirror,* July 25, 1891, p. 7.

"Last of Strike Cases Settled at Conference." *Billboard,* October 11, 1919, p. 5.

"Latest News of the Actors' Strike." *New York Dramatic Mirror,* August 21, 1919, pp. 1313, 1316.

Laurie, Joe Jr. *Vaudeville: From the Honky-Tonks to the Palace.* New York: Henry Holt, 1953.

"Leading Players Go Out, Closing Big Attractions." *New York Times,* August 8, 1919, pp. 1, 12.

"Leading Vaudeville Artists Forming Association of 100." *Variety,* January 7, 1911, p. 4.

Lee, Betty. *Marie Dressler: The Unlikeliest Star.* Lexington Kentucky: The University Press of Kentucky, 1997.

"Left Destitute in Port Jervis." *New York Dramatic Mirror,* October 12, 1895, p. 13.

"Legit Actors' Society Vote for Union Affiliation." *Variety,* June 2, 1916, p. 5.

"Legit Equitable Contract Adopted by Both Factions." *Variety,* October 5, 1917, p. 12.

"Legit Try-Out Contract Form Adopted by A.E.A." *Variety,* May 17, 1918, p. 12.

Lennards, M. F. "Francis Wilson Speaks." *Billboard,* November 15, 1919, pp. 10, 98.

"A Lesson for Legitimate Actors." *New York Dramatic Mirror,* February 23, 1901, p. 18.

"The Little Mice." *New York Dramatic Mirror,* October 6, 1900, p. 18.

"Loyal Acts Rewarded." *Variety,* February 23, 1917, p. 7.

"Major Doyle Tells Facts to Enlighten the White Rats." *Billboard*, March 11, 1916, p. 62.

"Managers Adopt Contract of Actors' Equity Assn." *Billboard*, June 16, 1917, pp. 4, 78.

"Managers Axe Still Falling on Members of the White Rats." *Billboard*, April 15, 1916, pp. 3, 62.

"Managers Cease to Treat with Actors." *Christian Science Monitor*, July 25, 1919, p. 5.

"Managers Checking Up on Who Aids N.V.A. Benefit." *Billboard*, May 26, 1917, pp. 6, 95.

"Managers Defiance Holds Up Strike Decision Till September 23." *Variety*, September 22, 1916, p. 6.

"Managers Give Artists Better Contract Than Asked For." *Billboard*, June 2, 1916, pp. 3, 59.

"The Managers' League." *New York Dramatic Mirror*, August 8, 1891, p. 4.

"Managers Make Two Requests for Conferences to End Fight." *Variety*, September 1, 1916, p. 5.

"Managers Much Worried by Artists' Aggressiveness." *Variety*, July 25, 1908, p. 8.

"Managers Not Hostile to Actors." *New York Dramatic Mirror*, June 10, 1916, p. 8.

"Managers Plan Salary Cut to Meet no Sunday Threat." *Variety*, November 10, 1916, p. 6.

"Managers Refuse Invitation for White Rat Conference." *Variety*, September 29, 1916, p. 3.

"Managers Said to Favor Settlement." *Christian Science Monitor*, September 4, 1919, p. 6.

"Managers Say Blacklist for Any Striking Actor." *Variety*, December 18, 1916, p. 6.

"Managers Securing Reports of White Rats Meetings." *Variety*, April 21, 1916, p. 5.

"Managers Tabbing Rats." *Variety*, March 24, 1916, p. 5.

"Managers Take Decided Stand Against Policy of Mountford." *Billboard*, March 11, 1916, pp. 3, 63.

"Managers Will Continue Fight Against Rats and Supporters." *Billboard*, May 5, 1917, pp. 2, 78.

"Marie Dressler." *Billboard*, October 4, 1919, p. 10.

"Mayor McClellan Signs Voss New Agency Bill." *Variety*, May 15, 1909, p. 4.

McArthur, Benjamin. *Actors and American Culture, 1880–1920*. Philadelphia: Temple University Press, 1984.

McCabe, John. *George M. Cohan: The Man Who Owned Broadway*. Garden City, New York: Doubleday, 1973.

"Miss Craigen's Broken Contract." *New York Dramatic Mirror*, September 29, 1890, p. 8.

"Mr. Gompers." *Billboard*, May 13, 1916, p. 6.

"Mobilizing Actors' Equity Association." *Billboard*, August 9, 1919, pp. 5, 14–15, 90.

Moderwell, Hiram Kelly. "Acting as a Trade." *New Republic* 6 (April 22, 1916): 310–312.

"More Arrests on Sunday." *New York Dramatic Mirror*, January 9, 1909, p. 17.

"More Attempted Strikes by W.R.A.U. Are Fiascos." *Billboard*, March 17, 1917, pp. 6, 8.

"More Money from Actors Is Plea of the Executives." *Billboard*, March 3, 1917, pp. 6, 79.

"More White Rats Strikes with Customary Results." *Variety*, March 16, 1917, pp. 6, 24.

"Mountford Back in Harness for Aggressive Campaign." *Variety*, October 22, 1915, p. 4.

"Mountford Back in New York Addresses Big Open Meeting." *Variety*, May 12, 1916, p. 5.

"Mountford Causes Ruction in Boston Labor Meeting." *Variety*, February 23, 1917, p. 7.

Mountford, Harry. "The White Rats' Year." *Variety*, December 12, 1908, p. 52.

"Mountford Has Fallen Down in Prevailing Chicago Opinion." *Variety*, December 22, 1916, p. 3.

"Mountford Stages Another Mutual Admiration Meeting." *Billboard*, May 20, 1916, pp. 6, 67.

"Much Ado About Nothing Furnishes Glee for Rats." *Billboard*, July 29, 1916, pp. 6, 83.

Mudge, R. C. "Benefits of Organization." *Variety*, December 15, 1906, p. 24.

"Mutually Accepted Contract by Managers and Artists." *Variety*, June 16, 1916, p. 3.

"National Vaudeville Artists." *Variety*, May 11, 1917, p. 5.

"National Vaudeville Artists, Title of New Organization." *Billboard*, May 6 1916, pp. 6, 78.

"New Actors' Society Making Some Headway." *Variety*, January 14, 1911, p. 8.

"New Agency Law Makes Personal Representatives." *Variety*, July 2, 1910, pp. 5, 23.

"No Bar to Negro Actors in Equity." *New York Dramatic Mirror*, September 4, 1919, p. 1391.

"Notes of the White Rats." *New York Dramatic Mirror*, June 13, 1908, p. 17.

"NYM Crinkle's Feuilleton." *New York Dramatic Mirror*, December 27, 1888, p. 1.

"Oh! Rats." *Billboard*, July 1, 1916, p. 6.

"Oklahoma City Strike Quiet." *Variety*, November 17, 1916, p. 6.

"Oklahoma Managers Send Defi to State Arbitration Board." *Variety*, September 15, 1916, p. 7.

"Oklahoma Strike Continues with Managers Watching." *Variety*, August 4, 1916, pp. 3, 6.

"Oklahoma Strike Lost." *Variety*, January 5, 1917, p. 7.

"Oklahoma Strikers Abandon Metropolitan; Deny Defeat." *Variety*, October 13, 1916, p. 6.

"Oklahoma's Unfair Lyric Turns Union, Without Rats." *Variety*, November 24, 1916, p. 6.

"An Old Question." *New York Dramatic Mirror*, September 20, 1896, p. 12.

"Old Union to Be Revived." *Variety*, January 28, 1911, p. 5.

"On Which Side Is Your Bread Buttered." *Variety*, October 13, 1916, p. 8.

"150 Houses Bar Salome." *Variety*, September 26, 1908, p. 3.

"$100,000 in Reserve for Rats' Investment Fund." *Variety*, August 1, 1908, p. 4.

"Organization Details." *Billboard*, May 20, 1916, pp. 6, 67.

"Outcome of Actors' Strike Still in Doubt This Week." *Variety*, August 15, 1919, pp. 3, 21.

"Outrageous." *New York Dramatic Mirror*, April 8, 1897, p. 12.

"Pacific Coast Managers Sign White Rats Contract." *Variety*, July 14, 1916, p. 3.

"Passage of Voss Agency Bill Promises Artists Protection." *Variety*, May 1, 1909, p. 6.

"Percy G. Williams' New Contract Form." *Variety*, March 23, 1907, p. 4.

"Performers Go on Strike." *New York Dramatic Mirror*, July 4, 1903, p. 16.

"Performers in Distress." *New York Dramatic Mirror*, October 27, 1906, p. 20.

"Photoplay Actors Fail to Form New Organization." *Variety*, July 25, 1913, p. 8.

"Pickets Barred." *Variety*, October 13, 1916, p. 3.

"Planning to Forbid Sunday Shows." *Variety*, September 14, 1907, p. 6.

"Plans for Affiliation." *Variety*, September 15, 1906, p. 2.

"Play Loyal Acts Is Order of Vaudeville Managers' Society." *Variety*, April 20, 1917, p. 7.

"Plays Without Actors?" *New Republic* 20 (August 27, 1919): 105–106.

"Police Inspect Sunday Concerts." *New York Dramatic Mirror*, March 14, 1903, p. 22.

"Preference to N.V.A. Acts." *Variety*, August 4, 1916, p. 6.

"President Mudge Marries May Belfort." *Variety*, November 2, 1907, p. 6.

"Procrastinating Players Losing White Rats Benefits." *Variety*, December 19, 1913, p. 8.

"Producers Getting Terrible Pounding." *Billboard*, September 6, 1919, pp. 5, 8.

"A Professional Question." *New York Dramatic Mirror*, October 2, 1897, p. 14.

"A Proper Protest." *New York Dramatic Mirror*, January 23, 1897, p. 12.

"The Proposed League." *New York Dramatic Mirror*, June 27, 1891, p. 5.

"Protecting Oklahoma City Aim of Chicago's Association." *Variety*, October 6, 1916, p. 6.

"Protection for Chorus Girls in Federation of Labor." *Variety*, November 21, 1913, p. 4.

"Protection for Our Actors." *New York Dramatic Mirror*, December 22, 1888, p. 6.

"Protection of White Rats Offered Women of Profession." *Variety*, December 28, 1907, p. 2.

"The Question of Opposition." *New York Dramatic Mirror*, August 15, 1908, p. 14.

"R. C. Mudge on White Rats." *New York Dramatic Mirror*, October 10, 1908, p. 19.

"The Rascals Must Go." *New York Dramatic Mirror*, June 25, 1892, p. 4.

"Rats Ask Minimum Scale for Chicago and Boston." *Variety*, November 4, 1911, p. 13.

"Rats' Awful Flop in St. Louis." *Variety*, February 23, 1917, p. 7.

"Rats Expel Two Members." *Variety*, October 17, 1908, p. 4.

"Rats Give Local Autonomy; Admit Women to Meetings." *Variety*, January 14, 1916, p. 5.

"Rats in Politics." *Variety*, August 15, 1908, p. 4.

"Rats Refuse Resignations." *Variety*, October 13, 1916, p. 3.

"The Real Mountford." *Billboard*, December 20, 1919, p. 48.

"Realty Interests in Actors' Strike." *Christian Science Monitor*, August 18, 1919, p. 5.

"Reorganization of Protective Association of Managers." *Billboard*, March 4, 1916, pp. 3, 71.

"Salaries Will Not Be Cut, Officially Says V.M.P.A." *Variety*, June 3, 1911, p. 17.

"Salary Cutting Sole Topic This Week in Vaudeville." *Variety*, October 17, 1914, pp. 3, 6.

Sargent, Epes W. "Percy Williams' View on the Organization of Vaudeville." *Variety*, April 28, 1906, p. 4.

_____. "Why the Vaudeville Artists of America Should Organize." *Variety*, February 24, 1906, p. 4.

_____. "Why the Vaudeville Artists of America Should Organize." *Variety*, March 10, 1906, p. 4.

_____. "Why the Vaudeville Artists of America Should Organize." *Variety*, March 24, 1906, p. 4

_____. "Why the Vaudeville Artists of America Should Organize." *Variety*, April 7, 1906, p. 4.

"Saturday March 9th, 1901." *Billboard*, March 9, 1901, p. 4.

"Scope of the Actors' Society." *New York Dramatic Mirror*, November 28, 1896, p. 14.

"Screen Club Gives Reel." *New York Times*, July 30, 1917, p. 9.

"Screen Club's Members Wary of Mountford and His Order." *Billboard*, March 25, 1916, pp. 3, 55.

"Second Annual Convention of White Rats at Chicago." *Variety*, July 30, 1909, pp. 9, 12.

Shannon, Carl L. "Oklahoma City Strike Going Along Without Much Change." *Variety*, August 18, 1916, pp. 6, 13.

_____. "Oklahoma Strike Settlement in Two Weeks Predicted." *Variety*, August 11, 1916, p. 5.

_____. "Strikers Pulling Acts Out in Oklahoma City Fight." *Variety*, August 25, 1916, p. 5.

"Show Business Resuming Old Trend After Settlement." *Variety*, September 12, 1919, p. 12.

Silverman, Sime. Editorial page. *Variety*, March 16, 1917, p. 9.

_____. Editorial page. *Variety*, March 30, 1917, p. 9.

_____. Editorial page. *Variety*, August 22, 1919, p. 9.

_____. "Merry Christmas." *Variety*, December 22, 1916, pp. 9, 20.

_____. "Mr. Fogarty and the Rats." *Variety*, September 26, 1914, p. 7.

_____. "Mountford's Rise and Fall." *Variety*, December 23, 1911, pp. 47, 122.

_____. "Strike." *Variety*, December 15, 1916, pp. 9, 19.

_____. "What the Actor Must Do." *Variety*, February 7, 1913, p. 6.

_____. "What the Actor Must Do." *Variety*, February 14, 1913, p. 8.

_____. "What the Actor Must Do." *Variety*, February 21, 1913, p. 8.

_____. "Why the Vaudeville Artists of America Should Organize." *Variety*, March 3, 1906, p. 4.

_____. "Why the Vaudeville Artists of America Should Organize." *Variety*, March 17, 1906, p. 4.

_____. "Why the Vaudeville Artists of America Should Organize." *Variety*, May 12, 1906, p. 4.

_____. "Why the Vaudeville Artists of America Should Organize." *Variety*, June 2, 1906, p. 4.

_____. "Why the Vaudeville Artists of America Should Organize." *Variety*, June 23, 1906, p. 4.

"Situation Unchanged." *Billboard*, August 26, 1916, p. 6.

"Sluts and Other Things." *Billboard*, August 26, 1916, p. 6.

"Small Time Forming Union with White Rats Agency." *Variety*, June 5, 1909, pp. 3, 11.

"Smaller Managers Protect the A.E.A.'s Contract Form." *Variety*, March 1, 1918, pp. 13–14.

Smith, W. M. "Oklahoma City Strike Going

Along Without Much Change." *Variety*, August 18, 1916, p. 6.

"Smoke of Burning Money Still Rises in Clouds." *Billboard*, August 30, 1919, pp. 5, 8.

"Speakers Urge Actors to Unionize the Stage." *New York Times*, January 14, 1905, p. 9.

"Special Representatives for Rats." *Variety*, June 27, 1908, p. 3.

"Startling Disclosures on Dwindling Rat Membership." *Billboard*, April 29, 1916, pp. 3, 67.

"State Board of Arbitration Is Considering Okla. Strike." *Billboard*, September 30, 1916, pp. 6, 78.

"Stop! Read!—And Reflect!" *Variety*, March 10, 1916, pp. 18–19.

"The Story of the Trust." *New York Dramatic Mirror*, November 13, 1897, p. 29.

"A Strike at Seattle." *New York Dramatic Mirror*, July 25, 1896, p. 14.

"Strike Costs Both Parties $1,500,000 in Three Weeks." *Variety*, August 29, 1919, p. 12.

"Strike Factions Deadlocked at End of Strife's Third Week." *Variety*, August 29, 1919, p. 3.

"Strike Fails, Says Loew." *New York Times*, March 10, 1917, p. 9.

"Strike Flivs Despite Pledge Equity Members Gave to Quit." *Variety*, August 1, 1919, p. 12.

"The Strike for Higher Salaries." *New York Dramatic Mirror*, June 17, 1882, p. 6.

"Strike in Chicago." *Variety*, August 15, 19191, pp. 17, 21.

"The Strike of the Vaudeville Actors." *New York Times*, February 23, 1901, p. 9.

"Strike of the White Rats." *Washington Post*, February 23, 1901, p. 11.

"Striking Actors Keep 9 Shows Dark." *New York Times*, August 9, 1919, pp. 1, 9.

"Striking Boston Artists Formed Into Actors' Union." *Variety*, August 20, 1910, p. 8.

"Strike's Aftermath Finds Chicago Conditions Normal." *Variety*, January 12, 1917, p. 6.

"Stuck to Rats; Forced Out." *Variety*, October 20, 1916, p. 6.

"Sunday Performances." *New York Dramatic Mirror*, July 3, 1886, p. 1.

"Sunday Performances." *New York Dramatic Mirror*, December 8, 1900, p. 14

"Supers Call Mass Meeting and Arrange for a Charter." *Variety*, September 1, 1916, p. 13.

"The Swindlers Must Go." *New York Dramatic Mirror*, July 16, 1892, p. 2.

"Theaters." *Christian Science Monitor*. August 21, 1919, p. 8.

"Theaters Stay Dark." *Washington Post*, August 9, 1919, p. 7.

"Theatrical Charter Confined to Rats by A. F. of L. Meeting." *Variety*, November 24, 1916, p. 3.

"Theatrical Interests Combine to Cope with Expected Strike." *Variety*, August 8, 1919, p. 6.

"Theatrical Litigation." *New York Dramatic Mirror*, April 11, 1885, p. 11.

"The Theatrical Protective Association." *New York Times*, July 22, 1864, p. 8.

"Theatricals Fiercest Fight Still Holding on Wednesday." *Variety*, August 22, 1919, pp. 3, 9.

"They Did Strike." *Billboard*, August 16, 1919, pp. 5, 12–13, 18.

"A Timely Hint." *New York Dramatic Mirror*, June 12, 1886, p. 1.

"To Non-Members of the W.R.A.U. and A.A.A." *Variety*, October 29, 1915, pp. 14–15.

"To Punish Fraud." *New York Dramatic Mirror*, July 9, 1892, p. 8.

"To the Actor and Actress of the U.S." *Variety*, October 22, 1915, pp. 12–13.

"To the Vaudeville Artist." *Variety*, March 24, 1916, p. 19.

"Trouble in a Company." *New York Dramatic Mirror*, October 14, 1893, p. 3.

"The Troubles in Vaudeville." *New York Dramatic Mirror*, March 2, 1901, pp. 18, 20.

"The Two Weeks Clause Again." *New York Dramatic Mirror*, December 6, 1890, p. 2.

"The Union and Mr. Conreid." *New York Times*, September 13, 1906, p. 6.

"A Union of Chorus Girls?" *New York Dramatic Mirror*, June 28, 1902, p. 15.

"Unionizing Again." *Variety*, October 22, 1910, p. 6.

"Unions Tackle Conreid with Chorus' Demands." *New York Times*, December 25, 1905, p. 4.

"United Agrees to Be Fair." *Variety*, March 9, 1907, p. 5.

"Unpaid Salaries." *New York Dramatic Mirror*, July 15, 1882, p. 6.

"Vaudeville Actors' Fund Suggested by Managers." *Variety*, March 4, 1911, p. 12.

"The Vaudeville Actors' Movement." *New York Dramatic Mirror*, July 14, 1900, p. 12.

"The Vaudeville Artists' New Association Now a Reality." *Billboard*, May 13, 1916, p. 14.

"The Vaudeville Comedy Club." *New York Dramatic Mirror*, June 8, 1907, pp. 8–9.

"Vaudeville Managers Are Not Against Organized Labor." *Variety*, October 20, 1916, p. 8.

"Vaudeville Managers' Ass'n Decide on Publicity Campaign." *Variety*, March 3, 1916, p. 5.

"Vaudeville Managers Confer." *New York Dramatic Mirror*, May 26, 1900, p. 17.

"Vaudeville Managers Talk on Proposed Unionizing." *Variety*, April 29, 1911, p. 13.

"Vaudeville Managers Won't Recognize Rats as a Union." *Variety*, September 2, 1911, p. 3.

"Vaudeville Protective Ass'n Is Artists' Secret Society." *Variety*, May 16, 1913, p. 4.

"The Vaudeville Situation." *New York Dramatic Mirror*, September 5, 1908, p. 17.

"Vaudeville Strike Declared Off." *Washington Post*, March 8, 1901, p. 3.

"The Vaudeville Troubles." *New York Dramatic Mirror*, March 2, 1901, p. 14.

"Vaudeville's Seamy Side." *Variety*, June 6, 1913, p. 6.

"V.M.P.A. Issues a Statement on Strikes and Unionism." *Variety*, April 22, 1911, p. 9.

"V.M.P.A. Will Give no Quarter to Rats." *Billboard*, December 2, 1916, pp. 6, 55.

Vreeland, F. T. "The Actors' Strike." *Nation* 109 (August 23, 1919): 243–244.

"Want Rats in Labor Union." *Variety*, April 20, 1907, p. 6.

"Wants All Agencies to Become Unionized Ones." *Variety*, June 11, 1910, p. 4.

"Warning Legitimate Players Against Picture Connection." *Variety*, January 6, 1912, p. 10.

"Waterbury's Sunday Stops." *Variety*, October 30, 1916, p. 6.

"Western Actors Join Union." *New York Dramatic Mirror*, August 6, 1904, p. 17.

"Western Vaudeville Man Agrees to Closed Shop." *Variety*, November 11, 1911, p. 5.

"What the White Rats Are Doing." *New York Dramatic Mirror*, March 30, 1901, p. 18.

"White Rat Bookings." *Billboard*, March 23, 1901, p. 24.

"A White Rat Loses Route Through Impassioned Speech." *Variety*, November 26, 1915, p. 6.

"White Rat Notes." *New York Dramatic Mirror*, August 1, 1908, p. 16.

"The White Rats." *Washington Post*, February 17, 1901, p. 26.

"White Rats Admit Defeat; Order Faces Bankruptcy." *Variety*, April 13, 1917, pp. 3, 7.

"White Rats After Irresponsible Agents." *Variety*, July 13, 1907, p. 2.

"White Rats and Labor Leaders Get-Together Meet in Boston." *Billboard*, February 26, 1916, pp. 3, 63.

"White Rats Annual Meeting." *Variety*, June 20, 1908, p. 8.

"The White Rats Are Standing Firm." *New York Times*, February 24, 1901, p. 7.

"White Rats Ask for Meeting for Submission of Its Demands." *Variety*, December 8, 1916, pp. 3, 13.

"White Rats Begin Crusade." *New York Times*, October 16, 1915, p. 11.

"White Rats Being Barred from Vaudeville." *Billboard*, April 1, 1916, pp. 3, 70.

"White Rats Desert Ranks in Fear of Cancellation." *Billboard*, April 8, 1916, p. 6.

"White Rats Draw Up Special Form of Contract." *Variety*, March 28, 1908, p. 3.

"White Rats Give Up *Player*; Using *Variety* for Its News." *Variety*, November 21, 1913, p. 3.

"White Rats in Death Throes and Beaten in All Walkouts." *Billboard*, March 24, 1917, pp. 3, 191.

"White Rats Introduce New Agency Measure in Albany." *Variety*, March 5, 1910, p. 9.

"White Rats Investigation by Union Labor People." *Variety*, May 18, 1912, p. 3.

"White Rats Make Important Move." *New York Dramatic Mirror*, February 2, 1901, p. 20.

"White Rats' Meeting Draws Crowd at Chicago." *Variety*, July 11, 1908, pp. 8, 21.

"White Rats Mortgage Clubhouse Furnishings for $5,000." *Variety*, December 29, 1916, p. 3.

"White Rats Move." *New York Dramatic Mirror*, April 3, 1907, p. 18.

"White Rats New Club House Astonishes, and Is Admired." *Variety*, December 13, 1912, p. 8.

"White Rats News." *Variety*, June 25, 1915, pp. 6–7.

"White Rats News." *Variety*, April 21, 1916, p. 16.

"White Rats News." *Variety*, September 22, 1916, pp. 15–19.

"The White Rats of America." *New York Dramatic Mirror*, June 30, 1900, p. 16.

"White Rats Recognize Claims of Insurgents." *Billboard*, March 4, 1916, p. 6.

"White Rats Rejoice." *New York Dramatic Mirror*, February 2, 3, 1901, pp. 18, 20.

"White Rats' Representative Declares Okla. City Unfair." *Variety*, July 28, 1916, p. 6.

"White Rats Reshaping Itself After Change of Direction." *Variety*, October 7, 1911, p. 9.

"White Rats Resign from Organization When Cancelled." *Billboard*, November 11, 1916, pp. 6, 63.

"White Rats Resort to Tactics of Ruffians." *Billboard*, March 24, 1917, pp. 38, 90.

"The White Rats Society Joins Labor Organization." *Variety*, November 12, 1910, p. 5.

"The White Rats Strike." *Billboard*, March 2, 1901, p. 9.

"White Rats' Strike Ended." *New York Times*, March 7, 1901, p. 2.

"The White Rats' Testimonial." *New York Dramatic Mirror*, September 15, 1900, p. 18.

"White Rats Theatres Pass to Feiber & Shea." *Variety*, March 2, 1912, p. 5.

"White Rats to Admit Women." *New York Dramatic Mirror*, January 26, 1901, p. 18.

"White Rats to Be Boycotted in Managers' Ass'n Threat." *Variety*, September 15, 1916, p. 3.

"White Rats' Union Tries to Stop Poli's Sundays." *Variety*, October 13, 1916, p. 3.

"White Rats Win Their Point." *New York Dramatic Mirror*, February 16, 1901, p. 20.

"Why Not Arbitrate?" *New York Dramatic Mirror*, October 28, 1882, p. 6.

"Why the Actors Joined Labor Federation." *New York Times*, June 4, 1916, p. SM8.

"Will Proceed in Accordance with Policies of A.F. of L." *Billboard*, June 17, 1916, pp. 3, 59.

"Willard Mack Elected Head of New Vaude Organization." *Billboard*, August 5, 1916, pp. 3, 71.

"Williams and Albee Talk." *Variety*, February 16, 1907, p. 6.

Wilmeth, Don B., and Christopher Bigsby, eds. *The Cambridge History of American Theatre volume 2: 1870–1945*. Cambridge: Cambridge University Press, 1999.

"W.R.A.U. Levies Assessment of 5 Percent on Workers' Pay." *Variety*, February 9, 1917, p. 5.

"W.R.A.U. Offers Protection to the Legitimate Player." *Variety*, December 12, 1913, p. 14.

"W.R.A.U. Will Resort to Conscription After May 26." *Variety*, March 31, 1916, p. 5.

"Year in Vaudeville." *Variety*, December 22, 1916, pp. 6, 118–119.

"A Young Actress Complains." *New York Dramatic Mirror*, September 29, 1894, p. 3.

Index